Colour Your Garden
with Australian Natives

COLOUR YOUR GARDEN
WITH
AUSTRALIAN NATIVES

GEOFF and BEV RIGBY

Look how the wildflowers grow . . .
not even King Solomon with all
his wealth had clothes as beautiful
as one of these flowers.

Luke 12.27

Kangaroo Press

To all who have loved
and encouraged us on
our journey

Acknowledgments

Many people have helped us to bring this book to fruition.

We wish to thank Diane Evans, Beth Bulluss, John Burgess, Nelda Marshall, Jim and Esma Rigby and Warwick and Roslyn Symons for their assistance in providing information, useful comments, discussions and encouragement during the various stages of preparation of the manuscript. We are indebted to Wendy Matthews for making corrections to the final manuscript.

The late Peter Althofer of Wellington and staff from the Botanic Gardens of Adelaide and Royal Botanic Gardens, Sydney have assisted in identification of plant species.

Col Tyndall, Paddy Lightfoot, and Bob and Margaret Wilson have supplied information on plant species and location of gardens of interest. We are also indebted to Paddy Lightfoot for the loan of his colour slides of *Boronia pinnata* and *Brachychiton acerifolius*.

Hazel Blackney, leader of the SGAP Hakea Study Group, Trevor Blake, leader of the Banksia Study Group; and Peter Vaughan, leader of the Brachychiton Study Group; have provided assistance and information on some of the species included in the book.

The continual interest shown by members of the Newcastle Group of the Society for Growing Australian Plants (SGAP) has been a source of encouragement during the preparation of the manuscript and is very much appreciated.

The information included in this book on botanical gardens, arboreta, wildflower gardens and flora reserves has been prepared from personal experiences together with discussions and information supplied from the various locations. In particular, we also wish to thank staff of the following:

Wollongong Botanic Garden and Wollongong City Council; Burrendong Arboretum, and Hazel and the late Peter Althofer; Hunter Region Botanic Garden and Sue Herd; Albury Botanic Gardens; Stony Range Flora Reserve; Ku-ring-gai Wildflower Garden; Illawarra Grevillea Park Society; Royal Botanic Gardens, Sydney; Mount Tomah Botanic Garden; Mount Annan Botanic Garden; Australian National Botanic Gardens and Herbarium, and Betty Collins; Kings Park Botanic Garden; Botanic Gardens of Adelaide and State Herbarium; Royal Tasmanian Botanic Gardens and Susan Wells; Flecker Botanic Gardens and David Warmington; City Botanic Gardens, Brisbane; Mt Coot-tha Botanic Gardens and Malcolm Cox; CSIRO Long Pocket Rainforest and Don Sands; CSIRO Division of Forest Research Arboretum, Atherton, and Geoff Tracey and Jan Weaver; Gallop Botanic Gardens, Cooktown; Darwin Botanic Garden and George Brown; Royal Botanic Gardens Melbourne; Cranbourne Botanic Gardens and Dr John Cunningham; The Wirrimbirra Sanctuary; Wagga Wagga Botanic Gardens and Nancy Hughes; Orange Botanic Gardens and Ken Pratt; Department of Conservation and Land Management of W.A.; Waite Agricultural Research Institute; University of Adelaide and Dr Jennifer Gardner; City of Ballarat; Department of Conservation and Land Management, W.A. (Goldfields Region); and Rockhampton City Council and Tom Wyatt.

Other books by the authors

Rigby, Geoff. *The Australian Gardener's Guide to Native Plants.* Treasure Press, 1989, 1990

Rigby, Geoff, & Lightfoot, Paddy. *Australian Native Trees and Large Shrubs Suitable for Planting in the Lower Hunter.* Society for Growing Australian Plants. Newcastle Group, 1985.

First published in 1992 by Kangaroo Press Pty Ltd
3 Whitehall Road (P.O. Box 75) Kenthurst 2156
Typeset by G.T. Setters Pty Limited
Printed in Hong Kong through Colorcraft Ltd

ISBN 0 86417 492 6

Contents

Foreword

Interest in the use and appreciation of native plants in home gardens has increased dramatically over recent years. An ever-increasing number of Australian plants are becoming available for cultivation and can be adapted to a range of home garden conditions.

When we first moved into our home, over 20 years ago, there were no gardens or trees. The original trees had been removed in preparation for building the house.

After seeing what could be done in some gardens, we developed a very keen interest in the propagation and cultivation of native plants and eventually established our own Australian garden. Over the years, this garden has changed. As we have learned more about the specific requirements of native plants, we have been able to incorporate a wider range of some of the more difficult to cultivate varieties. Our garden has changed the whole appearance of our home and is now a source of joy to us as we continue to develop it and enjoy its many facets.

In the early stages of developing the garden, we found it difficult to select the most suitable plants for a particular location or purpose, since information of this type was not readily available. However, from our experience in cultivating native plants, and our

observation of their growing characteristics and habits, we have developed an understanding of the essential features which are important in planning a native garden.

Plant features normally considered include size, shape, growth rate, foliage type, fragrance, flower shape, flowering period, suitability for cut flowers, and cultivation requirements.

In recent years, however, we have come to recognise the importance of colour when selecting plants. Not only are the colours of the flowers important, but the colours of foliage, fruits, nuts and barks are also valuable in ensuring year-round colour in the garden.

Just as much emphasis, therefore, should be placed on selecting plants, shrubs and trees for colour features and characteristics, as for some of the other features usually considered.

This book illustrates the range of colours which are associated with our beautiful Australian plants and will assist you to select the right plants for your purpose.

Emphasis has been placed on plants suitable for propagation and cultivation in home gardens. In general, plants indigenous to the local area are easiest

to grow and are more likely to survive in the home garden for long periods of time, provided some basic guidelines are followed. However, with a little extra effort to simulate the natural plant environments (as outlined in the individual descriptions) it is possible to cultivate a much wider collection of plants and take advantage of the greater range of colours and features available.

If suitable conditions cannot be created in the garden itself, we recommend the use of a variety of pots or containers in which the desirable conditions can be established.

In addition to the photographs in the early chapters of the book, we have included, in Chapter 8, details of a selection of botanic gardens, arboreta and wildflower gardens throughout Australia. These locations provide an excellent opportunity to see and enjoy a variety of plants growing in their natural environment, and to observe the colours and characteristics of the flowers and other features likely to be of interest in choosing plants for the garden.

After reading this book, we trust that you will share our enthusiasm for the outstanding beauty and colour of our unique native plants.

Geoff and Bev Rigby

The change in appearance of the authors' home, brought about by the native garden is very evident of these two photographs. The semi-formal layout makes use of sections of lawn between the several garden beds, which have generally been built up to provide good drainage. A range of trees and shrubs has been used to provide variation in height, texture and colour, as well as a year-round show of colour.

Introduction

And God said...

I have set my rainbow in the clouds,
and it will be a sign of the covenant
between me and the earth.

Genesis 9.12

Our Colourful Countryside

The eye-catching roadside displays of bushland colour are common features of the Australian countryside. The range of species and colours of our many native flowers varies from one location to another, and from season to season. Time taken to explore at closer range will often reveal many low-growing plants from a host of genera which were not at first apparent.

In spring, sandstone areas are host to a mixture of pink, red, orange and white flowers of *Boronia*, *Grevillea*, *Telopea* (waratah), *Banksia* and *Epacris*.

Well-drained sandy areas are ablaze with masses of white *Actinotus helianthii* (Flannel Flower) and pimelea; pink eriostemon, *Chamelaucium uncinatum* (Geraldton Wax), *Ceratopetalum gummiferum* (N.S.W. Christmas Bush) and red and green *Anigosanthos* (kangaroo paw).

On high mountain rocky outcrops, the long cream and white pendulous sprays of *Dendrobium speciosum* (Rock Lily) cover the host rockface, while yellow spikes of *D. gracilicaule* adorn the upper forest canopy. In another part of the forest, the masses of white flowers of *Clematis aristata* creep over the giant forest eucalypts.

In the protected, damp rainforest areas, attractive epiphytic *Platycerium* spp. (staghorn and elkhorn ferns) display their unusual light green, pendular fronds. The new green leaves of the dew-covered *Asplenium nidus* (Bird's Nest Fern), carefully wedged between branches high up in the *Allocasuarina torulosa* (Forest Oak), unfold to greet the early morning sun. In another part of the cool rainforest gully, the purple berries of *Acmena smithii* (Creek, or Narrow-Leaved Lillypilly) provide a tasty breakfast for the birds.

In the hot and dry inland areas, the red ironstone outcrops provide a matching backdrop for the unusual red and black upright flowers of *Clianthus formosus* (Sturt's Desert Pea). The woolly greyish leaves of this decumbent herb add to its beauty .

While the largest number of native flowers occurs during spring, many species provide colourful displays at different times of the year and some flower year round. The many species of *Acacia*, or wattle, offer an almost endless source of yellow flowers for most months of the year.

In plates 1–16, a selection of plants and flowers found growing naturally in the bush or along the roadside, has been included to illustrate the diversity of colours and other features available in our native flora.

This spectacular show of Flannel Flowers (*Actinotus helianthii*) at Tanilba Bay, N.S.W., is typical of similar massed displays which occur in the well drained sandy areas of many parts of Australia. These plants normally last for only a couple of years and often rely on a bush fire to germinate the seeds. Flannel Flowers can be grown with some perseverence in a home garden, provided very well-drained conditions are provided.

The well-drained coastal heathland near Forster, N.S.W., also supports masses of Flannel Flowers, *Eriostemon australasius* and numerous other small heath flowers.

Everlasting daisies often cover many hectares of countryside with a carpet of white, pink or yellow paper-like flowers. This display of pink and yellow everlastings near Mingenen in W.A. continues almost every year for several months from about August and is a real eye opener for visitors to that state. Everlastings are annuals and can be easily grown in the home garden from seed to give a most attractive multi-coloured rockery or bed display. They are readily dried and are excellent for dried floral arrangements. They are grown commercially for both the local and export cut-flower markets.

Several coloured forms of Geraldton Wax (*Chamelaucium uncinatum*) grow naturally in the Wireless Hill area near Perth. Similar displays of quite large trees can also be seen around other parts of Perth and W.A. Geraldton Wax has adapted well to garden cultivation and is now grown in many other parts of the country. A very well-drained location is essential.

The snow daisy of Australia (*Celmisia* spp.), which is found mainly in the alpine areas, is equal to any daisy in the world. A walk in the alpine region around Mt Kosciusko during summer will reveal the beauty of large areas of white snow daisies in amongst other alpine wildflowers.

Amongst the many native creepers, the False Sarsaparilla (*Hardenbergia violacea*) is one of the most prolific growers and flowerers. It is often seen covering many square metres of banks or trees with masses of bluish purple to purple flowers during spring. Provided a well-drained position is available, this creeper can be used very succesfully in home gardens to cover a bank, tree stump or fence. A white form as well as the purple form is available.

This cool, protected wet sclerophyll area in Wilsons Promontory, Victoria is similar to many areas of the continent. The sunlight and shade add further dimensions to the predominantly green landscape.

The new red foliage of *Nothofagus cunninghami* adds colour to this delightful forest landscape near Strathgordon, Tasmania.

The dry red ironstone country around Mt Newman, W.A., is brightened by a wide range of colourful and drought-resistant plants.

Common throughout the lowlands and on exposed sandstone plateaus around Kakadu National Park, N.T., is this attractive shrub *Calytrix extipulata*. Most plants in this area are fire tolerant as seasonal burning by the Aboriginal inhabitants has been part of the landscape for thousands of years.

W.A. is renowned for its extravagant wildflower displays, especially in spring. The banksias are no exception, as shrubs or trees of the various species splash the landscape with colour. Some species, although abundant, only grow in restricted areas as illustrated by *Banksia coccinea* around the Albany area.

This tall stand of Karri gums (*Eucalyptus diversicolor*), lining both sides of the road near Pemberton in W.A., provides a change of character from the lower growing species along the sand plains further north.

Probably the best known of all Australian plants, wattles, or acacias, are distributed throughout Australia. There are in excess of 500 species in this genus and it is possible to choose species which flower at different times throughout the year.

Native Plants for Home Gardens

In recent years an increasing number of Australian gardeners have come to appreciate the unique qualities, the beauty and the variety of the natural Australian bushland and more especially the native flora.

Through the efforts of many horticultural researchers and groups such as The Society For Growing Australian Plants, who are interested in encouraging the study, growing and propagation of Australian native plants, there has been an upsurge in the use of native plants in home gardens.

Although many species and varieties of our native flora have their own natural habitat and specific growing requirements, it is now possible to cultivate a large number of these in our home gardens.

Some species however remain difficult to cultivate under garden conditions and require very special conditions. For this reason it is advisable, at least in the early stages of planning a garden, to select species which have been shown to grow readily under the conditions available, and more especially, those indigenous to the local area.

In general most native plants prefer a well-drained environment, although there are obviously exceptions to this rule. Where these conditions are not available effective drainage can be provided by the use of built-up beds or containers.

Once the basic garden has been established, you may wish to try some of the more unusual species. Often success can be achieved by using pots or other alternatives which more closely simulate the natural conditions. The joy and satisfaction of being able to grow some of these unusual species or varieties is well worth the effort and helps in appreciating the diversity and beauty of our vast number of plants.

More specific details and guidelines to assist in the preparation of the garden and in the selection, propagation, planting, cultivation, and maintenance of native plants are included in Chapter 7. Careful planning of the species which you use in your garden will not only provide variety in shape, size, foliage, texture and fragrance but will also provide flowers with a range of colours throughout the year.

Grevillea biternata is one of the better grevilleas to cover a large area. Here it is shown growing on a bank along the Burwood Highway near Lilydale in Victoria, highlighting the potential of this plant for landscaping. It is very adaptable to most conditions and is fast growing. The red flowers of *G. lavandulacea* in this location provide an attractive contrast to the masses of white flowers of *G. biternata* and illustrate the versatility of the *Grevillea* genus.

An attractive feature using two purple-flowered groundcovers has been achieved in this small garden rockery. At the rear, trailing over the large rock, *Hardenbergia violacea* provides the back-drop for the beautiful *Dampiera diversifolia*. Note also how the bark mulch fills the gaps between the plants as they grow, as well as retaining moisture in the soil.

The aim of this book is to illustrate the variety of colours which can be created in a home garden with a range of Australian native plants. Particular emphasis has been given to plants which can be readily grown in home gardens. Information on desired conditions, size and shape, flowering time, colours and natural locations is included to assist in selection. While this information will provide basic guidelines, it is important to note that many plants have adapted well to locations and conditions different from their natural habitat. It is therefore worthwhile experimenting with some of the species from outside your area as your interests and enthusiasm develop.

Some species are not particularly tolerant of frosts, although many can be grown in cooler areas as long as they are protected from frosts until they become established. Very little research has been done on the effects of frost on Australian native plants. As a general rule, plants from mountain, alpine and inland areas are not susceptible to damage by frosts. Some rainforest and tropical or subtropical species have been grown successfully in frost-prone areas. Species which are distributed in different parts of the country often have some forms which are more tolerant of frosts than others. Local experience is invaluable in choosing suitable plants for some of the more difficult conditions and in identifying forms which have adapted to harsh conditions. We encourage you to seek advice from local native plant enthusiasts in your area. Some comments on frost-resistant species are included in the individual descriptions, although it is difficult to be specific about these details.

Many new cultivars have been produced in recent years, often from areas outside their parent natural locations, and add to the ever-increasing range of plants available for home gardens. These cultivars generally have the climatic and cultivation requirements of the parent plants.

Colour photographs of some individual specimen plants as well as flowers will also assist in planning your garden. Common names as well as botanical names are given for convenience.

For gardeners interested in learning more about this subject, assistance is readily available from organisations and nurseries specialising in the propagation and cultivation of native plants. Details of some of these, together with a list of botanic gardens and arboreta where plants can be seen growing are included in Chapter 8.

Large rocks have been used at the Burrendong Arboretum, near Wellington, N.S.W., to form large built-up beds with suitable drainage for some of the more difficult to grow Western Australian plants. This specimen of *Grevillea brachystylis* growing happily with several other more unusual plants clearly shows what can be achieved with this technique.

Other Features of Native Plants

Although the flowers provide the predominant source of colour, both in the natural environment and in the home garden, there are many other features of plants and trees which add colour to the garden. These include foliage, bark, nuts and fruits.

Flowers of many native plants are ideal for floral arrangements either as fresh flowers or often in dried form. Dried floral arrangements can be used for many months and even years. The natural colours are also often retained provided the appropriate steps are taken.

Flowers of many native plants provide a source of nectar for birds. A well-planned garden will attract birds to your garden, thereby adding additional colour and also assisting in the control of pests.

This beautiful large arrangement of fresh native flowers illustrates some of the striking colours and combinations which can be used to advantage. Several species of banksia have been used as the main feature of the arrangement.

1 Reds and Pinks

Stenocarpus

Up there, among those dark-green leaves,
Are most exciting things,
Like budding wheels, and flowers aflame,
And little seeds with wings.

No tree, I think, could ever have
More magical attire
Than scarlet flowers in clustered rings,
Like little wheels of fire.

Nuri Mass
Australian Wildflower Magic
(The Writer's Press, 1967)

It is often difficult to clearly distinguish betweeen the coloured flowers of many species and forms of plants of interest to the home gardener. Indeed it is also often difficult to separate the pinks and mauves.

Propagation from seeds can result in several coloured forms for the same species and this feature is very often the case with the pinks and reds. Several eucalypt species have a full range of floral colours from light pink through salmon to deep reds. One notable example is the Western Australian species *Eucalyptus ficifolia*; others include *E. leucoxylon* and *E. torquata*. Other genera which have ranges of pink and red flowers include *Crowea*, *Boronia* and *Grevillea*.

Pink-flowering plants are very popular for use in gardens or for floral displays and can be used to advantage with almost any colour combination. Red is a much stronger colour but nevertheless provides much interest in the garden and an opportunity to take advantage of the different flower forms of many interesting red-flowering plants.

The *Grevillea* genus probably has the greatest variety of red flower types and forms, with flowers ranging from prostrate species such as *G. gaudichaudii* through the small rockery shrubs like *G. baueri*; the medium-sized shrubs including the beautiful *G.* 'Robyn Gordon'; the larger spreading shrubs like *G. aspleniifolia*; and the taller species such as *G. banksii*.

The pinks and reds are prominent colours in new foliage or in bud covers, as illustrated in the section on colourful foliage in Chapter 6.

A well-planned garden can produce beautiful displays at various times of the year with pink flushes in combination with the soft pastel tones of white and even yellow, light blue, mauve and purple. Some care in the selection of plants will be well rewarded in the final result when flowering occurs.

The use of various specimens in large pots or tubs can also be most satisfying and provide a practical way of having colour in different locations by moving the pots around as desired. Several of the crowea species are particularly useful in this role, since in addition to offering several pink and red colour forms, they also have flowers for many months of the year.

Allocasuarina rigida N.S.W., Tas., Qld, S.A. Summer
The *Casuarina* genus (recently subdivided to create the *Allocasuarina* genus which is distinguished by its dark and shiny seed-like winged fruits) is well distributed throughout Australia. The flowers of the two genera are unusual, with the tiny red and brown male flowers growing in long spikes at the ends of the stems (giving the plants an attractive appearance when in flower). The red female flowers are arranged in a globular spike and mature into nut-like fruits. The flowers are pollinated by wind. Some species have both male and female flowers on the same tree. The attractive red flowers of *A. rigida* are typical of many of the species. Several fruits are also shown. This species, although not common in cultivation, grows to a small, rounded, bushy shrub or small tree. Both genera are adaptable to a wide range of conditions and deserve more attention as garden, street and park specimens.

Alyogyne huegelii (see also p. 55)
(Syn. *Hibiscus huegelii*)   S.A., W.A.
Lilac Hibiscus   Spring and summer
This genus is closely allied to the *Hibiscus* genus and has an upright habit with soft, lobed, dull green leaves. Flowers vary in colour from pink to yellow, white, lilac and purple, generally with a darker centre. They only last for one day, but many flowers are produced, giving a continuous display over several months. This species is hardy and has adapted well to garden cultivation, growing to 2 m high and 1.5 m across. Most soils are suitable, with a sunny position preferred to encourage profuse flowering. It is also tolerant of light frosts.

Anigosanthos 'Dwarf Delight'   Cultivar. Summer
Many cultivars of *Anigosanthos* species are now being made available for garden or pot cultivation. 'Dwarf Delight' is a hybrid between *A. flavidus* and *A. onycis*. It grows with a similar habit to *A. flavidus* but is generally more compact and not quite as tall. The branched flower spikes grow to 40 cm. It is a superb plant and bears apricot to red flowers in profusion. Like many of the cultivars, it appears to be less prone to the 'ink disease' often encountered with *A. flavidus*. Well-drained conditions and a sunny position are preferred.

Anigosanthos flavidus (see also p. 41) W.A. Summer
Yellow Kangaroo Paw

This red-flowering form is somewhat more colourful
than the more common yellow form and provides an
attractive and long-lasting flower display. It is a very
hardy garden specimen. All species of this genus thrive
in well-drained soils, although this species has adapted
well to a wide range of soils, including clay. Flowering
is improved if grown in full sun, where the flower
spikes can grow up to 2 m long. Clumps of this
vigorous plant can grow to 1 m across within a few
years.

Anigosanthos 'Regal Claw' (see also p. 35)
Cultivar   Spring and summer

Another of the excellent cultivars for garden
cultivation, A. 'Regal Claw' is a hybrid between *A.
flavidus* and *A. preissii* and has flower spikes up to 1.5
m long, with orange-red mutiple heads. Both the stems
and flowers are covered in fine red hairs. Like most
of the *Anigosanthos* genus, this plant makes an excellent
pot specimen provided a large pot is used. Division
of this vigorous grower is recommended every 2 to
3 years.

Bauera rubioides (see also p. 64) Eastern states, Tas.
Dog Rose   Spring and summer

Another of the very popular natives that have been
used extensively by landscape gardeners, this beautiful
shrub is difficult to better as a rockery or built-up bed
specimen. It tends to have a prostrate habit in full
sun, growing to 50 cm, with spreading branches up
to 1 m across. In shaded positions, the branches may
become tall and spindly. A dwarf form of *B. rubioides*,
var. *microphylla*, grows only to a height of 30 cm. A
hybrid between *B. rubioides* and *B. sessiliflora*, 'Ruby
Glow', is also available. All plants provide good pot
specimens. Flowers vary in colour from pure white
through delicate pinks to ruby red and petunia purple.
Double-flowered forms are occasionally seen. Good
watering is generally preferred to provide vigorous
growth. A range of soils appear to be suitable as long
as drainage is good. Sprigs of flowers last well in water
and are ideal in shallow bowls. A sunny position will
improve flowering.

Blandfordia grandiflora   N.S.W., Qld. Summer
Christmas Bell

The bell-shaped flowers of this species are on spikes
up to 50 cm long with as many as ten flowers on the
same stem. It is truly one of the most outstanding of
our native flowers. Dainty in appearance, it has grass-
like leaves up to 50 cm long and thick fibrous roots
which spread to form clumps of new leaves. Deep light
soil, free of lime, with a relatively even moisture
content is required. A sunny position is preferred.
Garden cultivation is not always easy but pot culture
provides an alternative.

Boronia ledifolia   N.S.W., Vic., Qld. Spring
Ledum Boronia; Sydney Boronia

One of the better-flowering species, *B. ledifolia* has
masses of large, deep pink, star-shaped flowers. Some
white flowering specimens have been reported. This
rounded shrub, growing to 1 m, has simple aromatic
leaves which appear in groups of three. As with most
of the *Boronia* species, a well-drained shaded position
with plenty of mulch is required to maintain a cool
root run.

Boronia mollis   N.S.W. Late winter to spring
Soft Boronia

This species has one of the longest flowering periods
of all *Boronia* species, with an abundance of deep pink
star-shaped flowers for several months. It grows as
a somewhat straggling shrub to 2 m with soft, hairy,
pinnate, highly aromatic leaves. Pruning after
flowering is recommended to maintain a bushy
attractive shape. Well-drained conditions and a cool
root run are recommended.

Boronia serrulata   N.S.W. Spring
Native Rose; Sydney Rock Rose

One of the most attractive of all the *Boronia* species,
the Native Rose is superb as a cut flower, especially
for small posies. The rather crowded vivid pink,
fragrant, cup-shaped flowers occur at the end of the
branches which carry rich green toothed rhomboidal-
shaped leaves. This small plant grows to about 1 m
and is a superb garden or pot specimen, provided well-
drained conditions exist.

Boronia 'Telopea Valley Star'   Cultivar. Spring

This plant is one of the many registered *Boronia*
cultivars. It has masses of star-shaped pink flowers
and grows as a handsome small shrub to 1.5 m. As
with all *Boronia* species, a well-drained and mulched
location in a semi-shaded position is necessary for
success.

Boronia pinnata   N.S.W. Spring and summer

This variable shrub generally grows to 1.5 m tall but
some forms with low spreading branches are in
cultivation. The pinnate, or feather-like, fragrant
leaves are rather thick and leathery. The dainty star-
like flowers vary in colour from deep pink to purple,
although the pink form is the most common. Multi-
petalled and white forms have been reported. Light
to medium soils and a semi-shaded position are
preferred.

Brachysema lanceolatum   W.A. Spring
Swan River Pea

Like the majority of Australian native plants, the Swan
River Pea likes well-drained positions. However it will
survive well under very dry conditions and is a
valuable garden plant for this reason. The bright red
pea flowers with silver calyces have a prominent keel
and are borne in clusters along the weeping stems.
This shrub, grows to 1 m high, but may spread to
2 to 3 m if sufficient space is available. However it
will also grow well in a limited space. The dark green
lanceolate leaves are silver on the underside and add
interest to this plant. A sunny position is preferred
and pruning is recommended to maintain an attractive
shape.

Callistemon brachyandrus N.S.W., Vic., S.A. Summer

In a well-drained location, this rounded shrub grows
to about 2.5 to 3 m high and makes a good
background plant. The small red flower brushes, 4
cm long, have yellow anthers. The long, pointed, dark
green leaves grow up to 4 cm long. This species will
withstand dry conditions. As with all *Callistemon*
species, a sunny position is preferred to enhance
flowering.

Brachychiton acerifolius   N.S.W., Qld. Autumn to
Illawarra Flame Tree   summer

One of the 12 species of the *Brachychiton* genus which
are all endemic to Australia, this large tree provides
an attractive display of red bell-shaped flowers. When
not flowering, the tree is evergreen with large, light
green leaves. Part or whole of the tree becomes
deciduous during the flowering period. Flowering
(often irregular) is from autumn through winter and
through to summer in some places. This tree grows
to 30 m and is hardy in most soils and aspects,
provided ample water is available. Growth may be
relatively slow in the early stages.

Callistemon chisholmii   Qld. May to August

The sparse, open habit of this little-known species distinguishes it from most other *Callistemon* species. It is found growing in sandstone areas along creek banks, is hardy and is well suited to a range of both dry and wet conditions. Growing to around 3 m tall and 1.5 m across, this sparse shrub has dark green, leathery leaves and dark red flower spikes up to 8 cm long and 3 cm diameter.

Callistemon citrinus (see also p. 64) N.S.W., Vic., Qld.
Crimson Bottlebrush   Spring
Lemon-Scented Bottlebrush

The bright red flower brushes of this form are popular with bees and small birds. The foliage is somewhat flat, stiff and dense. Pruning after flowering will maintain the appearance or yield an attractive hedge. The average height of this shrub is 2 m to 2.5 m, although shrubs up to 3 m are possible if one stem is retained and suitably trained. A semi-prostrate white flowering form, often sold under the name of *C. citrinus* 'Anzac', is also available.

Callistemon citrinus 'Briar Hill'   Cultivar.
September to December

Another of the flowering forms originating from *C. citrinus*, 'Briar Hill' grows to 3 m high with a spread of 3 m. It flowers profusely with red to purple flower spikes up to 12 cm long. The new foliage growth is light pink.

Callistemon linearis   N.S.W. Spring and summer
Narrow-Leaf Bottlebrush

This spreading shrub, growing to 2.5 m has rather stiff narrow leaves about 2 mm wide and up to 10 cm long. The red brushes are up to 15 cm long. They are showy and abundant and attractive to birds. The narrow leaves provide an attractive variation to the broader leaves of the other *Callistemon* species. This shrub will survive in somewhat heavy soils in a warm moist position in the garden.

Callistemon citrinus 'Harkness';   Cultivar.
'Gawler Hybrid'   September to December

Originating as a garden hybrid from Gawler in S.A., this shrub is probably one of the most attractive and widely grown garden species of recent years. Unlike its parent, *C. citrinus*, this hybrid has most attractive soft foliage with flowers which are generally larger (up to 25 cm long). As with most *Callistemon*, regular trimming will maintain an attractive form. The flowers are most attractive in floral arrangements. Propagation from cuttings is essential to preserve the hybrid form.

Callistemon citrinus 'Reeves Pink'   Cultivar.
September to December

This seedling arising from *C. citrinus* has attractive pink flower spikes to 10 cm long with gold anthers. The flowers generally occur in profusion in clusters. This form grows to around 3 m high with a similar spread.

Callistemon pachyphyllus (see also p. 52)   N.S.W.,
Wallum Bottlebrush   Qld. Spring and autumn

This somewhat uncommon salmon pink form of *C. pachyphyllus* is an attractive variation to the usual dark red or green forms, and grows to 1.5 m high and 1.5 m across.

Callistemon phoeniceus   W.A. Summer
Fiery, or Lesser Bottlebrush

Although a native of W.A., *C. phoeniceus* has adapted well to a range of conditions as shown by this beautiful specimen which has grown to a height of 4.5 m in a relatively dry clay area near Newcastle in N.S.W. It is a tall bushy shrub with dark green leaves and beautiful scarlet flowers with yellow tips.

Callistemon polandii   Qld. Summer

This large bushy shrub is ideal for coastal areas of eastern Australia where some protection from heavy frosts is available. It grows to 4 m high with a spread of 3 m and has elliptical leaves. The dark red flowers, 10 cm long and 5 cm in diameter, are tipped with yellow anthers.

Callistemon subulatus   N.S.W., Vic. Summer

An attractive shrub with many branches, *C. subulatus* has fine leaves up to 5 cm long and red flower spikes up to 6 cm long. Another of the species which grows along river banks, this slightly pendulous shrub is very adaptable to a wide range of garden conditions and locations. Regular pruning after flowering will maintain a compact specimen.

Callistemon viminalis   N.S.W., Qld. Spring
Weeping Bottlebrush

This tall bushy shrub has most attractive weeping willowy branches which are covered with scarlet-red flowers. The leaves are generally narrower than *C. citrinus*. Very old trees, like the specimen shown, can reach a height of 5 m to 6 m with a spread of 3 m to 5 m. However, the majority of garden specimens will normally only reach 3 m over a few years. Regular pruning is recommended to maintain a bushy appearance.

Callistemon viminalis 'Bob Bailey'   Cultivar.
August to October

This cultivar originated from seed collected from a cultivated plant at the Heatley State Primary School in Queensland. It is similar in shape to *C. viminalis*, growing to 5 m tall by 3 m wide. The light pink flowers appear in dense open spikes, 10 to 16 cm long by 6 cm in diameter. This species has proved to be drought tolerant in Townsville. Severe frosts may cause damage to new tip growth.

Callistemon viminalis 'Captain Cook'   Cultivar.
Spring

This cultivar is a hardy dwarf weeping shrub growing to 1.5 m and has masses of bright red brushes. It is a very useful shrub for gardens where small plants are required. Most soil conditions and locations are suitable, although severe frosts should be avoided.

Calothamnus quadrifidus   W.A. Spring to summer
One-Sided Bottlebrush; Net-Bush

The *Calothamnus* genus has unusual flowers which are generally borne on old wood and are often hidden within the foliage. This species is the most common and hardiest of the genus. Well-drained open sunny positions are best for these plants. This upright species has grey-green, pine-like leaves covered in fine hairs. The long flower spikes consist of bundles of deep red stamens on one side of the woody stem, often all year round. Some forms have creamy-yellow flowers but these are not common in cultivation. It grows to about 2 m and will tolerate dry conditions. A prostrate form is also available.

Callistemon viminalis 'Hanna Ray' Cultivar. Spring
Another of the adaptable cultivars of *C. viminalis*, this shrub grows to 3 m and has attractive weeping branches which are covered in masses of scarlet brushes. It makes a good garden specimen.

Calothamnus villosus   W.A. Spring to summer
Silky Net-Bush

Although confined naturally to W.A., this species is a relatively hardy one which has been grown with reasonable success in the eastern states. The red flowers usually grow along one side of the stem and the stamens are united into bundles. This plant is soft and bushy. The hairy pin-like leaves provide most attractive foliage which can be useful in a hedge. It will generally grow to around 3 m under a wide range of conditions but an open sunny position provides the best flowering conditions. The flowers are attractive to birds.

Callistemon viminalis 'Little John' Cultivar. Spring
A dwarf *Callistemon* cultivar, this small shrub only grows to about 1 m and has attractive grey-green leaves and dark red brushes. It is a valuable plant for small rockery beds or pots.

Ceratopetalum gummiferum (see also p. 78)   N.S.W.
N.S.W. Christmas Bush   Summer
This is a favourite among gardeners in the eastern states. It prefers a well-drained sandy loam, although excellent specimens have been grown in heavy clay soils where reasonable drainage exists. An open sunny position results in cream flowers, which open from November onwards. As each flower dies, its calyx enlarges and turns red and papery looking, with four to five sepals. Each flower contains a single seed which falls when ripe. Trimming can be carried out following the flowering season to maintain fresh new growth and subsequent flowers in the next season. The flowers and calyces are excellent for indoors and have long been used by nurserymen and florists as a popular Christmas cut flower. Excessive water can result in root rot and should be avoided. This shrub will readily reach a height of 3 m in 4 to 5 years.

Chamelaucium uncinatum (see also p. 65) W.A. Spring
Geraldton Wax

The pale pink and red flowering forms of this W.A. shrub are most attractive and useful as cut flowers. It is commonly cultivated in the eastern states where well-drained conditions are available. The fine needle-like foliage adds to the masses of flowers during spring. Garden specimens will grow to a height of 2 m to 3 m. The flowers are excellent for floral arrangements and last well.

Correa decumbens   S.A. Summer

All of the *Correa* species are ideal garden specimens as they are adaptable to a wide range of conditions and will flower in shaded positions, a feature which is not common to many other native plants. This species grows as a spreading semi-prostrate plant up to 3 m across with narrow dark green leaves, and narrow red and green tubular flowers. These flowers have yellow tips and usually appear in an upturned fashion. Well-drained, moist locations are preferred by this plant which can provide a useful rockery specimen.

Chorizema cordatum   W.A. Spring

Typical of the pea-flowered family, this plant is widely grown in gardens for its bright red or yellow flowers in spring. The flowers may vary, with shades of pink and orange. In garden cultivation, this species grows under a wide range of conditions, but prefers a protected, partly shaded and well-drained environment. It grows to a height of 1 m and the leaves are somewhat heart-shaped with toothed edges. It is also excellent for a pot specimen.

Correa 'Dusky Bells' Cultivar. March to September

This cultivar, originating from *C. pulchella* and *C. reflexa* has proven itself as an adaptable and most useful rockery specimen after many years of cultivation, sometimes under different names. Growing to around 75 cm tall and 2 m across, this small shrub has many branches with dull green leaves 3.5 cm long by 2 cm wide. The tubular flowers are pale carmine-pink, up to 4 cm long. This plant prefers part shade.

Clianthus formosus N.S.W., Qld., S.A., W.A., N.T.
Sturt's Desert Pea   Spring and summer

South Australia's floral emblem, Sturt's Desert Pea is one of Australia's most outstanding and famous flowers. It grows as a procumbent spreading annual, or in some areas as a perennial, with soft greyish pinnate leaves and red pea-shaped flowers with a prominent black boss, or bump, in the middle. The flowers are held on erect peduncles. Very good drainage is required in full sun. This plant is not easy to cultivate unless special care is taken to provide a deep sandy location. It has a long tap root and plants are best grown from seed in the final location. Some success has been achieved using an earthenware drainpipe filled with sandy soil. In such a location it provides a most interesting cascading plant.

Correa reflexa (see also p. 53)   All states.
Native Fuchsia   Autumn to spring

The red-flowering form of this attractive rockery species has a green cap and yellow-tipped stamens. This species has 20 or more forms, including various natural hybrids with *C. alba*, *C. decurrens* and *C. pulchella*. It is a hardy plant and worthy of a place in any garden.

Correa reflexa var. *reflexa*   NSW. Autumn to spring

This is an attractive large red-flowering variety with a green edge at the end of the bell-shaped flowers. It grows to 50 cm and is an excellent rockery specimen. Pruning after flowering will maintain a compact shape and provide increased new growth and subsequent flowers.

Crowea 'Festival'   Cultivar. Most of the year

One of the best of the *Crowea* cultivars, this neat small shrub, growing to 50 cm, has small narrow leaves and masses of pink flowers for many months of the year. It is a superb form for cut flowers which last for long periods indoors. This plant is ideal as a rockery specimen or as a pot plant. Pruning is recommended to maintain a bushy appearance. A well-drained, sunny position is desirable with a cool root run, although flowering will still occur in a shaded position.

Crowea saligna   N.S.W. Summer and autumn
Lance-Leaf Crowea

Growing naturally in sandstone areas of N.S.W., this small shrub reaches a height of 1m with a similar spread, although garden specimens tend to be somewhat smaller. The deep green leaves are aromatic and elliptical in shape. The star-shaped flowers are deep pink and have a waxy appearance. This species grows best on a well-drained slope with filtered sunlight from larger protective shrubs. A cool root run is important. It can be pruned quite heavily for cut flowers after flowering. The bush will shoot readily and remain compact.

Darwinia citriodora   W.A. Winter to summer
Lemon-Scented Myrtle

This native of W.A. grows to a height of 1 to 1.5 m with a similar spread, forming a somewhat rounded shrub. The leaves are most attractive and provide excellent greenery for indoor decoration. The leaves colour during winter with traces of purple-red. When crushed between the fingers, a pleasant lemon scent is given off. The blooms are not particularly striking. This shrub grows quite profusely and prefers a warm position. The plant shown has grown to a height of 1 m over 3 years in a clay soil built up with a small addition of sandy loam. Reasonable drainage results from the slope of the garden.

Dendrobium tetragonium   N.S.W., Qld. September
Tree Spider Orchid   and October

Another of the epiphytic orchids, this species has semi-pendulous stems which are long and wiry with a tetragonal shape. The broad leaves are sometimes twisted and up to 8 cm long. The spidery flowers are variable in colour, greenish-yellow with brown, red or purple. This plant provides an unusual specimen and is best grown on a small piece of tree branch or cork.

Diplolaena angustifolia   W.A. Winter and spring
Yanchep Rose; Native Rose

The *Diplolaena* genus is related to the *Boronia* genus but only has 4 species, all restricted to W.A. The flowers are aggregated into dense pendant heads up to 3.5 cm across and are surrounded by 3 or 4 series of green overlapping bracts. The stamens range in colour from crimson to pale orange. It grows naturally in the limestone areas around Yanchep and therefore prefers an alkaline soil. This small bushy shrub grows to 1.5 m. It has adapted well to cultivation in the eastern states in a semi-shaded position with very good drainage.

Eremophila glabra   N.S.W., Qld, Vic., S.A.,
Common Emu-Bush;   W.A., N.T.
Fuchsia Bush; Tar Bush   August to March

Many forms of this variable and widespread species
are available. Most of these have adapted well to
cultivation, provided drainage is adequate. A sunny
location is preferred to stimulate flowering. This small
shrub grows to 1.5 m, with tubular flowers up to 3
cm long. Flower colour can vary from orange or red,
to green or yellow. The leaves, up to 5 cm long, are
alternate and generally elliptical with pointed tips.

Epacris impressa   N.S.W., Vic., S.A., Tas.
Common Heath   Most of the year

The Common Heath is the floral emblem of Victoria.
It tends to have a straggly habit, reaching 1 m in
height. The dark green leaves have sharp points and
the tubular flowers appear all the way along the stem
to create a most attractive feature. Flower colour varies
from white to red, with the red form being most
outstanding. A very well-drained but moist soil is
required with a generous supply of mulch to maintain
a cool root run. A semi-shaded position is preferable.
Garden cutivation of the *Epacris* genus is not easy,
but the results are well worth the effort.

Epacris longiflora   N.S.W. Most of the year
Native Fuchsia

This somewhat straggly but robust shrub is slightly
branched and suited to a small rockery where drainage
is very good and moist well-mulched conditions can
be maintained. It grows to 1 m with heart-shaped
leaves which are sharp and pointed. The beautiful
crimson bell-shaped flowers have white tips and
appear along the branches. This is another of our truly
outstanding native flowers.

Eremophila longifolia   N.S.W., Qld., Vic.,
Berrigan; Emu-Bush   S.A., W.A., N.T.
                            July to December

Although a tree form of this species exists, it is rarely
seen in its natural setting. The species is widespread
throughout Australia and grows in almost all
conditions, although a relatively well-drained, sunny
position is preferable for garden cultivation where it
will grow to 2 m high and 1.5m across. It has rough
dark grey bark and pendulous branches with dull
green pointed leaves of variable size, up to 20 cm
long. The tubular flowers vary in colour from pink to
reddish brown or brick-red and are hairy on the
outside.

Eremophila maculata (see also p. 43) N.S.W., Vic., S.A.
Spotted Emu Bush   Spring and summer

The orange-red colour form of this species is usually
prolific during the flowering season. It is quite hardy
as long as good drainage is available. The group of
plants illustrated have grown to a height of 80 cm over
a period of 4 years and provide a valuable addition
to this built-up bed area.

Eriostemon australasius   N.S.W., Qld.
Pink Wax Flower   Late winter and spring

This attractive shrub grows as an erect plant to 1 m
high with narrow elliptical leaves and many large pink
star-shaped flowers which have a waxy appearance.
They are excellent cut flowers and are long lasting.
The natural environment for this species is in deep
sand, often in semi-shaded positions. Similar
conditions are required for garden cultivation as it can
be somewhat difficult to maintain for long periods.
Mulch around the roots helps to maintain a constant
temperature. Pruning after flowering is necessary to
maintain a compact plant.

Eucalyptus caesia 'Silver Princess' (see also p. 74)
W.A. Winter and Spring

This registered cultivar of *E. caesia* has a most attractive weeping habit with grey-green foliage and larger pink-red flowers which hang in loose clusters from the white-grey stems. The bud caps are grey and the large silver-grey fruits which immediately follow the flowers are sought after for interior decoration. This tree will grow to about 8 m and requires a well-drained location. It is adaptable to a wide range of soils.

Eucalyptus ficifolia   W.A. Summer
Red Flowering Gum

Another of the internationally known native trees, this rough-barked eucalypt grows to around 10 m and has spectacular brilliant red flowerheads. Other coloured forms ranging from white to salmon and pink are common, although unfortunately the colour is not known until flowering occurs. It normally has a dense crown with large dark green leaves. A very well-drained frost-free location is essential. Although some success has been achieved with coastal plantings, this tree has not enjoyed universal success as a garden tree in many parts of N.S.W.

Eucalyptus lansdowneana   S.A. Winter

A small spreading tree, growing to 5 m with a mallee appearance, *E. lansdowneana* has slender stems with pink or red flowers clustered around them. A well-drained sunny position is desirable for this small tree.

Eucalyptus leucoxylon 'Rosea' S.A. May to September

The pink-flowering form of the Yellow Gum or *E. leucoxylon* is commonly available under this name. It is an attractive small tree reaching around 9 m under moist conditions and has rich pink flowers over a long period. It is a hardy tree for most areas and provides a valuable small specimen for many gardens.

Eucalyptus macrocarpa   W.A. Winter
Mottlecah; Rose of the West

Another of the gems of W.A., the Rose of the West has truly outstanding flowers. Red and among the largest of all the eucalypts, they reach up to 10 cm in diameter. The large leathery leaves are silvery-grey and enclose the flowers along the sprawling branches. This mallee-type tree only grows to about 3 m. The woody fruits which follow the flowers are also quite large and attractive. It is not easy to maintain in cultivation, particularly in the eastern states, and requres a very well-drained light soil in a dry location.

Eucalyptus ptychocarpa   W.A., N.T. Winter

A small or medium-size tree, *E. ptychocarpa* has large deep green leaves and large clusters of red, or in some cases white, flowers in profusion. The tree does not always grow into a handsome shape, but nevertheless is well worthwhile trying in locations where good drainage and full sun are available. It is not commonly grown in the eastern states, but is grown very widely in the Brisbane area. It grows to 10 m and has large urn-shaped fruits.

Eucalyptus sideroxylon (see also p. 84) N.S.W., Qld., Mugga; Red Ironbark   Vic. Winter to summer

This species of ironbark has the hardiest, most deeply furrowed and blackest bark of the *Eucalypt* genus. It occurs naturally in areas with a rainfall of 30 cm to 60 cm a year, characterised by high summer temperatures. Growing in such a climate, with poor shallow soils, it is obviously a tough tree. However it is also quite an attractive tree in cultivation with its almost black bark and soft grey-green foliage. The pink and red-flowering forms are paticularly attractive, although white and cream forms are also quite common. This tree is adaptable to a wide range of locations and conditions, growing to 15 m after many years. These two specimens illustrate the attractiveness of this species as a street tree away from power lines.

Graptophyllum excelsum   Qld. Summer

The deep red, tubular flowers of this erect shrub, which grows to 3 m high, provide a most attractive display during summer. It is also an outstanding foliage plant, with its dark green shiny obovate leaves. A well-composted soil and a semi-shaded position in the garden are desirable.

Grevillea alpina (see also p. 36) N.S.W., Vic., A.C.T. Mountain Grevillea   Winter to summer

The Mountain Grevillea varies in habit from a semi-prostrate plant to a shrub reaching 1 m in height. The leaves may be rounded or linear and the pink, red, orange or yellow flowers appear as terminal clusters. The spidery flowers often have yellow tips. Flowering generally occurs over long periods and most forms of this species grow well under most garden conditions and are frost tolerant.

Grevillea aquifolium   Vic., S.A. Winter to spring
Variable Prickly Grevillea

The large dull grey-green holly-like leaves of this hardy spreading or upright plant create an attractive appearance among other taller garden shrubs or trees. The toothbrush flowers are bright red and like most grevillea flowers attract many birds to the garden. It is a hardy plant under most garden conditions with reasonable drainage and is resistant to frosts.

Grevillea aspera   S.A. Spring

Although tall, upright forms of this species exist, it generally grows as a compact shrub to 1 m, with beautiful cream and red flowers which occur in a tight pendant cluster. This flower was photographed at the Adelaide Botanic Gardens, and although the species is not in common cultivation, it has been grown in the eastern states where good drainage exists.

Grevillea aspleniifolia   N.S.W. Most of the year

This is one of the larger *Grevillea* species suitable for garden use and can grow to 3 m tall and have a spread of up to 4 m. The leaves are long and narrow and the red toothbrush flowers appear in profusion in spring but persist almost all year. Pruning will assist in maintaining a bushy, more compact shrub. This shrub is ideal for cold, frosty areas and requires a well-drained soil. Most soils are suitable.

Grevillea 'Australflora McDonald Park'   Cultivar.
Spring

The parents of this hybrid are *G. rosmarinifolia* and
G. alpina. It is an attractive low-growing plant to 20
cm tall and up to 1 m across. It has red and yellow
flowers which appear in clusters. The narrow leaves
are up to 2 cm long.

Grevillea barklyana N.S.W., Vic. Spring and summer
This species has two forms, growing either as a tall
tree to 8 m with broad-lobed leaves (Gippsland form),
or as a spreading shrub to 2 m high (Jervis Bay form)
with light green leathery oval leaves. The toothbrush
flowers of both forms have a mid-pink colour which
quickly fades as the flowers age. The tall form tolerates
some shade and moisture, whereas the smaller form
prefers a well-drained sunny position. The new foliage
has attractive red tips.

Grevillea baueri   N.S.W. Winter and spring
Occurring naturally along the N.S.W. coast and in
the Blue Mountains area, this dense attractive low
shrub has several forms varying from prostrate to 1
m tall. The leaves are dark green, crowded and often
waxy. The flowers are usually dark pink and white
and are borne in 3 cm to 4 cm clusters. This is a hardy
attractive rockery plant in cooler or non humid areas
and is frost hardy. The flowers will turn black in very
humid areas.

Grevillea banksii (see also p. 67)   Qld. Most of the year
Red Silky Oak

The red-flowering form of this popular grevillea is a favourite with many honey-eating birds and grows to
a height of 3 m with a spread of 2.5 m. The tubular flowers appear most of the year. This form of the species
is known as var. *forsteri*. *G. banksii* is normally a much taller shrub and only flowers during spring. This shrub
is tolerant of most conditions as long as reasonable drainage is available. The flowers are excellent for floral
arrangements.

Grevillea bipinnatifida   W.A. Winter and spring
Grape Grevillea

This prickly species from W.A. is the parent of many
handsome hybrids, including *G.* 'Robyn Gordon' and
G. 'Ned Kelly'. It also has several forms from the
prostrate form to the larger shrub reaching up to 2
m tall. The foliage can be bright green to grey-green
and the leaves are divided into many segments. The
early large toothbrush flowers are pendulous and
yellowish but colour to deep red with maturity. These
flowers can grow to 10 cm long. Regular pruning is
required to maintain a bushy appearance. It is a hardy
plant, provided drainage is good. The unusual foliage
is particularly attractive.

Grevillea 'Bonnie Prince Charlie'   Cultivar.
Spring and summer

Although the parents of this cultivar are not certain,
the flowers and growing habit are similar to those of
G. 'Australflora McDonald Park'. The red and yellow
flowers are quite striking and this plant makes an
excellent rockery or tub specimen, growing to around
50 cm tall and 50 cm across. The broad linear leaves
are up to 2 cm long. Propagation by cutting is essential
and a well-drained soil is preferred.

Grevillea 'Boongala Spinebill'   Cultivar.
                                        Spring and summer

A hybrid, probably between *G. bipinnatifida* and *G. caleyi*, this grevillea grows to 2 m high with a spread of 2 m as a dense shrub with narrow divided leaves to 12 cm long. New leaf growth is reddish-pink. The large dark red toothbrush flowers are attractive to honeyeaters. This is probably the hardiest of all the *Grevillea* genus for garden cultivation but has not been widely recognised.

Grevillea confertifolia   Vic. Spring

This small spreading shrub reaches a height of only 15 cm with a spread of 1 m and has beautiful mauve-pink terminal clusters of spider flowers which show up against the dark green fine foliage. It normally grows in the Grampian ranges at high altitude, and although not common in cultivation should be adaptable as a rockery specimen in a well-drained position where a ready supply of water is available.

Grevillea brachystylis   W.A. Spring and summer

The dazzling red flowers of this species have a very short black-tipped style and occur in spidery clusters along a stalk of 6 to 9 flowers. This small shrub grows to 60 cm tall with hairy narrow leaves to 6 cm long. Very good drainage is required and although several specimens have been seen by the authors in gardens along the east coast, it is often difficult to maintain these plants for long periods of time. However it is a plant worth trying, even as a tub specimen.

Grevillea dimorpha   Vic. Winter and spring
Flame Grevillea

This quick-growing heavy-textured species has two distinctive forms, each with distinctive leaves. Both forms grow to 1 m high and are well suited to most soils with good drainage. One form has broad dark green leaves with a silky underside, whereas the other has long narrow leaves. The bright red flowers appear in large clusters along the stem and are more prominent in the narrow-leaved form. This species is frost resistant and prefers a sheltered position. Both forms are shown for comparison.

Grevillea caleyi   N.S.W. Winter to summer
Caley's Grevillea

Another of the large spreading *Grevillea* species, this shrub makes an attractive specimen in gardens where ample space is available. It grows to 3 m high with a spread of up to 4 m, with soft, hairy fishbone-shaped leaves up to 15 cm long. The branches droop and tend to grow almost horizontally. The cherry-red to purple styles provide colour on the toothbrush flowers which are 4 to 5 cm long. The shrub is very attractive when the new bright pink foliage occurs. Cultivation is not easy unless very good drainage is provided. It likes plenty of water and an open sunny position. The species is frost tolerant.

Grevillea dryandri   N.T., W.A., Qld. Autumn and
Dryander's Grevillea   winter

An attractive hummock-forming shrub, *G. dryandri* is easily recognised by its striking flowers held on long stalks. As well as red, the flowers may also be apricot in colour. Its immature seed pods are covered in sticky resin which is often foraged by ants. The fishbone-type leaves are lime green. This shrub requires perfect drainage and is not often seen in cultivation, however.plants grafted onto *G. robusta* have proven to be quite hardy in cultivation. Grafting techniques show a lot of promise for difficult species such as *G. dryandri* and are worth a try by the adventurous gardener.

Grevillea 'Frampton's Hybrid'   Cultivar.
                                          Spring and summer

Although a somewhat scruffy tall shrub to 3 m, the red toothbrush flowers and dark green twisted or bent leaves of this hybrid make it interesting as a garden shrub. It is a hybrid between *G. barklyana* and *G. aspleniifolia* (or *G. longifolia*). Well-drained conditions and an open sunny position appear to be desirable for this species.

Grevillea gaudichaudii Cultivar. Spring and summer

Although not as hardy as one of the other superb grevillea groundcovers, *G.* 'Poorinda Royal Mantle', this species is more attractive both in leaf and flower colour. It is a spectacular natural hybrid between *G. laurifolia* and *G. acanthifolia* with deep purple-red toothbrush flowers. The leaves have several prickly lobes with beautiful red new growth. A spread of several metres can easily be achieved in 2 to 3 years. A well-drained, open sunny position is desirable for this excellent rockery or bank groundcover. It is also frost resistant.

Grevillea hookerana   W.A. Spring to summer
Toothbrush Grevillea

There are a number of forms of this species and flowerheads may vary considerably. The toothbrush flowers are typical of many *Grevillea* species and grow up to 50 to 75 mm long on branches bearing narrow light green divided leaves 50 to 75 mm long. This is one of the outstanding ornamental windbreak or hedge species. It is very hardy, growing up to 2.5 m high and 3 m across, but requires good drainage. The flowers attract many honeyeaters and are attractive in indoor arrangements.

Grevillea ilicifolia (see also p. 54) N.S.W., Vic., S.A.
Holly Grevillea   Spring to summer

The red mature flowers of this spreading, slow-growing shrub make it an attractive addition to a garden rockery or as a garden specimen on its own. Some forms grow to 2 m high and 2 m across, although some prostrate forms rarely exceed 50 cm in height. The stiff pointed-lobed leaves are covered with fine, silky hairs. A light well-drained soil in a sunny, damp position is preferable.

Grevillea 'Ivanhoe'   Cultivar. July to November

Probably a hybrid of *G. caleyi* and *G. aspleniifolia* or *G. longifolia*, this species is one of the best of all screening grevilleas, although it may be blown over in very strong winds when young. It reaches an average height of 3 to 5 m with a spread of 2 to 3 m and has attractive light green foliage with burgundy new growth. The pink to red toothbrush flowers appear mainly from July to November but there may be some for most of the year. This excellent shrub is resistant to frosts, drought and high humidity. Pruning is recommended to maintain a bushy specimen.

Grevillea johnsonii   N.S.W. Spring

Similar to *G. longistyla*, this is a most attractive plant with cherry-red and white spider flowers which appear in forks in the small branches near the tips of new growth. It grows to 3 m tall with 20 cm long fishbone-type leaves, finely divided. A very well-drained, sunny location is necessary for cultivation in the garden. It is not recommended for humid areas.

Grevillea juniperina   N.S.W. Most of the year
Prickly Spider Flower

The prostrate form of this grevillea provides a tough, almost flat groundcover of angular branches with narrow, prickly leaves. They are studded with yellow-ochre to orange-red flowers. This spreading plant grows to a width of 3 m over 2 to 3 years and is hardy in most garden situations.

Grevillea longistyla   Qld. Winter to summer

This species is often confused with *G. johnsonii* as it has similar flowers, although they are generally larger. The narrow bright green leaves are 15 to 25 cm long and are often divided into 3 or more segments. The red waxy flowers appear as erect cylindrical spikes and are attractive to many nectar-feeding birds. This shrub grows to 3 m tall and requires a well-drained frost-free sunny location.

Grevillea lanigera   N.S.W., Vic. Spring

The narrow grey leaves of this somewhat variable prostrate or low-growing shrub distinguish this species from many of the other *Grevillea* species with the more familiar green foliage. It has an open texture and the red and cream flowers are borne in small spider clusters. The prostrate form with its soft foliage is one of the most attractive of all the grevillea groundcovers and will spread to 2 m over a period of 3 years. Almost any soil or location is suitable for this under-utilised plant.

Grevillea 'Misty Pink'   Cultivar. Most of the year

Growing to a height of 2 to 3 m with a spread of 1.5 m to 2 m, this hybrid between *G. banksii* and *G. sessilis* is one of the more attractive of the recently introduced hybrids. The large pale pink flowers with cream styles appear in large erect heads up to 15 cm long. It is a vigorous shrub and deserves widespread use as a garden specimen particularly as it tolerates most soils in warmer areas where frosts do not occur. The silver-green leaves are soft and divided with many narrow lobes. Pruning is recommended to retain a bushy appearance and to encourage flowers. Young plants need to be protected from strong winds as they can be easily blown over. The flowers are superb for floral arrangements.

Grevillea lavandulacea   N.S.W., Vic. S.A.
                                              Most of the year

Although this species has variable growth habits and flower colours, the foliage has an attractive grey-green colour which provides contrast to other dark green plants. The red flowers of the excellent specimen seen here growing with *Correa reflexa* in the background outside the Penfolds Winery at Nuriootpa, in the Barossa Valley, South Australia, highlight the beauty of this species. It generally grows to around 1 m tall with a spread of up to 2 m, although some low-growing, compact forms are also available. The species has proven to be hardy in most well-drained, sunny positions.

Grevillea 'Ned Kelly'   Cultivar. Most of the year
(Mason's Hybrid)

This plant has similar parents to *G.* 'Robyn Gordon' (*G. banksii* and *G. bipinnatifida*), but is a little taller, growing up to 2 m. The large flowers are orange-red and appear all year round. The large leaves are light green and are divided into soft fern-like lobes. Well-drained conditions are preferable. Regular pruning will encourage fresh growth and profuse flowering. Along with *G.* 'Robyn Gordon', this plant is highly recommended for pride of place in any home garden.

Grevillea pilosa   W.A. Winter to summer

This stiff, slightly prickly shrub grows to 50 cm high and 1 m to 1.5 m across, with grey-green leaves on arching branches. The brownish, hairy buds open to pink or red hairy flowers. This tough shrub provides a showy display in well-drained soils. It is tolerant of both frosts and hot, dry conditions.

Grevillea 'Poorinda Royal Mantle'   Cultivar.
                                      Spring and summer

This delightful prostrate groundcover is apparently a hybrid between *G. laurifolia* and *G. willisii*. It has long stems which can spread up to 4 m to 6 m, as shown in the illustration. The leaves are generally lobed with pointed tips, and between 60 and 70 mm long by about 20 mm wide. The upper surface is smooth and dark green while the underside is grey with a dense covering of silky hairs. The red toothbrush flowers cover the plant in spring and summer. This cultivar makes an excellent specimen to cover a bank or a built-up area and will tolerate a range of soils and frosty conditions.

Grevillea 'Pink Surprise' Cultivar. Most of the year

With similar flowers to *G.* 'Misty Pink', this species grows to a very much taller shrub, often reaching 6 m high. The spectacular flowers, up to 15 cm long, appear on the upper parts of the tree, sometimes out of view or reach. The fishbone-type leaves are 30 cm long with many fine lobes. The flowers are a light pink inside and a silvery pink outside with light yellow styles. It is a rapid-growing shrub and needs protection from winds. Well-drained conditions and a sunny location are desirable. Pruning will assist in restricting the height of this highly recommended shrub. This plant is a registered hybrid between an undescribed species from Munduberra and Coochin Hills and *G. banksii*.

Grevillea rivularis   N.S.W. Most of the year
Carrington Falls Grevillea

As the common name indicates, this grevillea comes from a rather restricted area near the Carrington Falls in N.S.W. The pale pink to greenish-lilac toothbrush-type flowers are one-sided and about 4 cm long. It has often been called the 'blue-flowering grevillea' because of the lilac-coloured flower form. This rather prickly shrub grows to 2 m high with a spread of up to 3 m, with rigid and spiny divided leaves. It is a rapid-growing, hardy plant, tolerant of shaded conditions and most soil types.

Grevillea 'Poorinda Peter' Cultivar. Spring to summer

In some respects, this hybrid between *G. acanthifolia* and *G. aspleniifolia* or *G. longifolia*, is similar to *G.* 'Ivanhoe' although it is a lower-growing shrub, reaching only 2 to 3 m. The deep red flowers appear in clusters 5 to 6 cm long and the leaves are 15 cm long with many sharp saw-tooth lobes. Like *G.* 'Ivanhoe', this species is a useful screen or large hedge plant for well-drained areas. Full sun is preferred to produce profuse flowering.

Grevillea 'Robyn Gordon' Cultivar. Most of the year

Probably one of the most outstanding and popular native plants, this grevillea is a natural hybrid between *G. bipinnatifida* and *G. banksii*. This cultivar received its name from Mr David Gordon (in whose garden the hybrid appeared) in memory of his daughter who died tragically in 1969 at the age of 16. It is interesting to note that all plants now in existence are progeny of the original cuttings distributed by Mr Gordon, which demonstrates the way in which native species can be developed and re-established to protect endangered species if sufficient interest is taken. *G.* 'Robyn Gordon' is a prolific flowerer with individual flowers reaching up to 20 cm in length. The buds are carmine rose and the mature flowers crimson. It is a low sprawling shrub reaching a height of 1.5 m with a spread of 2 to 3m. This hybrid will grow under a wide range of conditions and has become very widespread in home and public gardens. It provides excellent year-round cut flowers and should be grown in every garden either as a single specimen, as a hedge or along a fence.

Grevillea rosmarinifolia   N.S.W., Vic. August to
Rosemary Grevillea   December

Although there are many forms of this species, the
branches generally tend to be almost horizontal and
sprawling with sharp, stiff, narrow leaves. The larger
forms grow to 2 to 3 m high and 3 m wide, and
although a number of smaller dwarf forms exist they
are not as hardy as the tall forms. The flowers are
normally rosy-red with a white spot on the anther lobe.
Cream and deeper red flowering forms also exist. This
species is a particularly hardy native and will readily
grow in a range of soils and conditions. It is well suited
for a hedge or fence cover and is widely cultivated.

Grevillea sericea   N.S.W. Most of the year
Pink Spider Flower

The narrow dark green leaves of this small erect shrub
bear white to deep pink spider flowers in erect clusters.
It is a most desirable garden specimen and likes a well-
drained, sunny position. Regular pruning is required
to maintain a bushy specimen. It grows to around 1.5
m and is frost tolerant. A deep pink flowering form
from the Collaroy Plateau is available in some
nurseries and is recommended as a garden plant.

Grevillea 'Shirley Howie' Cultivar. Winter and spring
This hybrid of *G. capitellata* and *G. sericea* is a very
popular garden specimen in Brisbane, although it will
readily grow in other relatively warm areas where
good drainage is available. It has dark green glossy
leaves and is covered in deep pink heads of spider
flowers. The flowers are most attractive in floral
arrangements. Pruning is desirable to retain a bushy
specimen. It is tolerant of frosts and suitable for coastal
plantings where protection from winds is provided.

Grevillea 'Sid Cadwell'   Cultivar. Most of the year
Although this hybrid has attractive deep red
toothbrush flowers, it is subject to root rot in some
areas. The prickly narrow divided leaves are up to
7 cm long and occur on horizontal spreading branches
with an overall spread of around 2 m. It reaches a
height of 1 to 2 m. Very well-drained conditions are
essential for this species.

Grevillea speciosa   N.S.W., Vic., Qld. Spring
Red Spider Flower

Previously known as *G. punicea*, this species is very
attractive and well worth a place in the garden. It
grows into an erect, leafy bush with round terminal
clusters of smooth red flowers with long spreading
styles. The leaves are dark green on top and paler
underneath. The specimen shown has grown well in
an open, reasonably moist position in a built-up
garden bed with a clay base. Good drainage is
necessary. It can grow to a height of 3 m over several
years.

Grevillea steiglitziana   Vic. Winter and spring
From the stony Brisbane Ranges in Victoria, this
spreading plant has dark green holly-like prickly leaves
which are woolly underneath. The deep red and green
toothbrush flowers appear in pendant clusters. As
shown by this specimen in the authors' garden, this
small shrub is suitable as a rockery plant or fence
cover. It is a hardy species and will withstand dry
periods, but reasonable drainage is preferred.

Grevillea thelemanniana   W.A. Winter and spring

A hardy plant from W.A. with a long flowering period, *G. thelemanniana* is a most attractive species, although it is not often seen in gardens in the eastern states. Several forms ranging in height from 1 m to low spreading groundcovers are available. The groundcover forms may have grey leaves and dark red toothbrush flowers or lime green leaves with lighter-coloured flowers. The leaves are slightly prickly. This species appears to be tolerant of a range of soils but is not suited to frosty conditions.

Grevillea tripartita   W.A. Winter and spring

The attractive erect sharp grey leaves of this species and the large showy red and yellow flowers along the branches make it a desirable plant for the home garden. This frost-resistant species grows to 2.5 m high and requires a well-drained, sunny, dry position.

Grevillea victoriae   N.S.W., Vic.
Royal Grevillea   Winter and spring

The leaves of this species are most unusual for a grevillea. They are grey-green on the top with a silvery underside and resemble camellia leaves. The pendant clusters of rusty-red flowers occur throughout the foliage and last for several weeks. The flower buds also add attraction to this species. Growing naturally in elevated cold areas, this plant will withstand heavy frosts and snow. It appears to be reasonably hardy provided well-drained conditions are maintained.

Hakea bakerana (see also p. 75)   N.S.W.
Winter and spring

A rounded shrub growing to 1.5 m tall, *H. bakerana* is distinguished by its large clusters of pink flowers on the old wood. These flowers are often hidden under the light green needle-like leaves which grow to 7 cm in length. The large fruits, 5 cm in diameter, which follow the flowers are an attractive feature of this species. It grows naturally in a limited area north of Sydney. A sunny, well-drained location is best for this neat, medium-sized shrub.

Hakea bucculenta   W.A. Winter and spring
Red Pokers

One of the most beautiful species of the *Hakea* genus, *H. bucculenta* grows as an erect shrub to 4 m high on red sand. The spectacular orange-red tapered flowers up to 15 cm long are borne on old wood along the branches. The leaves are narrow with a grass-like appearance. Most hakeas produce nectar which is attractive to honeyeaters. In cultivation this species requires an extremely well-drained position with low humidity. It has not been grown with great success along the eastern coast, except grafted onto more robust root stocks.

Hakea crassinervia   W.A. Winter and spring

Although this W.A. species is believed to be extinct in the wild, it has been established successfully at the Burrendong Arboretum, near Wellington, N.S.W. Many plants have been propagated from this specimen and distributed widely. The bright pink flowers appear in clusters at the leaf axils, often along the entire length of the branches, making a most attractive feature. This spreading shrub grows to 1.5 m tall and can spread to 3 m across. The elliptical leaves are rigid and grow to 4 cm long. This unusual plant has adapted well to cultivation in a well-drained position.

Hakea laurina   W.A. Autumn and winter
Pincushion Hakea

As with *Callistemon citrinus*, this widely admired shrub is also grown in several countries outside Australia as a street or hedge specimen. The shrub survives best in an open well-drained lime-free position where it will form an upright plant with a rounded head up to 3 m tall. New tip growth is frost tender and the foliage is slightly blue-green. Tiny flower buds appear early in December and open toward the end of August. The flowers have a faint pleasant scent which attracts birds. This shrub may be subject to die back resulting from root rot under continual rainy-cold conditions, although new growth generally occurs after the soil dries out. This tree is shallow rooted and can blow over in strong winds. The flowers are most spectacular and recommend this species as a valuable garden shrub.

Hakea multilineata   W.A. Winter and spring
Grass-Leaf Hakea

The reddish-pink tapered flower spikes of this hakea are similar to those of *H. francisiana*, *H. coriacae* and *H. bucculenta*. All are outstanding as flower specimens. This species grows to 3 m, often with one or two well developed trunks having smooth bark. The narrow flat leaves are blunt with a taper towards the base and grow to 12 cm in length. This frost resistant species prefers a warm dry position with very good drainage.

Hakea purpurea   Qld. Winter and spring
Crimson Hakea

The exquisite bright crimson-red flower clusters along the stems of the Crimson Hakea resemble those of some grevilleas. The species grows to 2.5 m tall and 1.5 m wide and has sharp needle-like foliage. It has adapted well to cultivation in an open well-drained sunny position and is able to withstand dry periods. It is frost resistant and, like most of the *Hakea* species, the flowers are favourites with honeyeaters.

Hakea trineura   N.S.W., Qld. Winter and spring
This most attractive species is variable in flower colour, with the N.S.W. form having red pendulous flowers and the Queensland form yellowish green ones. The oblong to narrow elliptical leaves grow to 16 cm long with reddish longitudinal veins and are covered with rusty hairs. As an erect shrub, this rare species grows to 6 m tall, is fast growing and adaptable to most soils, provided some drainage is available. It is not widely grown but deserves more attention as a garden or street tree. It is frost resistant.

Helichrysum bracteatum   All states except Tas.
Spring to summer

Many forms of this plant are commonly cultivated as garden annuals in rockery or larger garden beds. The basic species is a robust plant usually to a height of 30 to 60 cm with a solitary stem, but may have stems in groups of three or four, with broad, soft, woolly leaves. The branches end in pink, red, orange or golden-yellow papery flowers, 25 to 50 mm across. It prefers a light, well-drained soil in full sun and provides excellent flowers for indoor arrangements, either as fresh or dried specimens. Regular watering is required in dry summer periods. Unlike most native plants, these annuals respond well to reasonably heavy applications of conventional garden fertilisers.

Helichrysum cassinianum   S.A., W.A., N.T. Spring
(Syn. *Schoenia cassiniana*)
Pink Cluster Everlasting; Pink Everlasting; Casssini's Everlasting

A showy little annual producing many stems from a leafy base, this everlasting daisy grows easily and adapts to any soil, but requires full sun for best results. It is a valuable garden bedding or border plant and gives a splash of pink colour to a rockery during spring. It is also useful as a pot plant and for cut flowers. Propagation from seed is not difficult. It grows to 30 cm high with rough oblong leaves to 7 cm long.

Helipterum roseum   W.A. Spring

Another of the 'paper daisies', these attractive annuals are favourites in the cut-flower trade and provide an excellent garden display during spring. They grow to 40 cm high with smooth narrow leaves and pink or red papery flowers with yellow or black centres on erect stems. Massed displays of these beautiful plants will equal any garden-bed floral display. Shown here is a spring display at King's Park Gardens in Perth. A well-drained sunny area is ideal. As with *Helichrysum bracteatum*, these plants respond to a well prepared and fertilised or mulched soil.

Indigofera australis   All states. Winter and spring
Austral Indigo

Although this quick-growing plant is commonly seen in the bush, it has not been grown to any great extent as a garden specimen. It is a hardy species and will grow under most well-drained conditions, including in frosty areas. The spreading foliage is soft and elegant with a loose texture. The branches grow to 2 m and have small mauve-pink pea flowers in long heads. This under-utilised plant is recommended as an attractive garden specimen.

Kunzea ambigua (see also p. 69) N.S.W., Vic., Tas.
White Kunzea; Tick Bush   Spring

Although the common name refers to the normal white form of this species, the pink-flowering form is an attractive addition to any garden. The arching branches of this shrub with its fine light-green foliage make it well worth growing.

Kennedia prostrata   All states. Winter and spring
Running Postman

A vigorous and robust groundcover and climber, this species can cover an area of several square metres in one season's growth. These characteristics make it an ideal plant to hold the soil on a steep bank until other plants have grown sufficiently. Pruning is necessary to prevent this vine from becoming entangled in the branches and leaves of surrounding shrubs. Almost all soils are suitable for this plant. The bright red pea flowers form an attractive contrast to the deep green broadleaf foliage.

Kennedia rubicunda   N.S.W., Qld, Vic.
Dusky Coral Pea   Spring and summer

Another rapid-growing groundcover, this plant will quickly grow to a spread of 3 to 4 m. The bright pink-red pea flowers appear on the fine stems amongst the dark green crinkled leaves. A well-drained sunny or semi-shaded position is preferred, although dry conditions can be withstood. It is frost resistant but needs plenty of room to spread.

Kunzea baxteri   W.A. Winter and spring
Scarlet Kunzea

This is one of the W.A. species which has adapted well to garden cultivation and is a common sight in many gardens along the east coast. It is a relatively hardy plant, but prefers a well-drained, open, sunny position. The spectacular dense red bottlebrush-type flowerheads appear over a long flowering period and are most attractive to birds for their nectar. This species grows to 3 m high as a compact rounded shrub with narrow crowded leaves radiating from the stems in various directions. Pruning after flowering will help to maintain an attractive bushy shape. It is highly recommended for garden specimen planting.

Lambertia formosa   N.S.W. Most of the year
Mountain Devil; Honey Flower

These plants are popular with native birds as a source of nectar and provide a year-round supply. This species usually grows to 2 m tall with many branches originating from the ground. It has stiff dark green leaves which are narrow and have sharp points and a prominent vein in the centre of the leaf. The bright red flowers appear without a stalk and have seven heads surrounded by brownish bracts. The common name comes from the two-horned woody fruits which follow the flowers. They are often used in dried floral arrangements. A well-drained, sunny position is required for this hardy, frost-resistant plant which grows relatively slowly.

Melaleuca fulgens   W.A. Spring and summer
Scarlet Honey-Myrtle

The loose bottlebrush-like flowerheads of this medium-sized shrub are generally pink or red with attractive gold tips, although a beautiful salmon-coloured form is also available and well worth growing as a garden specimen. This form flowers during late winter and spring. An open, sunny and well-drained location with an ample supply of water is preferable. Pruning is required after flowering to retain a compact appearance and promote flowering in the following season. It generally grows as an erect plant to 2 m tall with narrow, concave grey-green leaves. The flowers attract birds.

Lechenaultia formosa (see also p. 37)   W.A.
Red Lechenaultia   Winter and spring

The red-flowering forms of this species are most attractive in a rockery or large tub, especially when grown as a group. Many different colour combinations are available in the several cultivars of this beautiful plant. Light sandy conditions with very good drainage are required. This species often tends to be short lived in cultivation and needs to be replaced regularly to maintain an annual feature. Propagation from cuttings is relatively easy and reliable.

Melaleuca hypericifolia   N.S.W. Summer
Hillock Bush

This spreading shrub or small tree has attractive slender arching branchlets which grow to 2 to 3 m long and create a most interesting feature in any garden. The oval leaves, up to 50 mm in length, appear in pairs. The flowers are dull to bright red in cylindrical spikes on old wood. This species will withstand a somewhat wet environment. Pruning is recommended after flowering.

Leptospermum lanigerum var. *macrocarpum*   N.S.W.
Summer and autumn

This hardy and unusual scrambling shrub is ideal as a rockery specimen. It usually grows to only about 1 m, has oblong leaves to 2 cm and large pink or white flowers with a prominent green centre. Most soil conditions and aspects are suitable for this plant.

Melaleuca lateritia   W.A. Spring and summer
Robin Redbreast Bush

Another of the W.A. species which has adapted well to garden cultivation in other states, the Robin Redbreast Bush has open, twiggy branches with fine, narrow, alternate leaves, 1 to 2 cm long. The orange-red bottlebrush-like flower spikes are 5 cm long and generally appear along the leafless part of the branches. It is a hardy shrub, growing to 2 m tall, preferring good drainage, but a moist position. Young plants require protection from frosts. The flowers are a good source of nectar for birds. Pruning is needed to establish and maintain a compact plant.

Melaleuca 'Paynes Hybrid'　　　Cultivar. N.S.W.
Spring and summer

A light-textured soil in an open well-drained location is required for this delightful small shrub which grows to 2.5 m tall. It has small grey-green leaves and crimson-scarlet bottlebrush-like flowers with golden tips. They often appear in clusters of several flowers and make a rather spectacular display. Another of the many bird-attracting species, this shrub can be grown as a single garden specimen or in a group, trimmed to provide a colourful hedge.

Oreocallis wickhamii　　　Qld. Spring
Tree Waratah; Red Silky Oak

A tall rainforest tree from Queensland, the Tree Waratah has large red waratah-like flower clusters emerging from the dark green canopy of leaves. This tree requires a warm sheltered position with plenty of room and moisture in a well-mulched soil to simulate rainforest conditions. The flowers are long lasting and attractive to birds. Although not common in cultivation, this specimen is well worth trying in frost-free areas.

Melaleuca radula　　　W.A. Spring to summer
Graceful Honey-Myrtle

Another of the open-textured *Melaleuca* species, the Graceful Honey-Myrtle also has large attractive bottlebrush-type flowers. They are borne at the bases or below the ends of the leafy branches and often occur in pairs. The new flowers are pinkish-mauve and fade to a dirty colour as they mature. This shrub grows to 2.5 m tall and has graceful branches with narrow, pointed leaves up to 5 cm long. Light to medium, well-drained soils are recommended in an open or partially-shaded location. It will withstand dry periods but prefers a moist environment. Pruning is essential to maintain a good shape.

Passiflora aurantica (see also p. 71)　　N.S.W., Qld.
Golden Passionflower　　　All year

The *Passiflora* genus has three or four indigenous species, all climbing plants with twining tendrils and large lobed shiny leaves. The large attractive flowers are salmon-pink with deep red centres and only remain open for one day. They have a conspicuous long divided style or stalk of pollen receiver. The fruit is large and edible but not very tasty. The common name, passionflower, relates to the arrangement of flower parts which resembles a crown of thorns, as worn by Christ at his Passion. A warm, sheltered, moist position is preferred for this climber which is ideal for a fence, trellis or tree cover. It must be protected from frosts.

Nematolepis phebalioides　　W.A. Autumn to summer
This W.A. genus has only two species and is closely related to the correas which are common in the eastern states. The flowers of this small shrub have five petals forming a tube with ten stamens with long hairs. It grows to 1 m as an erect plant with short, blunt, undivided leaves. The pendulous flowers are a beautiful apricot-red. This outstanding and unusual flower is well worth the little extra effort in cultivation. A very well-drained, light soil is essential. This species is recommended for tubs where the natural conditions can be established and maintained. Pruning is recommended to maintain a good specimen shape. Propagation from cuttings is generally reliable.

Pelargonium rodneyanum　N.S.W., Vic., S.A., W.A.
Magenta Storksbill　　　Spring and summer

Only three species of this genus are restricted to Australia. The soft leaves and magenta flowers are strongly scented. This dwarf species grows with a prostrate trailing habit up to 30 cm tall with the leaves forming rosettes. The flowers are carried on long slender stems. The species makes a most attractive specimen in a rockery bed or large tub where it can trail over or amongst the rocks or over the edge of the tub. This plant is growing in the rockery area of the Australian National Botanic Gardens in Canberra. It is frost resistant and prefers a light soil and dry conditions, preferably in an open, sunny position.

Pimelea ferruginea   W.A. Winter and spring
Pink Rice-Flower

Most of the species of this genus are restricted to the south-west of W.A., although several species are now widely cultivated in home gardens throughout the continent. This species grows to a rounded shrub to 1 m and has glossy oval leaves with masses of bright pink pincushion flowerheads at the ends of the branches. A well-drained soil is required in a sunny or partially shaded position. It is frost resistant and makes an excellent rockery or large tub specimen plant. Pruning after flowering is recommended to maintain an attractive compact shape.

Pimelea ferruginea 'Magenta Mist'   Cultivar.
Winter to spring

This cultivar of *P. ferruginea* grows to a rounded shrub with a height of 1 m. It has masses of magenta flowerheads.

Rhododendron lochae   Qld. Spring and summer
Australian Rhododendron

This is the sole species of this genus which occurs in Australia, and is only found naturally at altitudes above 1000 m in northern Queensland. It has been grown successfully in the warmer climates of N.S.W., mainly as a tub specimen. It grows to a height of 1 m and has glossy, ovate, dark green, textured leaves with outstanding brilliant red, tubular flowers which hang in terminal clusters. A cool, shaded position in a well-mulched, open soil with very good drainage is essential for success with this prize specimen. A mixture containing fine gravel with pine bark and peat moss is an ideal medium for this plant.

Schefflera actinophylla   Qld. Summer to winter
Umbrella Tree

There are only two Australian species of this genus, previously known as *Brassaia*. Found in the rainforests of northern Queensland, the Umbrella Tree has adapted well to the warm moist areas of N.S.W. where it is very common. It grows to 6 m tall and has small red flowers in dense spikes from the apex of the tree. The foliage is soft and shiny and needs adequate protection from strong winds and frosts. This species makes an attractive specimen tree and can also make an excellent indoor plant for several years in a tub or large pot. It should be grown well away from buildings to avoid damage by the somewhat invasive root system.

Stenocarpus sinuatus   N.S.W., Qld.
Firewheel Tree   Autumn to winter

Although located naturally in coastal gullies and rainforests, the popular Firewheel Tree can be grown in full sun where the orange-red flowers, resembling those of many grevilleas, can make a most attractive display. Another excellent species for specimen planting, this erect tree will grow to 10 to 12 m, provided protection from frosts is available. A plentiful supply of water is desirable. Growth may be very slow in the early years, and often the plant does not flower for several years after planting as a seedling.

Stylidium graminifolium　　N.S.W., Qld, A.C.T.,
Grass Trigger Plant　　　　　　Vic., S.A., Tas.
　　　　　　　　　　　　　　Spring to summer

The stylidiums or trigger plants are mostly Australian and derive their common name from the irritable column which reacts like a trigger and hits insects which alight on it on their back, transferring pollen which is then carried to adjacent plants. The column is formed by a combination of the anthers and the stigma. These triggers are only reactive on warm days. This species grows as a tufted plant, and although not common in cultivation can be grown with some success in a pot. The pink to deep magenta flowers are borne on stems up to 40 cm long. A well-drained, sunny position is required.

Telopea oreades　　　　N.S.W., Vic. Spring
Gippsland Waratah

This slender plant with open foliage grows to 3 m high and 3 m across. It has large egg-shaped or lance-shaped dark green leaves up to 30 cm long which are grey-green on the underside. The red flowers are rather loosely packed with red bracts at the base and occur in broad heads at the end of the branches. A medium moist soil is required in a protected, semi-shaded position. Competition from roots of other shrubs should be avoided.

Syzygium wilsonii　　　　Qld. Spring and summer
Powder-puff Lillypilly

One of the most attractive of all rainforest plants, the Powder-puff Lillypilly has adapted surprisingly well to cultivation in N.S.W. as far south as Sydney. A rich, well composted soil in a warm position with partial shade is ideal. A regular water supply is desirable to promote growth and flowering. The branches and foliage have a weeping habit with the fresh growth giving flushes of bright red-brown colour. It grows to 3 m tall and has beautiful large crimson red pompon flowers at the tips of the branches.

Telopea speciosissima　　　　N.S.W. Spring
N.S.W. Waratah

The red-flowering form of this species is the most familiar one and is the floral emblem of N.S.W. It grows as an erect shrub to 3 m tall and is well worth the effort to cultivate in the home garden. It is tolerant of a wide range of soils but must have a well-drained location. It has long, dark green, stiff leaves, strongly veined and with toothed edges. The dense, cone-shaped, dark red flower clusters are 75 to 100 mm across. Separate flowers are narrow, rose-shaped, opening from the base. Pruning is desirable to produce a more compact shrub and to encourage the growth of extra flowering stems. Branches and flowers are subject to borer attack which can be controlled with malathion. A close watch should be kept during autumn when the flowers are forming to ensure that borers do not attack the buds. Root competition from surrounding shrubs should be avoided. The flowers are excellent as cut specimens and last for several weeks.

Tecomanthe hilli　　　　Qld. Winter
Pink Trumpet Vine

This beautiful twining plant from the rainforest areas of north Queensland is one of the most attractive of all Australian vines. The clusters of large, deep pink, bell-shaped flowers last for several months and add a truly spectacular feature to any garden. The soft, dark green leaves contrast with the flowers. Worthy of much wider cultivation, this species likes a well-drained soil with plenty of water in a warm, frost-free position.

Telopea speciosissima × *Telopea mongaensis*
(*Telopea* 'Braidwood Brilliant')　　Cultivar. Spring
This registered cultivar developed at the Australian National Botanic Gardens in Canberra is a frost-resistant, multi-stemmed shrub growing to 2 m. It has a slightly less dense flowerhead than *T. speciosissima* and is similar in colour. A rich, well-drained soil in a sunny or semi-shaded location is required.

Templetonia retusa   S.A., W.A. Winter and spring
Cocky's Tongues

The *Templetonia* genus is entirely Australian, with eight species. The dark red pea flowers have ten united stamens. The foliage is light green with broad egg-shaped or oblong to wedge-shaped leaves with blunt ends and very short stalks. This shrub grows up to 2 m in height and 1.2 m across and has a somewhat open texture with angular branches. A light soil in a well-drained sunny or semi-shaded location is desirable. It is lime tolerant and will grow in exposed coastal areas and under dry and frosty conditions.

Tetratheca stenocarpa   Vic. Spring

A slender shrub with weak trailing branches to 1.5 m in length, this species produces masses of dark pink, or sometimes white, flowers. The flowers appear either singly or in groups of two or three in the axils of the upper leaves. The leaves are alternate and up to 1 cm long and 9 mm across. This plant occurs naturally on hillsides in mountain forest areas and requires a well-drained soil. It is not common in cultivation, but is worthy of consideration, as shown by this handsome specimen growing in the Australian National Botanic Gardens in Canberra.

Thryptomene saxicola W.A. Spring, most of the year
Rock Thryptomene

Although normally an erect shrub to 1 m in height, the Rock Thryptomene may often have rather pendulous branches. It provides excellent cut flowers and severe pruning has little effect on its growth and shape. The pink flowers appear prolifically in spring but can continue for most of the year in some areas, making it a valuable addition to the home garden. The site should be well drained with some protection where frosts occur.

Zieria smithii   N.S.W., Qld., Vic. Spring
The trifoliate dark green leaves of this rounded shrub are very aromatic, although the smell is not particularly pleasant. It grows to 1.5 m high and bears masses of small pink or white flowers in clusters. It is an attractive plant for small gardens and requires a well-drained, shaded position. It is frost resistant and benefits from pruning to maintain a compact appearance.

Woollsia pungens (see also p. 83)   N.S.W., Qld.
                                    Most of the year
Growing naturally in poor sandy soils, this species is best grown in a rockery bed with good drainage, in a partially shaded location. Plants benefit from regular watering. Reaching a height of 1 m over several years, this erect shrub has short prickly leaves with attractive red new growth. The small flowers appear most of the year and are either white or pink.

2 Oranges, Golds and Browns

I love a sunburnt country,
  A land of sweeping plains,
Of rugged mountain ranges,
  Of droughts and flooding rains,
I love her far horizons,
  I love her jewel-sea,
Her beauty and her terror—
  The wide brown land for me.

Dorothea Mackellar
My Country
© The Estate of Dorothea Mackellar
Reprinted with permission of Curtis Brown Aust Pty Ltd

Only a very limited number of native plants have flowers in this colour group; nevertheless, these include some outstanding garden specimens. Examples include *Banksia ericifolia* and *Banksia spinulosa,* two of the hardy eastern Australian banksias which are favourites with many home and landscape gardeners. The flowers last for several months and are useful in fresh and dried floral arrangements.

Honeyeaters are very much attracted to the nectar contained in the large flowers.

The gold-flowering species are commonly found in the vicinity of yellow-flowering species in nature, a feature which can be used to advantage in the home garden. Indeed it is often difficult to clearly distinguish between some of the yellows and oranges. Some flowers have combinations of the two colours or even change from yellow to gold as they mature. Examples include some of the *Banksia*, *Hibbertia* and *Pultenaea* species.

Several species produce flowers which turn brown at the end of their lives and often remain on the plant for many years. In some cases these are somewhat untidy but with some species, such as *Banksia robur*, they can make an attractive feature until the new season's flowers appear.

Anigosanthos 'Regal Claw' (see also p. 11) Cultivar.
Spring and summer

This cultivar is a cross between *A. flavidus* and *A. preissii* and produces large golden-orange flowerheads on tall spikes up to 1.5 m long. The flowers have a somewhat flattened appearance and, along with the stems, are covered with dense orange-red hairs. They last for several months and are a most attractive addition to a garden rockery where a well-drained, sunny position is available.

Prostanthera magnifica   W.A. Spring
Splendid Mintbush

As with many native flowers, it is difficult to describe the colour of the flowers of this plant accurately since it includes yellow, pink, white, brown and orange. The tubular flowers are borne in terminal heads on the heath-like shrub which grows to 1.5 m. It requires a well-drained, sunny position and is resistant to frosts. This plant is not common in cultivation but is worthy of more attention.

Banksia ericifolia (see also p. 75)   N.S.W.
Heath banksia   April to October

This most attractive shrub with fine green foliage usually remains fairly dense to ground level without any special attention, as shown in the photograph. This specimen has grown in full clay on a sloping bank to a height of 2.5 m in three years, with flowers appearing after the first year's growth. It is adaptable to a variety of situations from moist to fairly dry and semi-shade to full sunlight, but the best is a moist, well-drained sunny position. The large orange flowers can grow up to 25 cm in length and provide excellent specimens for indoor floral arrangements. Spent flowers should not be removed as they add character to the plant. Pruning can produce an attractive tall hedge. The Heath Banksia is a favourite of honeyeaters.

Banksia 'Giant Candles'   Cultivar. Winter and
                                              early spring

This cultivar is a hybrid between *B. ericifolia* and *B. spinulosa* and has one of the largest flowers of all the banksias, with the burnt orange spikes reaching up to 40 cm in length. The new narrow-leaved foliage is light green, turning to a dark green as it matures. This cultivar consistently produces many large flowers and is strongly recommended as a garden specimen for a reasonably well-drained location. It grows to a height of 2.5 to 3 m with a similar spread.

Banksia media   W.A. February to October
Southern Plains Banksia

The flowers of this compact shrub vary in colour from orange to golden-bronze to yellow and have a long cylindrical shape. It is probably the easiest of the W.A. banksias to cultivate outside that state and grows to 2 to 3 m high with small, shiny, toothed leaves. A light, well-drained soil in a sunny position is preferred and it will tolerate short dry periods. It is frost tolerant and has been grown successfully along exposed east coast areas.

Banksia spinulosa   N.S.W., Qld, Vic.
Hairpin Banksia   Autumn to October

This species grows well in soils ranging from light through to moderately heavy, provided good drainage is available. Soils containing lime can lead to yellowing of the foliage and poor growth. *B. spinulosa* is a very useful addition to any garden and usually grows into an attractive specimen that flowers profusely. The flowers, which grow up to 10 to 20 cm in length, are an excellent food source for bees and nectar-feeding birds. As with many of the other *Banksia* species, the Hairpin Banksia provides excellent cut flowers. It grows to 2 to 4 m high with long narrow leaves and large cylindrical orange flowers with black styles. This species will grow readily in semi-shade or an open position to produce a compact symmetrical shrub. Pruning is not necessary if the plant is not in a confined position.

Banksia robur (see also p. 51, 75)   N.S.W. Qld.
Swamp Banksia   Winter and spring
As the common name implies, this shrub inhabits damp swampy locations and is ideal for a wide range of soils in the home garden. The early green flowers change to bronze and finally brown as they age and are most attractive for floral decorations, either fresh or dried. Full sun will promote prolific flowering. This species is well worth a position in your garden, especially in a damp location where not too many other native plants will grow. It grows to a height of 1.5 to 2 m.

Grevillea alpina (see also p. 20) N.S.W., Vic., A.C.T.
Mountain Grevillea   Winter to summer

The orange-flowering form of this shrub is not often seen in cultivation. However it provides a most useful garden shrub where plants can be obtained. Only a relatively few *Grevillea* species have orange flowers.

Grevillea floribunda　　　　　N.S.W., Qld.
　　　　　　　　　　　　Winter and spring

Various forms of this species exist, ranging from erect and somewhat straggling plants up to 1.5 m high to lower, semi-prostrate spreading forms. The orange or brown-green flowers appear in pendulous woolly clusters from the branches. This species prefers a well-drained, sunny position in the garden.

Grevillea robusta　　N.S.W., Qld. Summer
Silky Oak

A medium to large tree growing to 10 to 20 m over many years, the Silky Oak has large, thin, divided leaves up to 15 cm wide by 30 cm long, shining dark green above and pale below. The older leaves fall as young leaves appear after flowering. The leaves spread in flat crowns on short shoots from the upper side of woody branches. In early summer these bear large golden-brown combs which form flat clusters covering the tree. This tree is one of the hardiest of the *Grevillea* genus and will adapt to most conditions. It requires plenty of room.

Grevillea 'Honey Gem'　Cultivar. Most of the year
This registered cultivar between *G. banksii* and *G. pteridifolia*, is a vigorous plant, often reaching 2 m in a couple of years. It will eventually grow to 3 to 5 m with fishbone-type leaves up to 30 cm long and 25 cm wide. The one-sided orange-brown toothbrush-type flowerheads grow to 15 cm long and tend to be borne horizontally. This shrub has a somewhat rounded and dense appearance and is becoming very popular in home gardens. A well-drained, sunny location is preferred. Pruning will help to maintain a compact specimen.

Grevillea buxifolia　　N.S.W. Most of the year
Grey Spider Flower

The open habit of this shrub is a common sight in the bushland around Sydney. The crowded oblong leaves are hairy and bear terminal heads of grey and brown flowers almost all year round. The unusual flower colour makes this hardy species invaluable for floral arrangements. In a well-drained position this plant is reliable as a garden specimen and grows to a height of 1 m. It is frost resistant and benefits from pruning to produce a bushy specimen.

Hibbertia stellaris　　　　　W.A. Spring and autumn

Probably the daintiest of the *Hibbertia* genus, this small shrub, growing to 30 cm high has fine bronze-tipped foliage and small orange flowers. It can be a frustrating plant in cultivation and requires a well-drained but moist position. It is probably easier to maintain as a pot specimen or in a rockery area where these conditions can be achieved. Nevertheless it is still worth the effort because it is such a beautiful subject.

Grevillea pteridifolia　　　　　Qld, N.T.
Fern-Leafed Grevillea　　　　May to September

A common feature along the roads and seasonally flooded grassy flats in the Kakadu National Park, the Fern-Leafed Grevillea is one of the largest *Grevillea* species in the area, growing as a sparsely branched shrub to 5 m high. It has long silver, narrow-fingered leaves and large golden toothbrush-type flower spikes up to 15 cm long. They produce copious quantities of nectar which attracts many birds. Although common in Queensland gardens, this species has not been cultivated to any great extent in the southern states. A well-drained soil in a sunny position is preferable for this frost-tender shrub. A prostrate form also exists and could be useful for sloping banks.

Lechenaultia formosa (see also p. 30)　　　W.A.
Red Lechenaultia　　　　　Winter and spring

The orange-yellow flowering form of this small rockery plant makes a most attractive rockery feature as shown by this specimen at the Burrendong Arboretum near Wellington in N.S.W. This species is also ideal as a pot specimen. It requires a well-drained position. Unfortunately it is often short lived, but is easily propagated from cuttings.

3 Yellows and Greens

Rock-Lily

The rock-lily's pale spray,
like sunlight, halts my way
up through the unpierced hush
of birdless blue-grey bush.

Out from you, rock, my friend,
I lean and, reaching, bend
the scentless pale spray back
to me and see the black
spots in each orchid flower.

Roland Robinson
Selected Poems
© The Estate of Roland Robinson 1989
Reprinted with permission, Collins/Angus & Robertson Publishers

The flowers of some species of several plant genera are both green and yellow or change from green to yellow as they mature, and it is sometimes difficult to clearly distinguish between the two colours. For this reason green and yellow flowers have been combined in this chapter to avoid duplication of species descriptions.

We normally associate green with the foliage of plants, and some of the photographs at the beginning of the book illustrate the variations in greens which occur in foliage. However Australian plants also have a range of attractive green flowers which, like foliage, display combinations of different shades of green.

The majority of green-flowered species come from a small number of plant genera, including *Banksia, Correa, Callistemon, Eucalyptus* and *Grevillea*. Although limited in number, the green-flowered species can add interest to the garden, especially in combination with the contrasting greens of foliage and with other coloured flowers.

Birds are always an added attraction in any garden and the flowers of many native plants can entice birds to the garden. Green-flowered species appear to be particularly attractive to some birds, especially honeyeaters.

When we think of yellow flowers, our attention automatically turns to the *Acacia* or wattle genus. The Golden Wattle (*Acacia pycnantha*) with its brilliant yellow fragrant flowers is the national floral emblem of Australia. The yellow flowers of the wattles are a familiar part of our countryside: coast, swamps and inland, seashore and high mountain tops, all have their own quota of wattles.

There are over 600 species and there is a wattle, usually several, for every type of soil, climate, situation and setting and it is not difficult by judicious selection to have at least one in flower all year round, even in a small garden. Wattles are also a familiar sight in other countries where they are grown for cut flowers and for perfume.

Other genera which feature an abundance of yellow flowers include *Hibbertia, Banksia, Eucalyptus, Hakea, Helychrysum* and *Melaleuca*.

Bright yellow flowers are invaluable in dark or shady spots in the garden to brighten up an otherwise dull appearance. This feature is a real advantage of yellow-flowering species which commonly flower in the winter months when other colours are somewhat scarce.

A limited number of species have the rare distinction of combining green and yellow with black to produce most unusual and distinctive flowers. One noteworthy example is the Black Coral Pea (*Kennedia nigricans*).

Predominantly Yellow

Acacia amblygona   N.S.W., Qld. Late winter to spring

A spreading, rather stiff shrub with triangular, pointed phyllodes and masses of golden balls in solitary heads on short stalks, *A. amblygona* grows to about 2 m in medium to heavy soils and makes a very showy specimen. It likes a sunny open position with reasonable drainage.

Acacia amblygona 'Australflora Winter Gold'
Vic. Winter to spring

This cultivar originated from a batch of seedlings of the usually upright form of *A. amblygona* grown by Molyneux Nurseries in Montrose, Victoria. This prostrate form reaches a height of only 30 cm with a spread of about 2 m. The rich yellow flower clusters, consisting of pompon globular heads 5 mm in diameter, are borne on stalks 10 mm long. The phyllodes taper to a sharp point at the base. This cultivar is useful in an elevated rockery bed where it can spill over a bank or group of rocks, as shown by this specimen at the Australian National Botanic Gardens in Canberra.

Acacia baileyana (see also p. 81)   N.S.W.
Cootamundra Wattle   Winter to spring

One of the most popular of all wattles, *A. baileyana* is widely cultivated as an ornamental tree spreading to 4.5 to 9 m and reaching 8 to 9 m in height. Branched clusters of brilliant yellow flowers, 20-25 per head, occur in a massive display above the short ferny blue-green foliage. This species is well suited to a wide range of conditions.

Acacia decurrens N.S.W., Qld, Vic., A.C.T. Spring
Black Wattle

Normally growing to a height of 10 m, this handsome wattle can be trimmed to a tall shrub. The feathery dark green leaves enhance the dense profuse clusters of golden-yellow, perfumed flowers. This tree is found growing in light to medium soils on the coast, mountains and in rainforest. It can tolerate relatively dry conditions but is slightly frost tender. Like many wattles, it is very fast growing.

Acacia drummondii   W.A. Summer
Drummond's Wattle

This wattle is a very useful shrub where space is limited. Care is necessary to select a suitable spot since it is tender to frost, wind and hot summer sun. Larger shrubs can provide shelter where plants can develop to perfection. Growing to a height of up to 1.5 m it can adapt readily to a sloping wall or large rockery or can make an interesting tub specimen. Flower buds for the following spring form in summer along the entire length of the stem. Most soils are suitable, where drainage is good, but an ample supply of water is necessary in dry periods. Light pruning after flowering helps to maintain bushy and long-lived specimens.

Acacia fimbriata   N.S.W., Qld. Spring
Fringed Wattle

This rather bushy tree or small shrub has somewhat pendulous branches and branchlets giving a graceful appearance. The small narrow phyllodes are grey-green and fringed with small hairs. The small brilliant yellow flowerheads appear in dense clusters and are very sweetly perfumed. This species can withstand a reasonable amount of moisture as it grows naturally in valleys and along streams. The specimen shown has grown to a height of 4.5 m over 4 years.

Acacia flexifolia   N.S.W., Qld, Vic. Winter
Bent-Leaf Wattle

An attractive dense rounded shrub with narrow leathery phyllodes, *A. flexifolia* has small, solitary, dainty flowerheads. It is normally found on slopes and inland in light to medium soils in dry open situations. This species only grows to a height of around 1.5 m and is frost tolerant.

Acacia floribunda   N.S.W., Qld, Vic. Spring
White Sallow Wattle

One of the graceful wattles, this tree generally does not reach the natural height of 4 to 5 m in cultivation. It has a drooping habit with slender, soft, light green phyllodes. Flowers are very profuse in loose pale yellow rods. Preferring a damp shaded position, this tree will grow in light to medium soils. This species is grown widely in North America.

Acacia glaucescens   N.S.W. Late spring
Coastal Myall

The blue-green leaves of this medium-sized tree, up to 20 m high, together with its vertically ridged, rugged, fibrous bark, make it an attractive specimen where space is available. The sickle-shaped phyllodes have a velvety silver-grey sheen. Flowers are pale to medium yellow in spikes 20 to 60 mm long in pairs or clusters. The specimen shown has reached a height of 10 m over several years in a semi-shaded position. It is well suited for street or park plantings.

Acacia iteaphylla   S.A. Autumn to winter
Port Lincoln Wattle

A beautiful dense, small tree with weeping branches, this wattle has narrow blue-green pointed phyllodes and pale yellow flowerheads in clusters on slender stalks. The wide silver-grey seed pods hanging in bunches are an added attraction while immature. Light to medium soils are suitable so long as good drainage is available. Although found growing in hot dry conditions it responds well to watering under cultivation, where it can grow to a height of 5 m.

Acacia prominens   N.S.W. Spring
Golden Rain Wattle; Gosford Wattle

This is a delightful tall shrub or tree, up to 8 m, with a weeping habit and light green phyllodes. The dense golden flowerheads appear in clusters of balls and are very profuse. Unlike most wattle flowers the blooms are completely unaffected by rain. Well grown specimens can reach a height of 6 to 9 m and are a magnificent sight especially in flower. The flowers are highly scented. Most soils and locations are suitable.

Acacia longifolia   N.S.W., Qld, Vic., S.A., Tas.
Sydney Golden Wattle;   Winter to spring
Sallow Wattle

This most adaptable fast-growing wattle will vary its habit to suit the situation. In normal situations it is a quick-growing straight tree to 5 m, whereas in exposed locations it can become twisted. It has long bright green phyllodes and profuse golden rod-like flower spikes. Most soils are suitable, provided drainage is good. This is one of the hardiest of the wattles and is well suited to seaside gardens since it can tolerate salt spray.

Acacia rigens   N.S.W., Vic., Tas.
Nealie; Needlebush   Winter to spring

This many-branched, tall, rounded shrub has stiff, sharply-pointed, bluish foliage and small clusters of fluffy, deep yellow flower balls. Found in medium to heavy soils on slopes and inland, this species typically grows up to 2 m. It is frost resistant, well suited to inland gardens and requires little water once established.

Acacia podalyriifolia (see also p. 81)   Qld. Winter
Queensland Silver Wattle

Although a fast-growing tall shrub or small tree, up to 8 m high by 5 m across, this species can be rather short lived and subject to attack by leaf-eating insects. However its bluish-green phyllodes, which can be narrow or sometimes almost round, together with its fluffy flowerheads make it one of the most attractive of all wattles. The seed pods are very flat and attractively crinkled. This species is commonly grown in many N.S.W. gardens under a wide range of conditions. Like many wattles, it can provide a quick ornamental cover.

Acacia saligna   W.A. Spring to summer
Golden Wreath Wattle; Orange Wattle

Formerly known as *Acacia cyanophylla*, this is a fast-growing wattle with widely spreading and weeping foliage. The flowerheads are large and golden yellow with up to 70 flowers per head. In full flower this small tree which reaches 6 to 7 m in height is quite profuse and spectacular in spring, though it seldom flowers all over simultaneously. It is resistant to winds and salt spray. Originally only found in W.A., it is now widely cultivated in many areas of N.S.W. and other states. It is one of the few acacias which germinates in nature without assistance from bush fires.

Acacia vestita   N.S.W. Spring to summer
Hairy Wattle; Weeping Boree

This graceful wattle with free-flowering, weeping branches and hairy foliage prefers an open, well-drained position, although it can tolerate heavy clay soils provided good drainage is available. The specimen shown has grown well in a heavy clay base soil with a 30 cm layer of sandy loam added to form a built-up bed. It forms a large, slightly spreading, bushy shrub up to 3 m in height with a similar spread. When in flower it is one of the most beautiful wattles. Its weeping branches give the plant an attractive appearance when not in flower. The species is generally free from pests and diseases and is also fairly resistant to root rot fungus.

Anigosanthos flavidus (see also p. 11) W.A. Summer
Yellow Kangaroo Paw

This plant is an excellent example of the adaptability of some of the W.A. plants for cultivation in other states. It is widely cultivated in home gardens, adapting to most conditions. The common name of this delightful native comes from the shape and woolly exterior of the flowers, which are excellent for interior decoration. All species of this genus thrive well in well-drained soils, although they can withstand wet clay soils. Flowers appear regularly during the flowering season and the branched stems can reach up to 2 m in length. Flower colour varies from dull green to yellow-red and even orange. This species is often subject to black blotches ('ink disease') on the leaves. Unfortunately a cure has not been found, but the leaves can be cut back to ground level after flowering has ceased to yield fresh green growth free of the disease.

Banksia integrifolia (see also p. 52, 75) N.S.W., Vic.,
Coast Banksia; White Honeysuckle Qld. All year
Like many of the banksias, the flowers of this species change colour as they age. In contrast to the green fresh flowers shown below, the more mature flowers are a pale yellow. This feature highlights the versatility of the banksias in providing a range of colours throughout the flowering season.

Banksia marginata N.S.W., Qld. March to October
Silver Banksia

Although this shrub will grow up to 6 m over many years, it commonly reaches only 2 m under garden cultivation, particularly if planted as part of a group of shrubs. The flowers are smaller than the majority of the banksias (up to 90 mm long). However they provide an interesting contrast to the other forms and appear profusely, with varied colour tones as the flowers change from yellow to brown with age. They are often crowded with bees and are suitable for indoor flowers.

Banksia oblongifolia   N.S.W., Qld. March to June
Probably one of the most attractive banksia species of the *integrifolia* group, this tall shrub grows naturally in a range of sandy clay to sandstone soils to 3 m tall and is well suited to garden cultivation. The leaves, which are generally 5 to 8 cm long and 1.5 to 2 cm wide, are often rusty on the upper surface with many short hairs on the underside. The long pale yellow cylindrical flowers are up to 15 cm long and 6 cm diameter and are borne terminally on the branchlets. Although rather slow growing, this species makes an attractive garden specimen.

Banksia serrata (see also p. 52, 86)   N.S.W.
Saw Banksia   March to June
Another of the banksia species which produces flowers changing in colour from green to yellow, *B. serrata* is well worth a spot in the garden where sufficient space is available. Mature trees can easily reach a height of 3 to 4 m.

Boronia megastigma   W.A. Spring
Brown Boronia

Although the common name suggests a brown flower, this species has highly fragrant cup-like flowers varying in colour from all yellow to dark brown with yellow inside. Like all boronias, this species is not easy to grow in cultivation and is often short lived under garden rockery or pot conditions. Nevertheless it is a most attractive plant and worth a try, especially as a pot specimen. It has been grown for many years for cut flowers and for its perfume. Several cultivars of this species with various colour combinations have been produced. It grows to a height of 70 cm.

Bossiaea foliosa   N.S.W., Vic.
Leafy Bossiaea   November to February

The *Bossiaea* genus is represented in all states and consists of some 50 species. Although not widely cultivated these plants provide interesting garden specimens where well-drained, slightly moist conditions exist. Some protection of the roots and partial sun is preferable. The small, single yellow pea-shaped flowers of this species are borne on very short stalks. The dense foliage adds to the attraction of this small shrub which grows to around 1 m high and 1 m across. It is an excellent rockery plant.

Bulbine bulbosa   N.S.W., Qld., Vic., Tas., S.A.
Bulbine Lily;   September to December
Wild Onion; Native Leak

This genus contains some 30 species, with only 3 of these occurring in Australia. They are bulbous plants with succulent linear leaves to 40 cm long and are ideal for rockery beds or containers, where a plentiful supply of water is available. The yellow star-like flowers are borne on erect, soft stems up to 50 cm long, and gradually mature along the stem. The foliage is poisonous to stock.

Carpobrotus sp. N.S.W., Qld. Spring and summer
Coastal Pig Face

Growing along the seashore, the carpobrotus, or pigface, is a fleshy creeping plant with long triangular leaves and flowers up to 75 mm in diameter. Flowers range in colour with various shades of yellow and pink. An open sunny position is necessary to ensure flowering. It is an ideal subject for the seashore. This yellow-flowering form was photographed in the sandy area around Wireless Hill near Perth.

Cassia artemisioides   N.S.W., S.A., N.T.
Silver Cassia   Winter to spring

A beautiful bushy shrub with a low branching habit and silver-grey foliage. The common name comes from the fine silky-white down which covers the bush. The bright yellow buttercup-type flowers have a delicate perfume. The shrub grows quickly to a height of 2 m and is ideal for a dry hot spot in the garden. Good drainage and protection from frosts are required. Since the plant grows rapidly it benefits from regular pruning to maintain a bushy appearance.

Conostylis aculeata   W.A. Spring and summer

Like most of the species of this genus, *C. aculeata* grows into an attractive clump of rather spiny leaves with woolly yellow flowerheads on stems which are mostly shorter than the leaves. The plant grows generally to a height of around 30 cm and is fairly hardy. It has adapted well to cultivation in an open, sandy, well-drained location and also makes an excellent pot specimen. The specimen shown is growing under these conditions in a rockery at the Burrendong Arboretum, near Wellington, N.S.W.

Craspedia glauca   All States. Spring and summer
Billy Buttons

Globular heads of yellow flowers appear on the erect stems, up to 30 cm high, of this plant. The light green leaves have a rosette shape, generally at ground level. This species requires a sunny open position for good results. Almost any soil is suitable as long as it is not too wet. Although it may be treated as a perennial under some circumstances, this plant is generally grown as an annual. Massed displays are most attractive. This species is synonymous with *C. uniflora.*

Dendrobium gracilicaule N.S.W., Qld. July to August

With a mass of dull or light yellow flowers with red blotches on the outside sepals, this orchid, found naturally on rainforest trees and sometimes on rocks, is an ideal specimen for cultivating on a paperbark tree branch, piece of treefern or pot. It is hardy but requires protection from frosts. The 15 to 20 mm diameter cup-shaped flowers appear on short drooping racemes. The leathery leaves generally occur at the end of the cylindrical stems which may be up to 130 mm long. The flowers are sweetly scented.

Conostylis seorsiflora   W.A. Spring

Growing with a spreading mat-like habit, this small rockery plant has light green, thin, flat leaves. The solitary, yellow, star-like flowers appear in amongst the foliage which grows only to a height of 5 cm. It is an excellent rockery or pot specimen and prefers a semi-shaded position with watering in the dry months. It grows by suckering and can be trained to form an interesting border around a rockery bed.

Dendrobium speciosum   N.S.W., Qld., Vic. Spring
Rock Lily; King Orchid

There are two varieties of this species: the Rock Lily or Orchid and the variety known as 'hillii' or King Orchid which grows on trees. The pseudobulbs are large and thick, tapering to the top and about 30 cm long. The leaves are oval, large and stiff. The tree-growing variety has leaves growing to 90 cm long. The different forms have a wide variation in flower colour, from almost white to cream and yellow. The flowers grow on long racemes and are strongly perfumed. The tree variety has smaller flowers which are more numerous than the rock-growing variety. Both are easily grown either attached to a board or tree trunk or alternatively in a pot containing bark and charcoal. They require a semi-shaded to full sun position to give a good display of flowers. The beautiful specimen shown is attached to the base of a tree and experiences morning sun.

Eremophila maculata (see also p. 18) N.S.W., Vic., S.A.
Spotted Emu Bush   Winter and spring

One of the more popular species of this genus, the Spotted Emu Bush is an erect shrub well suited to dry conditions. Garden cultivation is possible as long as good drainage is provided. The height of this species is variable but it commonly grows to 1 m. The leaves are hairy and sometimes sticky. The flowers vary in colour from red-brown to pink and lemon. The latter colour is most attractive against the small dark green leaves. Regular pruning is necessary to maintain a compact specimen.

Eucalyptus dwyeri   N.S.W. July to November
Dwyer's Gum

This is a mallee or small tree, up to 5 m, from the
western slopes of N.S.W. with smooth creamy white
or light grey bark. The flowers are white to yellow
and are followed by small fruit.

Eucalyptus robusta (see also p. 74)   N.S.W., Qld.
Swamp Mahogany   Winter

An excellent species for park or garden planting where
sufficient space is available, the Swamp Mahogany
has a most attractive dense crown of thick dark green
leaves and bears cream to yellow flowers in profusion.
The species normally inhabits swampy areas and
consequently is well suited to heavy sodden soils and
will tolerate coastal exposure. It has also adapted well
to drier soils. It is a medium-sized tree, reaching 15
m in height, and has coarse fibrous bark. It is quick
growing.

Eucalyptus erythrocorys (see also p. 74)   W.A.
Illyarie; Red Cap Gum   Winter

This is one of the most spectacular of all our flowering
eucalypts with its large yellow flowers with grooved
red operculum and large angular fruits. It is a frost-
tender small tree growing to 9 m in drier areas.
Although not universally successful in the eastern
states, large numbers have been grown in the Swan
Hill area of Victoria and around Adelaide in South
Australia.

Goodenia ovata   N.S.W., Vic., Qld., S.A.
Hop Goodenia   Spring and summer

Only reaching about 1.5 m, this semi-erect shrub has
light green toothed leaves and large yellow flowers.
It is one of the most common species of the genus and
generally prefers some shade and a moist condition
for best results. It is frost tolerant and can adapt to
a range of common garden soils. The plant has a
trailing habit and can be used to advantage in a
rockery or to cover a moist slope.

Eucalyptus kruseana   W.A. Autumn to winter
Kruse's Mallee

This is a very attractive neat compact shrub, growing
to a height of only 3 m with blue-grey rounded leaves
and creamy-yellow flowers in clusters near the end
of the branches. It is a hardy, frost-resistant tree and
will grow in most soils in a sunny position.

Grevillea 'Coochin Hills' Cultivar. Spring and summer

A tall, erect shrub, *G.* 'Coochin Hills' grows to a
height of 2 m and has leaves up to 25 cm long which
are deeply divided into many very narrow pointed
lobes. The creamy yellow flowers are sometimes
variable in appearance.

Grevillea dielsiana   W.A. Spring and autumn

One of the most prickly of all grevilleas, this shrub growing to 2 m tall by 2 m diameter has breathtaking flowers. The flowers are borne in terminal toothbrush heads and may be coloured red through to yellow. Some forms have several colours in the one flower. It is rarely a dense or compact shrub and requires pruning to avoid it becoming very straggly. A well-drained position is required. Care needs to be exercised with the sharp dead leaves.

Grevillea 'Honeycomb'   Cultivar. Spring

One of the *Grevillea* forms from Coochin Hills and Munduberra, this fast-growing tall shrub can reach 5 m high and 2 m wide. It has glossy, light yellow flowers in dense erect brush-type heads up to 15 cm long. The leaves have a fishbone shape and are bright green. This species is subject to blowing over and requires some form of protection. Although not common in cultivation, it is a plant well worth considering for the home garden.

Hakea cinerea   W.A. September and October

This shrub is worthy of cultivation for its form and colour. The 10 to 15 cm stiff, ash-green leaves give the 2.5 m high upright shrub a glaucous appearance. The yellow flowers are also very attractive and are borne on the upper branches. The more mature flowers turn orange, giving a mixture of yellow and orange flowers on the shrub at the same time. Well-drained, sunny conditions are required.

Grevillea 'Sandra Gordon' Cultivar. April to October

This natural hybrid originating from the same property as *G.* 'Robyn Gordon' is a hybrid between *G. pteridifolia* and *G. sessilis*. It is frost resistant and fast growing up to 3 m tall with a spread of 2 to 3 m . The large attractive golden yellow-orange flowers will attract numerous honeyeaters as they drip nectar. Regular pruning is recommended to maintain a bushy plant. The flowers are excellent for indoor decoration. The plant requires some protection from strong winds as the roots are rather shallow.

Grevillea sessilis   Qld. Winter to spring

A large shrub with attractive dissected foliage, this species has cylindrical creamy-yellow flowers which appear during the cooler months. It tolerates heavy soils but grows best in well-drained situations. The new growth is a striking bronze colour and the erect habit make this plant a most desirable addition to any garden. It grows to a height of 3 to 4 m, but pruning will ensure a more bushy shape.

Hakea leucoptera   N.S.W., Qld., Vic., S.A., N.T.
                                                    Summer

Originating in the dry areas of several states, this open shrub which may be erect or spreading in habit can grow to 3 m high. The leaves are often hairy and the cream-yellow flowers are borne in clusters around the branches. This is a very hardy species for dry areas and makes a good screen or hedge plant provided it is pruned suitably.

Hakea suaveolens   W.A. Autumn and winter
Sweet-Scented Hakea

This vigorous rounded shrub or small tree has most attractive, prominent, globular, white to yellow flowers and narrow, divided, sharp leaves. Like many of the hakeas, this large shrub reaching up to 5 m will adapt to a range of soils and locations, including seaside gardens. Pruning will assist in maintaining a shapely shrub. Dry periods can be tolerated and it is also tolerant of frosty conditions.

Hakea sulcata   W.A. Spring

An open rounded shrub, *H. sulcata* has furrowed needle-like leaves with globular yellow to pink flowers neatly spread along the branchlets. This shrub will grow to 1.5 m high with a spread of 1.5 m . Specimens of this species have been readily cultivated in N.S.W.

Helichrysum apiculatum (see also p. 82)   All states.
Common Everlasting   Spring to autumn

This prostrate, spreading perennial herb has cotton-like silver-grey leaves and clusters of small golden-yellow flowerheads over a long flowering period. These flowers last very well as cut flowers and the glaucous leaves add to the contrast. Some forms of this species are frost hardy. It is an excellent plant for a rockery and also as a quick-growing groundcover in most soils. It is tolerant of dry conditions but benefits from a regular watering in dry locations. Heavy pruning is quite acceptable to maintain a manageable specimen. It is very readily propagated from cuttings or from rooted runners.

Helichrysum bracteatum 'Diamond Head'   Cultivar.
Summer and winter

This cultivar was located in the Diamond Head area of New South Wales where it forms a compact plant 20 cm high and 50 cm across. The light green foliage is soft and slightly hairy with the small leaves measuring about 5 cm long and 5 mm wide. The papery yellow flowers are borne above the foliage on stems 10 to 12 cm long. The flowers have a carnation-like perfume. Most soils are acceptable and a sunny position with adequate water during dry spells is preferred.

Helichrysum bracteatum 'Cockatoo'   Cultivar.
Winter and spring

Another of the *H. bracteatum* cultivars, this perennial herb is also an excellent rockery or pot specimen, providing large pale lemon-yellow flowers. Plants typically grow to a height of 50 cm with a spread of up to 1 m. The grey-green felty leaves contrast with the papery flowers. It is a quick-growing plant and requires pruning to maintain fresh leaf growth.

Helichrysum bracteatum 'Dargan Hill Monarch'
Cultivar. Spring and summer

This perennial cultivar of *H. bracteatum* has glorious large yellow flowers for many months of the year. Plants will very quickly grow to cover an area of 0.5 to 1 square metre with a height of about 30 cm. As with other cultivars of this species, it readily adapts to a range of conditions and will respond well to relatively heavy feeding. Regular watering in dry periods is required and constant pruning will help maintain an attractive feature plant. Although generally regarded as a perennial, it is advisable to replace the plant every couple of years to maintain an attractive, bushy appearance. The flowers are excellent in dried arrangements.

Helichrysum bracteatum 'Montrosa Nana'
All states except Tas. Spring to summer

This robust annual usually grows to a height of 30 to 60 cm with a solitary stem, but may also have stems in groups of three to four, and broad leaves. The branches end in large golden yellow papery flowers 25 to 50 mm across. This cultivar prefers a light well-drained soil and provides excellent flowers for indoor decoration either as fresh or dried specimens. Regular watering is required in the dry months.

Helichrysum ramosissimum Qld. Spring and summer
Yellow Buttons

This species was originally included with *H. apiculatum* but has recently been separated as a different species. The orange-yellow heads are 6 mm across and occur in small clusters. The grey-green leaves are 1 to 2.5 cm long and hairy on both sides. This plant is another excellent rockery or pot specimen which suckers readily.

Helichrysum rutidolepis   N.S.W., Vic., Tas., S.A., A.C.T., Qld. Summer and autumn

This species is similar to *H. scorpioides*, the Button Everlasting, and has pale yellow flowerheads up to 1.5 cm across on the tips of the unbranched woolly stems. This delightful perennial plant forms attractive clumps up to 30 cm tall and 1 m across and is ideal as a rockery specimen or border plant. Although not commonly found in home gardens, it is adaptable to most soils and can be grown from seed, cuttings or division. A moist position is preferable.

Hibbertia aspera   N.S.W., Vic., S.A.
Most of the year

The bright yellow flowers of this spreading plant are produced most of the year. It grows to a height of 60 cm and 1 m across and has dark green leaves. It is one of the hardier species and will grow under most conditions. The flowers tend to be somewhat sparse compared to some of the other species which flower in profusion.

Hibbertia cuneiformis   W.A. Spring and summer
Cut-Leaf Hibbertia

Another of the erect *Hibbertia* species, this small shrub reaches 2.5 m high and is the tallest of the genus. The toothed, dark green leaves and bright yellow flowers are typical of the *Hibbertia* genus. Suited to most areas with good drainage, it is resistant to frosts and suitable for protected coastal areas. Like all *Hibbertia* species it provides an attractive display of yellow flowers among other garden plants.

Hibbertia dentata   N.S.W., Qld., Vic.
Spring and summer

A slender climbing plant, *H. dentata* will readily twine around a tree trunk or fence to make an attractive specimen bearing large yellow flowers to 4 cm in diameter along the stems. The dark green toothed leaves appear slightly insignificant when the plant is in full flower. They are sometimes subject to attack by insects and need to be protected. This plant makes an excellent specimen in a pot with a wire or wooden frame for the twining stems to cover. It requires a well-drained location and partial shade.

Hibbertia obtusifolia   N.S.W., Vic., Qld., Tas.
Showy Guinea Flower   Spring

This spreading bush grows up to 50 cm in some cases, although the specimen shown is a prostrate form and ideally suited as a rockery plant. The arresting bright yellow flowers are most attractive and contrast well with the apple-green linear to oblong leaves. A shady area and summer watering is required in dry areas. It provides an excellent cascading plant in a pot.

Hibbertia pedunculata N.S.W., Vic. Most of the year

Spreading up to 60 cm, this semi-prostrate species has yellow flowers on long peduncles above the narrow dark green leaves. It is an outstanding rockery plant and groundcover in most conditions, provided that it is not too wet. The spreading stems often take root, providing additional plants if desired.

Hibbertia empetrifolia N.S.W., Qld., Vic., Tas., S.A.
Spring and summer

This species is one of the hardiest of the *Hibbertia* genus, and grows to a height of 60 cm with a spread of up to 1.5 m . It has a spreading habit and can readily climb up adjacent shrubs or dead branches, a most pleasing sight when it is covered in deep yellow flowers. The elliptical leaves are dark green. Requiring good drainage, this species is one of the most reliable for cultivation but prefers a sheltered, semi-shaded position and watering during dry spells. It is also frost resistant.

Hibbertia vestita   Qld. December

This is a small shrub deeply branched from a short woody stem at ground level and reaching a height of 30 cm with a width of 60 cm. The plants are rounded in shape but tend to become straggly and irregular in groups. A sandy slightly damp position is ideal. The species is becoming endangered in its natural habitat by urban development and garden cultivation is to be encouraged.

Hibbertia scandens   N.S.W., Qld. Spring,
Climbing Guinea Flower   summer and winter

Growing naturally in sand dunes, this vigorous creeper is useful for trailing up a fence or over a log feature amongst other plants. The large showy yellow flowers up to 70 mm in diameter are carried on creeping fleshy stems with broad dark green leaves. This is a very hardy and adaptable plant and will grow in most areas except where heavy frosts occur.

Hymenosporum flavum   N.S.W., Qld. Spring
Native Frangipani

Originating in rainforest, this medium-sized tree, up to 10 m, has an erect, open habit with shiny leaves and large, tubular, highly perfumed flowers of cream and yellow. The flowers appear in terminal clusters. This species makes an attractive specimen for a street tree or garden feature specimen in the warm coastal areas, provided adequate water is available.

Isopogon anemonifolius   N.S.W., Qld.
Broad-Leaf Drumsticks   Spring and summer

This upright shrub has divided flattened leaves with a reddish tinge during the cooler months. The prominent terminal clusters of yellow flowers are followed by rounded seed cones. The foliage is very useful as greenery in floral arrangements and is long lasting. This shrub reaches a height of 2 m, prefers a well-drained sunny position and is frost resistant. It is a hardy species for the home garden and responds well to regular trimming.

Isopogon dawsonii   N.S.W. Spring
Nepean Cone Bush

The pale yellow flowers of this tall shrub are tinged with pink and are silky-haired. Reaching 3 m in height, it has many branches with flat divided leaves. The flowers are followed by silky-grey seed cones which provide additional interest for this unusual garden specimen. It will grow under most conditions.

Melaleuca incana (see also p. 82)   W.A. Spring
Grey Honey-Myrtle

Distinguished from other species of this genus by its blue-green foliage with attractive tips, *M. incana* is likely to attract attention in any garden. Although it can grow rapidly to a height of 1.8 m over 4 to 5 years, the shape can be controlled by pruning. This shrub adapts to a wide range of conditions, although strong winds should be avoided and watering should be maintained during long dry periods to give lush growth and profuse flowering. The beautiful primrose yellow flowers, which are soft and graceful like the foliage, grow up to 25 mm in length. Flowers and foliage are pleasant to arrange in long sprays and last well in water.

Melaleuca quinquenervia (see also p. 86) N.S.W.,
Broad-Leaved   N.T., Vic.
Paperbark   Summer to autumn

One of the larger melaleucas, growing up to 10 m, this species is very adaptable and popular. It is resistant to salt spray and winds as well as brackish water, and occurs in swamps and on shores of lakes. An open moist soil is preferable, although the specimen shown has grown in a relatively dry clay-based soil. It is a useful tree for ornamental purposes as well as street plantings. The cream-yellow bottlebrush-like flowers are quite attractive and a favourite with birds.

Oxylobium robustum   N.S.W., Qld.
                      Spring and summer

The flowers of this genus make a bold display in any garden. This species, like most in this genus, makes an attractive plant for home gardens provided it is trimmed heavily after flowering to maintain a bushy appearance. It is a rounded shrub growing to 2 m and has long narrow leaves to 5 cm. Clusters of bright yellow pea flowers are produced on the branch ends. A well-drained, protected area is ideal.

Persoonia chamaepitys (see also p. 83)   N.S.W.
                                  Summer

An unusual groundcover from the Blue Mountains area of N.S.W., *P. chamaepitys* has most attractive, light green foliage, resembling pine needles. The yellow flowers are almost hidden amongst the foliage. Well-drained soils and a sunny or partially shaded location are desirable.

Phebalium ambiens   N.S.W., Qld.
                                    Spring and early summer

The main characteristic of most flowers of the
Phebalium genus, which contains some 45 species, is
the prominent anthers of the fluffy clusters. Only a
limited number of species have been successfully
cultivated. This species grows to 2.5 m high and 1
m across with large oblong leaves to 10 cm long. The
flowerheads are white to yellow. This is one of the
easier-to-cultivate species, requiring good drainage
and a partially shaded location. A generous coverage
of mulch will assist in keeping the roots cool.

Phebalium squamulosum   N.S.W., Qld., Vic., S.A.
Scaly Phebalium   Spring

The narrow elliptical leaves of this small shrub have
a silver underside. Several subspecies exist and
consequently the plants are quite variable in growing
habit, although generally growing to about 2 m in
height. It has bright cream to yellow terminal flowers
in clusters. A lightly shaded, slightly moist position
with good drainage and a cool root run is preferred.
It is a most attractive rounded and compact shrub.

Phebalium whitei   Qld. Spring

This rather small species grows as an erect shrub to
50 cm tall, with dark green oblong leaves to 5 cm long.
The golden-yellow flowers are the largest of the
Phebalium genus and are most attractive. While this
plant is valuable as a garden specimen, it has not been
grown extensively in cultivation. This specimen was
photographed at the Australian National Botanic
Gardens in Canberra.

Pomaderris elliptica   N.S.W., Vic., Tas.
(Syn. *Pomaderris pilifera*)   Spring and summer

The 40 species of the *Pomaderris* genus are characterised
by the large heads of bright yellow or cream flowers.
Most are relatively hardy in cultivation, provided good
drainage is provided. This species grows as an erect
shrub to 2 m high and 2 m across. The elliptical leaves
are blunt at the end and vary in size up to 10 cm long.

Pultenaea daphnoides N.S.W., Qld., Vic., S.A., Tas.
Large-Leaf Bush Pea   Spring

A moisture lover, this shrub comes from forests and
woodlands where good drainage and well-mulched
conditions exist. The 2 m-tall plant provides a bright
display of colour with terminal clusters of yellow and
red pea flowers. It has dark green wedge-shaped leaves
with a small point. This is one of the most common
species of the genus.

Ranunculus lappaceus   All states except W.A.
Common Buttercup   Summer

This widespread perennial herb is distinguishable by
its creeping branches with soft spreading hairs on the
stems, lobed leaves and shiny yellow flowers. The
plants will weave amongst other shrubs in a rockery
and will grow under a wide range of conditions
provided a plentiful supply of water is available.

Senecio linearifolium   N.S.W., A.C.T., Vic.
Spring and summer

The *Senecio* genus consists of some 30 species in Australia, which are not generally cultivated to any extent since they are often considered as weeds. However their hardy nature and vivid yellow flowers make them attractive for some locations. This species is a large spreading shrub up to 4 m in height and 5 m across with bright yellow flowers. It is hardy in almost any soil and conditions and can make a carefree screen plant.

Synaphea polymorpha   W.A. July to September
Albany Synaphea

This shrub grows to 70 cm tall with reddish stems and yellow flowers in short spikes set among the upper leaves. The upper leaves are smaller and less rigid than the lower leaves which reach up to 20 cm long. The leaves are light green. The species grows in the white sand areas in the Albany district of W.A. Although rare in cultivation it has been grown in South Australia with success. This species has the distinction of being one of the first two Australian plants to receive botanical names.

Tristaniopsis laurina   N.S.W., Qld., Vic. Summer
Kanooka or Water Gum

Growing to 15 m, this medium-sized tree has narrow glossy leaves which redden in colder areas and make an attractive feature. Although the tree grows naturally under very wet conditions along streams, it is sufficiently adaptable to withstand full sun and relatively dry conditions. Small yellow flowers occur along the stalks at the base of the leaves.

Predominantly Green

Xyris spp.

About 15 species of the *Xyris* genus are found in Australia. Growing as small tufted herbs in wet locations, they have yellow flowers with three petals. They are not common in cultivation but could provide an attractive aquisition around a small garden pool or in pots where suitable conditions can be maintained. The attractive small flowers are short lived.

Anigosanthos viridis   W.A. Spring and summer
Green Kangaroo Paw

The narrow, rounded leaves of this species are quite distinctive compared to other species. The bright green flowers appear on green stems up to 0.5 m long. Forming a compact clump, this plant is fast growing and is an ideal specimen for a pot or rockery area. It can tolerate moisture.

Banksia robur (see also p. 36, 75)   N.S.W., Qld.
Swamp Banksia   Autumn and winter

Although the natural habitat of this species is in swamps, it will adapt readily to a wide variety of soils and conditions in the garden. The ideal position is in a damp corner but it will tolerate a much drier location provided some water is available. The large stiff serrated leaves (up to 30 cm by 12 cm) have a flannel-like undersurface which contrasts with the feathery yellow veins of the older leaves. This shrub will grow up to 1 to 2 m in height with a spread of at least 2 m as a mature specimen. Flower buds are a bluish-green but turn yellow-green as they open. Spent flowers, which may last for many years, form an interesting feature of the shrub and are ideal in dried arrangements. Pruning will produce a compact, tighter form.

Banksia serrata (see also p. 41, 86)   N.S.W.
Saw Banksia   March to June
This large-leaved specimen is handsome in all seasons with large hard greenish brushes. Like some of the larger *Banksia* species, this one reaches small-tree proportions in its natural state, but in cultivation in home gardens will generally attain a height of only 1.5 to 2 m over several years. The light green, shiny leaves with prickly serrated edges grow up to 150 mm in length.

Banksia integrifolia (see also p. 41, 75) N.S.W., Vic.,
Coast Banksia; White Honeysuckle   Qld. All year
Found naturally on the cliffs and dunes of the eastern coast from Port Phillip in Victoria to southern Queensland, the Coast Banksia will withstand strong winds and sea spray. It is a versatile tree that is found in the high country as well as on mountain slopes. One of the larger banksias, it can reach a height of up to 8 to 10 m. The masses of honey-laden green to pale yellow flower spikes up to 150 mm long attract birds and bees. The flowers are stalkless. The woody seed capsules split into two, releasing a pair of paper-thin winged seeds. The leaves are dark glossy green, silver lined with matted felt-like hair. A prostrate form of this species is also available and can be used to advantage to cover a sloping bank or in a rockery.

Banksia integrifolia var. *compar*   N.S.W., Vic.
April to September
This variety of the Coast Banksia comes from southern Queensland and northern N.S.W. and has broad ovate leaves which are shiny above. The early green flowers often change to a pale yellow as they mature. This variety can adapt to a wide range of conditions and soils. It grows to a height of 8 to 10 m, with a spread of 1 to 1.5 m.

Callistemon pachyphyllus (see also p. 14) N.S.W., Qld.
Wallum Bottlebrush   Spring and autumn
Like several of the *Callistemon* species, *C. pachyphyllus* has several flower colour forms including green and pink. However it is the apple-green form which has made it popular for garden cultivation. The slender weeping branches with narrow leaves also add to its attractiveness. It has a rather open habit, reaching a height of 1.5 m and a diameter of 1.5 m . It is found in swampy areas and will tolerate poorly drained soils and salty conditions. As with colour forms of many plant species, it is essential to propagate plants from cuttings to ensure that the colour is reproduced.

Callistemon pallidus   N.S.W., A.C.T. Vic., Tas.
Lemon Bottlebrush   Summer and autumn
The geenish-yellow flower spikes of this species grow to 10 cm long with a slightly open arrangement of flowers. It is a hardy shrub, reaching 3 m in height, and is widely grown in a range of locations and soils, including water-logged and exposed conditions. There are only a limited number of green or yellow-flowering *Callistemon* species and these make an interesting and pleasant contrast to the more usual pink and red-flowering species.

Callistemon pinifolius   N.S.W. Spring
With narrow pine-like leaves, and apple-green (with yellow tips) or red flowers, this hardy shrub will grow to 1.5 m high by 1.5 m diameter. It prefers full sun and a moist environment. The green flowers are quite outstanding and are unusual for indoor decoration. Most callistemons benefit from pruning after flowering to maintain a bushy compact plant.

Callistemon pityoides (syn. *Callistemon sieberi*)
Alpine Bottlebrush   N.S.W., Qld., Vic., A.C.T.
Summer

This species is somewhat variable, depending on its natural habitat. The alpine form is rounded and grows to 2 m , whereas the form from marshland areas grows with an erect habit. Branches tend to be arching with fine, dark green, needle-like leaves. The greenish-yellow flower spikes grow to 5 cm long with a compact arrangement of flowers in the spike. Moist soils and a partially shaded location are desirable for this useful plant. Pruning is recommended to maintain a compact appearance.

Correa reflexa (see also p. 16) All states except N.T.
Native Fuchsia   Autumn to spring

This widespread plant shares its common name with *Epacris longiflora* and has some 20 or so different forms. It adapts to a wide range of conditions, growing naturally from mountain forests to dry mallee scrub. Its forms vary from semi-prostrate up to heights of 1.3 m . With leaves varying in shape and nature, they may be rough and heavy to almost smooth above and furry underneath. Flowers are tubular to heel-shaped with light protruding stamens, and yellow-green to crimson-red with yellow to green tips. Although unusual, the green forms are not generally as attractive as the other colour forms. Most soils are suitable so long as reasonable drainage is available, however watering is necessary during the growing season to establish healthy growth. Most *Correa* species will flower in shaded or semi-shaded positions, and this is one of the main attributes of this genus. Regular pruning will maintain a compact plant and increase the number of flowers.

Correa bauerlenii   N.S.W. Autumn to winter
Chef's Cap Correa

The greenish-yellow pendular flowers of *C. bauerlenii* are a most attractive feature in any garden. Growing to a height of 1 m, this plant has thin, slightly hairy, shiny leaves on red stems. As for most correas, a partly shaded moist condition in the garden is preferred. The flowers in winter are a welcome sight when others are scarce.

Correa reflexa var. *nummularifolia*   Vic,
March to September

This dwarf shrub, growing to 30 to 50 cm by 1 m has round to oval leathery leaves which are very hairy underneath and have a rusty appearance. The tubular greenish-white flowers are about 2 cm long and are generally abundant. The red-tipped anthers add to the attractiveness of the flowers. This variety is suited to well-drained coastal locations and is an excellent rockery specimen for a partially shaded or sunny aspect.

Correa glabra   N.S.W., Qld., Vic., S.A.
Rock Correa   May to August

The pendular, long tubular flowers of the Rock Correa can grow to 3 cm long and are commonly pale green, although golden or red colour forms can also occur. This species is somewhat variable in growing habit, but generally has a dense upright to spreading appearance, reaching 2 m with a spread of up to 2 m. The glabrous leaves are 1 to 4 cm by 0.5 to 2 cm and often have a wavy edge. This species adapts to most soil types, including coastal locations, and to partial shade or full sun.

Cymbidium suave N.S.W., Qld. August to October

One of the three species of native cymbidium, this epiphytic orchid roots in hollows or forks of the host tree. It is common around Sydney, but is not readily noticed as it is often tucked away in the crook of a hollow limb above eye level. The flowers are usually green to green-gold and are rarely more than 1 cm in size. They are carried profusely on crowded spikes and make a handsome display. The leaves are grass-like, long and slender. This orchid does not have a pseudobulb and requires considerable attention in cultivation as it has no reserve. Filtered overhead shade beneath a tree is desirable. Over-watering can result in loss of the plant.

Eucalyptus lehmanni (see also p. 74)   W.A.
Lehmann's Mallee;   July to September
Bushy Yate

The Bushy Yate grows as a rounded tree to 5 m tall and 4 to 5 m across. The large, shaggy, ball-like clusters of green flowers are most attractive. Preferring a well-drained sunny location, this hardy species has adapted to a wide range of soils and is grown in many parts of Australia. It is useful as a screen or windbreak and is tolerant of salt spray.

Hakea petiolaris   W.A. Autumn and winter
Sea Urchin Hakea

Grey-green elliptical leaves make this tall, erect, fast-growing shrub attractive as a garden specimen. Early flowers are green-yellow but change to dull red pincushion flowers with white styles as they mature. This species makes a hardy feature, screen or background shrub reaching a height of up to 5 m.

Kennedia nigricans   W.A. Spring
Black Coral Pea

The most vigorous of the *Kennedia* genus, this fast-growing groundcover is excellent for covering unsightly banks or fences. It will quickly overrun an area of up to 6 m diameter. The large dark green trifoliate leaves and unusual black and greenish-yellow flowers add an attractive touch to the area covered by the plant. Most soils are suitable although it is only moderately frost resistant. This plant should only be grown where there is ample space as it can quickly cover other low-growing plants in its way.

Grevillea ilicifolia (see also p. 23) S.A., Vic., N.S.W.
Holly Grevillea   Spring

An upright or spreading shrub, *G. ilicifolia* has holly leaves with attractive red tips on the new growth. The toothbrush-type flowers are initially green, turning to red as they mature. It is a relatively hardy plant in most soils and requires a sunny position.

Homoranthus darwinioides N.S.W. Most of the year

A most attractive small shrub for a container or rockery, *H. darwinioides* can grow to a height of 80 cm but is often semi-prostrate with arching branches and grey-green aromatic leaves. The small, pendulous, green and yellow flowers redden on ageing. Although this species is able to withstand dry conditions in sandy as well as heavy clay soils, a sunny or partially-shaded, well-drained position is preferred. It responds well to pruning by becoming denser and more floriferous.

Telopea Speciosissima 'Wirrimbirra White' Cultivar
(see also p. 73)   Spring

This unusual natural hybrid of the N.S.W. waratah was found in the Wirrimbirra Wildlife Sanctuary, near Bargo, N.S.W. It has been propagated from the original specimen and several excellent plants are growing in the Australian National Botanic Gardens at Canberra. Although the mature flower is a cream-white colour, the early bud growth is an attractive light green.

Grevillea venusta   Qld. Autumn to spring
Byfield Spider Flower

While this plant has a fascinating flower, its foliage has a lush, light green appearance and is well suited for use as a background or screening plant. The olive-green and yellow spider flowers have a dark brown style and are borne in a small brush head. In cultivation this shrub can reach 3 m and prefers a well-drained position in full sun or partial shade.

Homoranthus flavescens N.S.W. Spring and summer

The foliage of this plant is unusual and distinctive. The silver to grey leaves are crowded on the upper side of the spreading horizontal branches with some forms having an attractive reddish tinge to the foliage. The overlapping layers of foliage lead to a most attractive shrub of symmetrical form and a spreading, almost semi-prostrate habit. The flower buds develop near the ends of the branches. Individual flowers are quite small and vary in colour from green to yellow and finally dull red. Although found naturally in semi-shaded positions, this species will grow in full sun. The foliage may become somewhat sparse under these conditions. It is well suited as a rockery specimen or as an under-shrub in a bed with taller shrubs. It will grow in heavy as well as lighter soils to a height of 60 cm with a spread of 1 m over 3 years, as shown in this photograph.

4 Blues, Purples and Mauves

Around the lower edges
  There waves a bed of reeds,
Where water-rats are hidden
  And where the wild-duck breeds;
And grassy slopes rise gently
  To ridges long and low,
Where groves of wattle flourish
  And native bluebells grow.

Henry Lawson
Reedy River

Blue-flowering species are limited to a few genera. These are generally groundcovers or small shrubs and are ideal rockery or pot specimens, although not all species are easily cultivated or reliable as long-lived plants. This disadvantage can be overcome to some extent by growing the plants as tub specimens under conditions which closely simulate their natural environment.

Although not particularly valuable as cut flowers, some blue-flowering species provide spectacular displays during spring and summer. Probably one of the most outstanding of these, especially when grown in a massed display, is *Lechenaultia biloba* with its small brilliant blue flowers which pack together at the extremities of the fine foliage.

The spreading prostrate nature of plants such as *Dampiera diversifolia* and *Scaevola aemula* makes them invaluable species in planning colour and variety in a garden rockery. Both of these species are easily propagated and cultivated, provided appropriate conditions are established. Their spreading foliage will readily cover a small sloping bank or creep among rocks in a garden bed. They also make excellent specimens in hanging baskets or pots where the foliage can hang freely over the edge.

Blue flowers provide an interesting contrast against the dark green leaves of some of the species. They also create a striking effect when used in combination with almost any other coloured flowers in the garden.

It is often difficult to draw a distinct dividing line between the blue, purple and mauve flowers of many native plants. It is sometimes only possible to describe some flowers as mauve-pink since some species have flowers with many shades from the lighter mauves to the rich deep purples.

The range of purple and mauve-flowering plants is much more extensive than that of the blue-flowering species. One of the most noteworthy genera with mauve to purple flowers is the *Prostanthera* or mint bush

genus with some 100 different species spread throughout Australia. The massed displays of flowers on some species in spring give a most attractive appearance, almost completely covering the dark green foliage. Many mint bush species are readily grown in a variety of locations and soils. The strong fragrance of some is an additional reason for growing one or more of these plants in your garden.

The *Orthrosanthos* or morning iris genus is unusual as a garden lily with its beautiful deep blue-purple flowers held on upright stems. Although the flowers only last for one day, they are an attractive addition to a garden rockery.

The native daisy species, such as *Brachycome multifida*, are very useful plants for garden rockeries or larger beds. Massed displays with several plants in a clump can provide an attractive display of mauve-purple flowers for many months of the year.

One of the uncommon genera with several attractive garden species is the *Thomasia* genus. These plants are especially noteworthy since they only grow to a maximum height of 0.5 to 1 m and will thrive and flower readily under shaded as well as sunny conditions, a feature not often found in natives. The large flowers of *Thomasia grandiflora* are spectacular.

Purple patches of several vines and groundcovers are common in many bushland areas during spring. This colour display is provided by several species of *Hardenbergia* and *Kennedia*, which often cover very large areas. Some of these are ideal for covering banks, fences or pergolas in home gardens where adequate space is available.

Other blue, purple or mauve-flowering genera include *Sollya, Melaleuca, Wahlenbergia, Westringia, Eremophila, Verticordia, Hibiscus* and *Viola*.

The wide variety of flower forms and colour combinations, together with the different growing habits, give still more variety for consideration when planning your garden.

Alyogyne huegelii (see also p. 10)   W.A., S.A.
(Syn. *Hibiscus huegelii*)   Spring and summer
Lilac Hibiscus

The lilac flowers of this colour form are a valuable addition to any garden. This species generally flowers profusely over several months. It is a hardy, fast-growing plant and well worth a spot in your garden.

Brachycome multifida   N.S.W., Qld., Vic.
Most of the year

One of the daisy family, *B. multifida* deserves a place in every native garden, making an excellent rockery specimen. A well-drained open sunny position gives best results, although a shaded position will normally suffice. This plant grows to a maximum height of approximately 30 cm and provides a colourful display when several plants are grown in a clump. The specimen illustrated, growing in the rockery at the Australian National Botanic Gardens in Canberra, highlights the value of this plant for rockery use. A well-mulched area around the plants will help to retain moisture and control weed growth.

Callistemon citrinus 'Mauve Mist'   Cultivar.
November to January

This cultivar is an outstanding mauve-flowering, medium-sized shrub. It originated as a seedling from *C. citrinus* 'Reeves Pink' and is similar in colour, except for the definite mauve tinge in its flowers. Most garden soils and conditions are suitable for this much-branched shrub which grows to 3 m by 3 m. The flower spikes, up to 10 cm long, are usually borne in profusion as dense terminal clusters. Pruning is recommended to maintain a bushy specimen.

Calectasia cyanea   Vic., S.A., W.A.
Blue Tinsel Lily   August to December

The outstanding floral characteristics of the flowers of this species make it highly sought after for this purpose . It grows as a dwarf shrub to 50 cm and a spread of 1 m, with many erect stems and relatively short branches. The narrow leaves grow to 1.5 cm and the shiny bluish-purple flowers to 3.5 cm diameter. The flowers have 6 open petals and generally appear as solitary terminal flowers. A moist, well-drained soil is required in a partially shaded position, where some root protection is available. This species responds well to cultivation in a large pot or container. The variety *intermedia* shown here from South Australia and Victoria is more common in cultivation. The yellow anthers of this variety turn brown with age, whereas the anthers of *C. cyanea* turn red as they age.

Callistemon 'Purple Splendour'   Cultivar.
November to January

One of the lower-growing forms, *C.* 'Purple Splendour' grows only to around 2 m in height. It has deep mauve flower spikes which make it attractive as a garden specimen in almost any location.

Dampiera diversifolia   W.A. Spring and summer

This prostrate perennial groundcover, growing up to 1 m in diameter, produces a mass of tiny purple-blue flowers. Although it can withstand a range of conditions, a well-drained site with afternoon sun, free from winds and protected from more vigorous plants is necessary to ensure a good display. An adequate supply of water is necessary during dry periods. This species also makes an attractive plant for a pot or hanging basket.

Carpobrotus   glaucescens   N.S.W.,   Qld.
Coastal Noonflower   Spring and summer

The thick, fleshy, grey-green leaves of this spreading succulent plant are a common sight on coastal sand dunes. In these locations, the roots provide an effective means of retaining the sand, and the plant is also useful for this purpose in seaside places. This species is a very hardy groundcover for open sunny positions, where it will also grow over rocky areas. The large purple or sometimes pink flowers show up against the large leaves.

Dampiera purpurea   N.S.W., Qld., Vic. Spring

In common with many species of this genus, *D. purpurea* has a suckering habit with erect branches which can reach up to 1 m. The leaves on the sparsely branched stems are larger than those of some other species and are covered with hairs. The deep purple flowers are borne at the tips of the branches. A well-drained rockery position with filtered sunlight is preferable for this attractive plant.

Eremophila nivea   W.A., S.A. Spring

The beautiful soft silver-grey foliage together with the lilac-purple tubular flowers make this plant one well worth attempting to grow in your garden. It requires a light to medium soil with good drainage, and excessive humidity and moisture can result in fungal problems. The new growth is covered in white hairs. Pruning after flowering is recommended to maintain a compact appearance. This plant is not particularly common in cultivation but makes an outstanding contrast specimen in amongst dark green-foliaged plants in a rockery. It is necessary to provide water during long dry periods. This species grows to a height of 50 cm with a spread of 30 cm.

Halgania cyanea   N.S.W., Qld., Vic., S.A., W.A.,
Rough Halgania   N.T. Most of the year

One of the limited number of plants with deep blue flowers, this species has dull green toothed leaves 2 cm long and grows to 40 cm high with a spread of up to 1 m. Preferring dry areas, this frost resistant hardy plant will tolerate most conditions as long as good drainage is available. It has a tendency to sucker and will benefit from regular watering in dry periods.

Hardenbergia violacea   Eastern States.
False Sarsaparilla;   August to November
Purple Coral Pea

Often found growing in rocky areas and up tree trunks, this vigorous groundcover is ideally suited for sloping banks. The branches are scrambly with leathery leaves 3 to 9 cm long. Masses of purple-violet flowers almost entirely cover the foliage during the flowering season. This species is also useful to cover a dead tree stump or fence and will cover an area of several square metres in one growing season. Pruning is necessary to keep growth under control in areas where space is limited. A less vigorous form with fewer flowers is also available. Most soils with reasonable drainage are suitable. A sunny position will promote profuse flowering.

Hemiandra pungens (see also p. 69)   W.A.
Snakebush   Spring and summer

Amongst the several forms of this species, the prostrate groundcover form shown here growing at Wireless Hill, near Perth in W.A., is the most attractive for garden use. This form spreads up to 1 m across and has rigid, pointed, light green leaves and masses of small, tubular, mauve flowers along the branches. A sunny, protected and very well-drained location is essential to successfully grow this attractive cascading rockery plant.

Kunzea parvifolia   N.S.W., A.C.T., Vic. Summer

This spreading plant reaches a height of 1.5 m with a spread of up to 3 m. The fine, heath-like, dark green leaves are hairy when young. The fluffy, mauve-pink flowers appear along the pendulous branches in profusion. This is one of the hardier species for well-drained, open, sunny positions.

Lasiopetalum baueri   N.S.W., Vic., S.A., Tas.
                              Spring and summer

The *Lasiopetalum* genus is endemic to Australia with some 30 species, and is closely related to the *Thomasia* genus. This species is a low-growing shrub, up to 70 cm in height, with narrow, grey-green, slightly hairy leaves up to 5 cm long. The cup-like, mauve-pink to white flowers need to be viewed from underneath to appreciate their beauty. Like many *Thomasia* species, this plant will flower well in shady positions and is a very welcome addition to a garden rockery. This species is hardy in a well-drained location and benefits from regular pruning to maintain a compact plant.

Lechenaultia biloba 'White Flash'   Cultivar.
Winter and spring
This registered cultivar of *L. biloba* has a white centre and brilliant blue outer flower. It makes an outstanding rockery specimen where suitable conditions are available, as seen here in the rockery area of the Australian National Botanic Gardens in Canberra.

Lobelia membranacea   Qld. Spring and summer
An ideal rockery specimen, this suckering prostrate plant will cover an area up to 1 m in diameter in a damp location. It is frost hardy and bears masses of bright blue flowers against the light green leaves. Flowering is encouraged by plenty of light. Propagation is easy either from rooted suckers or cuttings.

Lechenaultia biloba   W.A. Winter to summer
Blue Lechenaultia
This outstanding display of Blue Lechenaultia at the Burrendong Arboretum illustrates the unique beauty of this W.A. treasure. Although some specimens may reach 30 cm to 50 cm, this species is often prostrate with fine leaves. The soft blue-green leaves are 3 to 10 mm long and approximately 1 mm across. The flowers are up to 20 mm across and may vary in colour from brilliant blue to white; they almost entirely cover the plant when in full flower. Excellent drainage and a light soil are essential for successful cultivation of this plant. Pruning will help to maintain a compact bush. It is often short lived in the eastern states, but is easily propagated from cutting to maintain continuity. It also makes an excellent pot specimen.

Melaleuca decussata   Vic., S.A. Spring and summer
Naturally found in damp locations, this shrub is quite hardy and can tolerate dry areas in cultivation. It performs better when water is applied during the drier months. It grows into a rounded shrub up to 2 m high and 2 m across with drooping branches and grey-green foliage. The small mauve bottlebrush-like flowers fade quickly after opening. Most soil conditions are suitable for this hardy shrub. Heavy pruning can be tolerated.

Melaleuca nesophila   W.A. Spring
For several months of the year this rapidly growing, hardy species produces delightful, globular, dense purple flowerheads up to 25 mm in diameter, tipped with yellow anthers. These flowers last well indoors. The dull green leaves are 10 to 15 mm long and 6 to 9 mm in width. This species will stand strong winds and salt spray, and a wide range of soils is suitable so long as drainage is good. Pruning will maintain a compact appearance. When grown among other shrubs it can reach up to 3 m, providing a useful variation in height. It is frost tender. Plants grown from seed may not flower for several years. This shrub is grown widely in the U.S.A.

Melaleuca armillaris   N.S.W., Qld., Vic.
Bracelet Honey-Myrtle   Spring and summer
This mauve-pink flowering form of the Bracelet Honey-Myrtle is an attractive alternative to the normal white form. Plants of this species will reach 3.5 m in 2 to 3 years and make an effective wind break or dividing hedge with little attention.

Melaleuca squamea   N.S.W., Vic., Tas., S.A.
                              Spring and summer

Another of the *Melaleuca* species preferring moist conditions, this open, erect shrub is well suited to poorly drained soils and is frost resistant. The small mauve flowers are borne at the tips of the arching branches. The soft, pointed, oval, leaves grow to 8 mm in length. Pruning will maintain a compact shrub to a height of 2 to 3 m.

Pratia pedunculata (see also p. 72) N.S.W., Qld, Vic.,
Trailing Pratia   Tas., S.A. Spring and summer

One of the attractive mat-type native plants, The Trailing Pratia will make a good groundcover rockery specimen in a damp, poorly drained location. The light blue, star-shaped flowers almost entirely cover the soft light green, oval leaves. It is frost resistant and can be used to form a lawn in a small shaded area where it is difficult to grow a conventional lawn.

Melaleuca thymifolia N.S.W., Qld. Spring and summer
Thyme-Leaf Honey-Myrtle

This small shrub is ideal for small gardens and is especially useful in wet locations, growing to 50 to 60 cm high. It can be used to create variation in height in a clump amongst other plants, in a rockery or as a groundcover with light trimming. The small clusters of stemless flowers are rich mauve. It will thrive in almost any soil with little attention. A light trimming is recommended to maintain an attractive specimen.

Prostanthera hirtula N.S.W., Vic. Spring and summer
Hairy Mint Bush

The prostrate form of this plant, shown here, forms an ideal specimen for rockeries with its slender branches spreading to 50 cm. The leaves up to 6 mm are lance-shaped to linear and appear in pairs along the branches, becoming shorter or even absent near the end of the branches. The leaves and branches are rough with short bristles. The deep mauve to pink flowers appear in pairs without stalks in the upper leaf axils. The specimen shown is growing in a well-drained sandy loam. The upright forms of this plant can grow to 2 m.

Orthrosanthus laxus   W.A. Spring
Morning Iris

The deep blue flowers of this perennial plant appear along the stem and only last for one day. A slightly shaded position with good drainage is preferable, with a regular supply of water in dry periods. Plants are easily propagated from the fine seed and can readily be grown in the eastern states. The plant has a tufted appearance, reaching 40 cm in height, and is ideal along the edge of a rockery bed or as a pot specimen.

Prostanthera incana   N.S.W. Spring
Hoary Mint Bush

The soft leaves of this spreading shrub are rounded and hairy. The mauve flowers appear in clusters towards the end of the branches. This hardy species is one of the more popular garden forms, growing to 2 m. A semi-shaded position with good drainage is desirable. Propagation from cuttings is not difficult.

Prostanthera rotundifolia   N.S.W., Vic., Tas., S.A.
Round-Leaf Mint Bush   Spring

As indicated by the common name, this species has rounded leaves which are sometimes toothed and up to 1 cm long. The purple or pink flowers are borne in profusion on the rounded, compact shrub which grows to 1.5 to 2 m with a spread of 2 m. It is a relatively hardy and frost-resistant shrub where drainage is good and a summer supply of water is available. The leaves are aromatic. Like all prostantheras, this shrub will benefit from regular pruning.

Scaevola albida (see also p. 73) N.S.W., Qld, Vic.,
                                        S.A. Spring and summer

This suckering groundcover has soft, bright green leaves with light blue, fan-shaped flowers. It is a hardy rockery specimen wherever reasonable drainage is available and is easily propagated from rooted suckers or cuttings. Pruning will maintain a desired shape. This plant makes an attractive specimen in a hanging basket with the foliage trailing over the edge. It is also useful to cover a sloping area in a rockery.

Prostanthera ovalifolia   N.S.W., Qld. Spring
Purple Mint Bush

This bushy plant with its dense texture is probably one of the most popular species for cultivation. The rosy mauve flowers provide a glorious display of colour, almost completely hiding the dull green, oval leaves. This shrub will grow to 2.5 to 3 m over a few years. A well-drained position is necessary as it is subject to collar rot. There are many varieties of this species available. The leaves are strongly aromatic.

Solanum brownii   N.S.W. Spring and summer

This genus has some 80 species distributed throughout Australia and consists of a range of shrubs and herbs. Relatively dry, well-drained conditions and at least part sun are best for cultivation. This species grows as a bushy shrub to 3 m high and 3 m across with soft grey leaves to 10 cm across. The purple flowers contrast attractively with the soft foliage. It is particularly useful as a screen plant.

Thomasia macrocarpa   W.A. Spring
Large-Fruited Thomasia

The large heart-shaped leaves of this species are soft and somewhat like a small grape leaf. Plants grow to 60 cm and the abundant mauve-pink flowers make an attractive combination with the interesting leaves. The flowers tend to face downward and need to be lifted to show their beauty. A well-drained, light soil and a semi-shaded position are desirable for this somewhat unusual and attractive plant. A light pruning after flowering will maintain a compact specimen.

Scaevola aemula   N.S.W., Vic., Tas., S.A., W.A.
Fairy Fan Flower   Spring and summer

The spreading nature of the *Scaevola* species, together with the attractive fan-shaped flowers, make them ideal rockery border plants. This species spreads up to 1 m with some upright shoots which may reach 30 cm. The bright green, toothed leaves are almost covered by the mauve flowers, which are useful in a small indoor vase arrangement. This frost-resistant plant prefers a well-drained location with adequate water in dry periods. It is a hardy plant for the garden.

Thomasia pygmaea   W.A. Spring

This small rounded shrub is one of the most attractive of all small native plants for rockery areas. During spring the small, rounded, dark-green leaves are absolutely covered by masses of small, mauve-pink, papery flowers. The flowers are also long lasting for indoor arrangements and excellent for pressed flowers. A well-drained light soil is desirable for either a rockery or pot, where the plant will grow to a height of 30 cm.

Thomasia rhynchocarpa   W.A. Spring

A spreading shrub with a height of 50 cm and a spread of 70 cm, *T. rhynchocarpa* has oblong leaves to 25 mm long and mauve-pink flowers. Like most *Thomasia* species, a well-drained, semi-shaded position is preferable for this plant. The flowers are small, but attractive. The low spreading habit makes for an attractive rockery specimen.

Thomasia petalocalyx W.A., S.A. Spring and summer
Paper Flower

A low spreading shrub with a soft furry appearance, this species reaches a height of up to 1 m. Small sprays of mauve-pink flowers cover the branches from late October to January. The oblong crinkly leaves, 20 to 40 mm long, are smothered with small, straight, brownish hairs. This species is suited to most reasonably well-drained soils and requires little attention apart from pruning to maintain an attractive bushy shape. The flowering period is lengthened if the plant is grown in a semi-shaded area. The flowers are ideal for floral arrangements. The specimen shown has grown to a height of 5 cm over 3 years in a semi-shaded rockery bed.

Thomasia sarotes   W.A. Spring

This species is similar in many ways to *T. pygmaea*, but does not produce as many flowers and has a more open appearance. Regular pruning after flowering is required to maintain a compact plant. It is a useful plant for use as a border in a well-drained, semi-shaded rockery bed, where it will only grow to around 30 cm. The small size also makes it attractive as a pot specimen.

Thysanotus patersonii   All states except Qld.
Fringed Lily   Spring and summer

Generally regarded as a vine, this species is a weakly twining, tuberous-rooted plant and will grow in a spiralling fashion around other plants. It has small leaves which quickly wither. The attractive purple flowers with three petals have long fringed margins. These plants are not very common in cultivation but can be easily grown from seed.

Viola betonicifolia   N.S.W., Qld, Vic., Tas., S.A.
Wild Violet; Purple Violet   Spring and summer

This *Viola* species grows as an erect tufted plant up to 12 cm with blue to purple flowers springing directly from the root. The long arrowhead-shaped leaves with blunt points grow from 25 to 100 mm long and are generally up to 12 mm wide. This plant will grow in a range of soils and prefers a moist semi-shaded area. It makes an attractive rockery or pot specimen.

Viola hederacea   N.S.W., Qld, Vic., Tas., S.A.
Ivy-Leaf Violet   Spring to winter

This creeping perennial with broad smooth leaves is the most widely distributed native violet, thriving in damp, shady positions. The patch of these shown provides an attractive display of flowers almost all year round in a cool damp position which is not suited to cultivation of other plants. These plants creep over the ground and root on the leaf node, covering an area of several square metres in 2 to 3 years. The blue and white flowers grow on slender stems and make a delicate indoor display in a small bowl.

Wahlenbergia communis   N.S.W., Vic., Tas.
Grass-Leaf Bluebell   Spring and summer

This group of plants growing in the rockery at the Australian National Botanic Gardens in Canberra shows the erect nature of this herbaceous plant, which grows to a height of 30 to 50 cm. Masses of purple-blue flowers appear on slender stems. A light soil with good drainage and a sunny position are required for this colourful plant. Propagation is easily achieved from seed or by division of the underground root stems.

Westringia eremicola N.S.W., Qld, Vic., A.C.T., S.A.
Spring and summer

Growing with an erect appearance to 1.5 m, this hardy shrub has light green leaves in groups of 3 along the soft branches. It produces mauve flowers for several months of the year. Most soils are suitable where reasonably well-drained conditions exist. Full sun is preferable, although the species will flower in a semi-shaded position. Under these conditions, it is especially important to prune the shrub regularly to maintain a compact specimen.

Westringia longifolia   N.S.W., Vic. Summer

This tall, erect shrub with soft, narrow, linear, light green leaves can be an attractive garden specimen. The flowers are pale mauve in summer and long lasting. This plant will grow to 1 m over a period of 3 years. A well-drained, sandy loam and a sunny or semi-shaded position are desirable, and regular pruning will help to retain a bushy specimen. It is very frost tolerant.

5 Creams and Whites

Flannel Flower

Petals white, and whisper soft,
Gently tipped with green—
Flannel flower, there's witchery
Wherever you are seen.

Nuri Mass
Australian Wildflower Magic
(The Writer's Press, 1967)

Like the yellows, white flowers are a most valuable addition to any garden, bringing light to dark and shaded areas and giving contrast to the various shades of green foliage. The brilliant terminal white flowers of *Pimelea ligustrina* surrounded by its light green leaves makes an outstanding feature in any garden or as an indoor floral arrangement. The massive natural display of soft white flannel flowers in their bushland settings is a sight unequalled in any other country of the world.

The whites and creams often blend well with other colours such as yellow and pink and ease the transition from the softer colours to the stronger blues and reds. White flowers can also make the brighter and stronger colours more outstanding and brilliant when grown next to them.

The choice and location of white-flowering species is therefore a most important consideration in planning the layout of a home garden. A rockery garden bed may appear very ordinary if all of the flowers appeared at the same time and were all white. Whereas by careful selection of plants with different flowering times and floral colours, the effect can be significantly enhanced.

Several Australian species have white as well as coloured flower forms and this feature provides additional opportunity for landscaping and garden bed design. Suitable species include *Bauera rubioides*, *Grevillea banksii* and *Eucalyptus sideroxylon*. It is essential to propagate new plants vegetatively to ensure that the desired colour form is reproduced.

White native flowers have been popular with florists for many years as they add contrast and character to floral arrangements. The demand for these flowers, together with the interest in new species for this purpose, has added impetus to the search for new plants for garden cultivation.

Some of the larger white-flowering species also have plant forms which allow a choice in size and shape for the same basic flower. One striking example is *Baeckea virgata* which has a large medium-sized shrub form as well as a semi-prostrate form which only grows to a height of 50 cm. These different forms permit this species to be grown as a specimen shrub as well as a rockery plant or miniature hedge along a garden path.

Actinotus helianthii (see also p. 7)   N.S.W., Qld.
Flannel Flower   September to December

This robust bushy annual has one or more erect stems from 30 to 60 cm tall. The lower stems are clothed with rather short, divided, velvety or woolly grey leaves, whereas the upper stems are essentially leafless, sometimes branched, having one or more white flowers up to 75 mm across. The flowers are white with a pale green centre with petal-like bracts having the appearance of flannel. These flowers are superb specimens for indoor arrangements, adding texture and colour to any group of natives. The plants require a sandy loam with excellent drainage. Little success will be achieved in heavy soils. A large pot can be used very successfully if these conditions are not available in the garden.

Ammobium alatum   N.S.W. Summer

A hardy perennial from the tablelands area of N.S.W., this plant grows in a clump to 30 cm diameter with branched flower stems up to 50 cm long. It has silvery-grey leaves with yellow flowers surrounded by white papery bracts. Most soils and locations can be tolerated by this plant in full sun.

Bauera rubioides (see also p. 11)   Eastern states.
Dog Rose   Spring and summer

The white form of this species is reasonably common in garden beds,and like the pink form, is a very useful rockery, pot or bed plant. It is very attractive when in flower and grows rapidly into a handsome shrub, to 50 cm, with spreading branches. It is highly recommended for garden cultivation.

Baeckea virgata   N.S.W., Qld, Vic., N.T. Summer
Twiggy Heath Myrtle

An erect shrub with small, flat, dark green leaves and small 2 mm white flowers occurring singly amongst the leaves, *B. virgata* makes a most attractive show when in flower. The natural form generally grows to 3 m tall although several dwarf and prostrate forms are available. The dwarf forms are excellent as a border along a garden path. This plant will grow under most conditions in an open position. The tall form should be pruned regularly to maintain a bushy specimen. The foliage and flowers are very good for floral arrangements.

Callistemon citrinus (see also p. 13) N.S.W., Qld, Vic.
Crimson Bottlebrush;   Spring to December
Lemon-Scented Bottlebrush

Widely known outside Australia, this plant adapts readily to any position or soil including wet conditions, even near the sea. Although the natural species has bright red flowers, it hybridises readily and several white-flowering forms are available. The foliage is somewhat stiff and dense and the leaves are broad and leathery with a lemon scent when crushed. The flowers are favourites with birds. Pruning after flowering will retain the appearance or makes an attractive hedge. The average height of the natural species is 2 to 2.5 m, but the hybrid forms may vary in size and habit. The white form of this species is often sold as *C. citrinus* 'Anzac'

Burchardia umbellata   N.S.W., Qld, Vic., Tas.,
Milk Maids   S.A., W.A. September to December

A dwarf perennial herb with leaves to 0.5 cm long, this lily is commonly found growing in open forest areas. It is ideal as a container plant in home gardens. The white flowers to 2.5 cm diameter occur in terminal umbrels on scapes, or on leafless peduncles (20 to 30 cm long) which originate from near the ground. The flowers are commonly reddish underneath. The *Burchardia* genus is endemic to Australia with only two known species. Well-drained conditions and full or partial sun are recommended.

Calytrix tetragona   N.S.W., Qld, Vic., W.A., S.A.,
Fringe Myrtle   Tas. August to November

Although there are some 50 species of this endemic genus, very few are seen in general cultivation. The attractive star-like flowers have five petals and provide an outstanding display of colour. This species is quite variable in shape and size, ranging from low, spreading forms to upright plants reaching 1 m tall. Flowers vary in colour from white to deep pink with the calyx retaining a red colour well after the flowers have matured. A well-drained, sandy soil in a sunny location is required for cultivation.

Chamelaucium uncinatum (see also p. 16)   W.A.
Geraldton Wax   Spring and summer

A well-known and very popular spreading shrub, Geraldton Wax has small, linear, dark green leaves about 12 mm long with hooked ends, and grows to a height of 2 to 3 m. The clusters of large flowers appear in white, pink and in some cases red. These are excellent and long lasting for indoor arrangements and have been grown for many years by nurserymen for this purpose. Although a native of the Geraldton area of W.A., this species has adapted well to soil and weather conditions on the east coast. A well-drained position is essential.

Clematis aristata   N.S.W., Qld, Vic., Tas. Spring
Traveller's Joy; Old Man's Beard

The massive displays of starry white flowers produced by this vigorous climber are a common sight in many bushland areas during spring. It can cover whole trees with its twisting branches and light green toothed leaves. The flowers are followed by feathery fruits which become very fluffy as they mature, hence the common name of Old Man's Beard. This climber can rapidly cover a fence or wall and prefers a moist, sheltered position in sun or semi-shade, and a well-drained soil.

Correa alba   N.S.W., Vic., W.A. Autumn and
White Correa   throughout the year

Occurring naturally on rocky sea cliffs as well as in dunes, this compact shrub grows only to a height of approximately 1 m. The branches and underside of the foliage are covered with dense, greyish, matted, woolly hairs. The leaves are oval to nearly circular, 20 to 40 mm long, and have a pleasant aromatic scent when crushed. They have been used as a substitute for tea. The terminal flowers are white with four separate waxy petals which curve outwards. These flowers are quite unlike the flowers of other *Correa* species. A well-drained sunny position is preferable.

Correa 'Ivory Bells'   Cultivar. June to December

This cultivar originated in San Francisco and its parents are reputed to be *C. alba* and *C. backhousiana*. It is an attractive small spreading shrub, growing to 1 m in height and up to 2 m across, although it will take many years to reach these dimensions in a home garden. The elliptic to ovate leaves are approximately 3 cm by 2 cm, are dull green above and pale greenish underneath. The tubular flowers are ivory to tan. Most well-drained soils and a partially shaded or full-sun location are suitable for this attractive plant. Pruning is beneficial in maintaining a compact specimen.

Cryptandra scortechinii   N.S.W., Qld.
Ball Cryptandra   Winter and spring

This small dense shrub is a superb specimen for any native garden. The woolly, rounded heads of lovely white flowers are very long lasting and are excellent for cut flowers. It has a rounded habit, growing to 1 m high and 60 cm diameter. A well-drained position with full sun is preferable. This species can also be used as a container plant.

Dendrobium cucumerinum   N.S.W., Qld.
Cucumber Orchid   November to February

This creeping epiphytic orchid is found mostly on casuarina tree trunks and limbs in its natural location. The leaves are fleshy, gherkin-like in appearance, up to 5 cm long and often attract more attention than the greenish-white to yellowish flowers with purple streaks. Plants of this species are readily cultivated on a tree limb or piece of cork.

Dendrobium linguiforme   N.S.W., Qld.
Tongue Orchid   Late spring to early summer
This creeping epiphytic orchid has thick oval leaves up to 20 to 40 mm, fluted on the top with short creeping stems. The delicate white to cream spidery flowers appear on numerous short racemes. Like many of the *Dendrobium* species, this plant is easily established on a paperbark branch or a piece of tree-fern. The specimen shown has been growing for several years in the authors' garden attached to a paperbark tree fork.

Diplarrena moreae   N.S.W., Vic., Tas. Late spring
Butterfly Flag
This is a beautiful addition to any garden and forms a stocky tussock with blue-green leaves about 30 cm long. In the late spring months the plant produces wiry flowering stalks up to 90 cm tall, and over the next couple of months occasional white iris-type flowers appear. These are very frail but lack nothing in beauty. They reach their best development in the morning and quickly shrivel on hot or windy days. The species grows naturally in heavy clay or rock situations usually in cooler, protected areas. Best results are achieved in gardens where protected wet clay conditions exist.

Epacris microphylla   N.S.W., Qld, Vic., Tas.
Coral Heath   Autumn to spring
A common inhabitant of the coastal heathlands, this upright plant has very small prickly leaves with white flowers clustered along the upper stems. Reaching a height of 1 m, this plant will grow readily in most soils including wet areas, provided adequate drainage exists. A partially shaded location is preferable to full sun.

Eriostemon myoporoides   N.S.W., Qld, Vic.
Long-Leafed Wax Flower   Winter and spring
The leaves of this hardy shrub have a slightly waxy appearance. It will thrive in a wide range of climatic conditions to form a shrub which is often wider than its height with dense growth right down to the ground. In colder areas the flowers open about the end of June, gradually increasing through the winter until early September when the shrub is dotted with white flowers. Both heavy and light soils are generally tolerated. Light pruning can produce a dense plant or informal hedge. Sprigs of flowers can be used indoors, although the leathery leaves have a strong aromatic scent. This handsome shrub will grow up to 2 m and is a valuable addition to any garden.

Eucalyptus curtisii   Qld. Summer
Plunkett Mallee
One of the most floriferous of all the eucalypts, the Plunkett Mallee has beautiful large heads of cream-white flowers at the end of the branches. It is a valuable small tree, reaching 7 m in cultivation, and has long pointed shiny green mature leaves. The tree is hardy, frost resistant and has attractive smooth silver-grey new bark. It is highly recommended for small gardens and as a street tree where taller eucalypts are unsuitable.

Eucalyptus globulus (see also p. 74)   Vic., Tas.
Tasmanian Blue Gum   Winter and spring
Known extensively for its most attractive blue-grey juvenile leaves, the Tasmanian Blue gum is a very tall tree reaching 30 m. The floral emblem of Tasmania, it has large cream flowers which attract many birds. The grey-green juvenile leaves are replaced by very long, glossy, dark green leaves as the tree matures. This change may not occur for several years after planting. It generally has a single straight trunk. The mature grey-green bark is shed in long ribbons giving the trunk an attractive appearance. This is a tall forest tree, to 30 m, and is only suitable for use in locations where sufficient room is available.

Eucalyptus nicholii (see also p. 85)   N.S.W.
Narrow-Leaf Black Peppermint   Autumn

Probably one of the most popular large trees for home gardens or the street, *E. nicholii* does not usually grow to more than 12 m. It has an attractive rough bark and rather irregular branches which have a tendency toward a weeping habit. The many creamy flowers are borne in groups of seven along the branches. The fruits are small and hemispherical with a flat or slightly raised disc. *E. nicholii* is especially popular overseas where its fine light green foliage and rounded compact crown are much admired and the pink to plum-coloured tint of the new leaves is used as a background to floral displays. It grows naturally on shallow soils overlaying slates but will grow in a wide range of soils. It is frost resistant and moderately drought resistant. The specimen illustrated has grown into a most attractive tree to a height of 10 m over 8 years.

Grevillea banksii (see also p. 21)   Qld.
Red Silky Oak   Most of the year

This very quick-growing large shrub with attractive large grey divided leaves is one of the more reliable grevilleas and readily adapts to a wide range of conditions in the warmer climates but it is frost tender. Although the normal colour form has red flowers tipped with yellow, a white form is also common in cultivation. The flowers are very beautiful and attract honeyeaters. This species is very hardy and can stand heavy pruning.

Eucalyptus polyanthemos   N.S.W., A.C.T., Vic.
Red Box   September to December

This eucalypt is a medium-sized, spreading woodland tree to 16 m with rounded dull grey-green foliage. The white flowers contrast attractively with the interesting leaves. The bark may vary in colour from grey, cream, pink or brown over much of the trunk and branches. It is a hardy tree for colder climates and grows to a height of 16 m.

Grevillea biternata   W.A. Spring

This plant has become well established as a valuable groundcover for banks or beds in exposed positions. Its white flowers almost entirely cover the thick foliage, which is attractive in its own right. This species can quickly cover an area up to 4 square metres in approximately 2 years. The free-flowing branches are suited for trailing over a built-up area such as would be formed with a sleeper retaining bank. The occasional vertical branch can be cut off to retain the prostrate habit. Good drainage is preferred, although a wide range of soils and clays are generally acceptable. The flowers attract honeyeaters to the garden.

Grevillea australis   N.S.W., Vic., Tas. Spring

This is a common shrub of the snow country on the mainland and Tasmania growing to a height of about 1 m, although a completely prostrate form has been observed in the Mt Barrow area of Tasmania. The small, scented, white flowers add little to the appearance of the plant, but its dark green, shiny, foliage is sufficient to recommend its use as a garden specimen. It is frost hardy and prefers a well-drained location.

Grevillea rosmarinifolia var. *lutea*   N.S.W., Vic.
     Late winter and spring

This species is generally regarded as one of the hardiest of all grevilleas and will grow under most conditions, with a preference for reasonable drainage. This variety grows as a rounded shrub to 2 m high and has abundant creamish flowers. The needle-like foliage is somewhat prickly and dark green.

Grevillea vestita   W.A. Winter and spring

The soft grey-green leaves of this spreading shrub are wedge-shaped and very attractive. It makes a good screen plant, growing to 2 m high and 2 to 3 m across in most soils and locations. The soft white feathery flowers appear in the leaf axils and are generally borne in profusion over several months. The foliage and flowers are very good for floral arrangements.

Hakea oleifolia   W.A. Spring

Like many of the *Hakea* species, the white flowers of this erect shrub, which grows to 5 m high and 2 m across, are borne in small axillary clusters along the stems. The flat, oblong leaves grow to 5 cm long and, unlike those of most hakeas, are soft to touch. This shrub grows in semi-shaded or open situations and would be useful for seaside plantings.

Grevillea 'White Wings' Cultivar. Winter and spring

This attractive, hardy shrub has flowers and foliage somewhat like *Grevillea biternata* although the habit is quite different as it grows to a height of some 1.5 to 2 m over a period of only two years. Flowering is quite profuse with the small white flowers held in tufted clusters along the branches. The rigid leaves are divided into 3 narrow lobes, each subdivided into 3 to 5 segments with an overall length of 5 cm. They are slightly perfumed. This species prefers a well-drained position and benefits from pruning. It is thought to be a hybrid between *G. biternata* and *G. phanerophlebia*.

Haloragodendron racemosum   N.S.W. Summer

A fast-growing rounded shrub to about 1 m high, *H. racemosum* has cream flowers which show up well against the dark green leaves. It is not common in cultivation, requiring well-drained conditions and a full-sun or semi-shaded location.

Hakea florulenta   Qld. Summer

This is one of the broad-leaved species found naturally in the Wallum and Brisbane metropolitan areas of Queensland, but is rarely seen in cultivation. The white flowers are borne in profusion from the leaf axils along the branches. The species has a prominent lignotuber. It grows to a height of 3 m with a spread of 2.5 m.

Helipterum anthemoides N.S.W. Late winter to spring
Chamomile Sunray

Like many of the daisies, this bushy little shrub (50 cm high by 30 cm across) likes a rich composted soil with good drainage and some shade during hot weather. The roots should be kept cool with mulch. The grey-green leaves have short hairs and smell strongly of chamomile when crushed. The wine-red buds open to beautiful snow-white everlasting flowers. The branched stems should be pruned after flowering to give a soft cushion appearance. This is an ideal plant for rockeries, hanging baskets or pots, where the foliage will cascade over the rim to make an attractive feature. Flowers are excellent for dried arrangements and the fragrant leaves can be used in potpourri.

Helichrysum diosmifolium   N.S.W., Qld.
Pill Flower; Sago Flower   Winter to summer

This erect shrub, growing to 2.5 m tall is a common sight along the roadside in N.S.W. and Queensland. It has an open habit in its natural setting, but can be pruned in cultivation to a more compact shape. The leaves may be blue-green to dark green and narrow or elliptical in shape and are stalkless. They are rough on top and woolly underneath. The foliage is aromatic when crushed. The handsome white flowers appear in clusters and are long lasting, making excellent cut fresh or dried flowers. This species is not in general cultivation but is very hardy and tolerant of a variety of soils. It is worthy of more widespread use. Root protection is desirable. It can be readily propagated from cuttings.

Hemiandra pungens (see also p. 57)   W.A.
Snakebush   Spring and summer

The prostrate form of this somewhat variable plant is most commonly cultivated as a garden specimen. The small spreading shrub is a very good rockery specimen, growing to a diameter of 1 m with rigid, pointed leaves. Flower colour is variable from mauve-pink to almost white with pink-spotted throat. An extremely well-drained position with full sun is essential for this plant.

Isotoma anethifolia   Qld. Summer

In warmer climates this herbaceous plant reaches a height of 30 cm and can be grown as a perennial. However in colder areas it may not survive beyond one year. It has masses of star-like white or pink flowers with dainty light green foliage. The old foliage should be heavily pruned after flowering to give fresh new growth and abundant flowers in the next season. The sap from this plant can irritate the skin and should be avoided.

Kunzea ambigua (see also p. 29) N.S.W., Vic., Tas.
Tick Bush; White Kunzea   September to November
Growing to a height of 2 to 3 m, this shrub has masses of small creamy-white, honey-scented flowers in heavy sprays. In sandstone and granite-based soils it grows into a rather stiff, upright, spreading shrub with fibrous, furrowed bark. The seed capsules are distinctive but remain on the plant only until they mature. Light pruning will help to shape and develop a bushy specimen. The flowers are attractive to honeyeaters. This is a hardy shrub which prefers a well-drained soil and either full or partial sun.

Leptospermum flavescens 'Cardwell'   N.S.W., Qld.
Winter and spring

This shrub is a truly outstanding specimen with its weeping foliage absolutely covered with masses of white flowers along the arching branches. The 1.5 m tall shrub has light green, oblong leaves and grows well in a sunny, well-watered position. It is frost tolerant and responds well to pruning after flowering.

Leptospermum flavescens 'Pacific Beauty' N.S.W., Qld.
Winter and spring

This semi-prostrate form of *L. flavescens* is well suited as a rockery plant growing to a height of only about 80 cm with a spread of 1 m. It has a cascading habit with fine lacy foliage. The new growth is an attractive pink colour. The plant is smothered in winter and spring with large white flowers with a pale green centre. It is a hardy shrub and tolerant of salt spray. Pruning is recommended to maintain a bushy appearance.

Libertia paniculata   N.S.W., Vic., Qld. Spring
This tufted plant has grass-like leaves and white flowers on slender, branching stems which grow to 50 cm in length. Most soils are generally suitable. A partially shaded location is desirable. Additional plants can be cultivated by division of the parent plant.

Melaleuca linariifolia 'Snowstorm'   N.S.W., Qld.
Spring and summer
This is a registered cultivar of the species and a profuse flowerer. Masses of white flowers cover the bushy shrub which grows to 3 m and has light green foliage. As with other profuse-flowering forms, this plant is attractive to honeyeaters. A sunny and moist position is ideal for this specimen or screen plant.

Lophostemon confertus   N.S.W., Qld.
Brush Box   November to December
This species is widely grown as a street tree or separate specimen, under a wide range of conditions. It is a straight-trunked tree, with a dense conical crown, often attaining a height of 30 m in warmer areas, although in colder areas it seldom exceeds 10 to 15 m. The young shoots have white or silky hairs and exude a milky juice when broken. The elliptical leaves are glossy green above and dull green below. Feathery clusters of cream-white flowers are a favourite with honeyeaters.

Melaleuca alternifolia   N.S.W., Qld. Summer
As shown by this large tree growing in the Australian National Botanic Gardens in Canberra, the dark green leaves and masses of bottlebrush-like white flowers make it a most attractive asset in a garden where sufficient space is available. It grows as a bushy shrub to a height of 6 m with a spread of 4 m and has papery bark. It is a hardy plant for poorly drained conditions and will tolerate shade as well as open sun.

Micromyrtus ciliata
Fringed Heath-Myrtle   S.A., Vic. Late winter and
spring
This well-known shrub varies in habit from prostrate to upright and is a most interesting addition either as a groundcover or an individual specimen. It is graceful in appearance, with long tapering and arching branches which may reach up to 1 m in length. Overall height seldom exceeds 1 m. In full sun this plant makes a spectacular rockery specimen, with masses of small cup-shaped flowers which vary in colour from white to flush pink and red and remain on the plant for several weeks. The tiny leaves and flowers are some of the smallest of all native garden shrubs. Once established, it stands drought well, although adequate watering ensures lush and continuous growth during the first couple of years. Flowers are excellent for indoor arrangements in shallow bowls and are long lasting. If allowed to dry out slowly, the stems will retain enough colour to be used to advantage in floral arrangements. The leaves are aromatic when bruised. Light, fine soils and good drainage are preferred.

Myoporum viscosum   N.S.W., Vic., S.A. Summer
Sticky Boobialla

Growing as a rounded shrub to 2 m high and a spread of 1.5 m, this species has narrow leaves up to 7 cm long and white flowers 1 cm in diameter. In a well-drained, sunny position in the garden it is a hardy plant and is resistant to salt spray.

Olearia floribunda N.S.W., Vic., A.C.T., Tas., S.A.
Spring to early summer

Another of the daisy family, *O. floribunda* is a shrub growing to 1.5 m high and bears small white daisy flowers. Like most of the *Olearia* species, it will become woody unless pruned regularly. It is one of the native plants which responds well to fertilisers, producing lush growth. It is hardy and suitable for most soils.

Olearia microphylla   N.S.W., Qld. Late winter and
Bridal Daisy Bush   spring

This small erect shrub reaches 1 m high and a width of 60 cm and produces masses of small white daisy flowers among the tiny dark green leaves. A sunny or partially shaded position with well-drained conditions in a rockery or large pot is preferable for this frost-resistant plant. Regular pruning is recommended.

Pandorea pandorana N.S.W., Qld, Vic., Tas., W.A.
Wonga Wonga Vine   Spring

Native vines and creepers are very useful for growing on pergolas, fences, dead tree stumps or even over a bank. The Wonga Wonga Vine is no exception and is a vigorous woody climber with shiny leaves. Clusters of creamy white bell-shaped flowers appear in profusion and almost completely cover the foliage. This specimen covering a large tree at the Australian National Botanic Gardens in Canberra has not quite reached its best flowering period. Most soils are suitable, although a moist composted soil is preferable. It is frost resistant and prefers a semi-shaded position, although it will also grow in full sun.

Passiflora aurantia (see also p. 31)   N.S.W., Qld.
Golden Passionflower   All year

The native *Passiflora* species are commonly herbaceous or woody vines which climb with the aid of tendrils. The light green leaves are alternate and generally 3-lobed. The attractive white to salmon-pink flowers with deep red centres are bisexual and normally have 5 petals and 5 sepals. Although the flowers only open for a day, they are produced all year and give a very interesting touch of colour to a fence or trellis. A warm, sheltered, moist position in a frost-free area is preferred.

Pimelea ligustrina   N.S.W., Vic., Qld, Tas., S.A.
Tall Rice-Flower   Summer

The elliptical or lanceolate leaves of this open shrub are light green and up to 5 cm long. The white heads of pincushion-type flowers appear on slender stems, sometimes with a drooping appearance. It usually grows up to 2 m tall and is a hardy plant in a well-drained area. Flowering and rounded growth can be promoted by pruning at the end of the flowering season. This plant will grow and flower well in a semi-shaded as well as a sunny position.

Pittosporum undulatum (see also p. 76)   N.S.W.,
Sweet Pittosporum;   Qld, Vic., Tas., S.A.
Mock Orange   Spring

One of the most widely cultivated and hardiest of all native trees, the Sweet Pittosporum will tolerate almost any condition so long as adequate moisture is available. A sunny position will produce more flowers than a shaded one. It is a fast-growing bushy tree to 8 m, with waxy, dark green mature leaves and sweetly perfumed, cream-white flowers. The fruits are light orange and sticky when open. They attract many birds. The new leaves are light green and contrast with the more mature dark green leaves.

Pratia pedunculata (see also p. 59)   N.S.W., Qld,
Trailing Pratia   Vic., Tas., S.A.
Spring and summer

In wet areas, this prostrate creeping plant will form a close mat up to 1 m across with soft green oval leaves and masses of star-like white or pale blue flowers. It is an ideal groundcover for poorly drained conditions in a rockery or tub, especially in cold or frosty areas.

Pseudanthus pimeleoides   Qld. July

Plants of this small shrub grow in open sunny forests on steep hillside slopes, normally at fairly high altitude. The natural soils are mainly clay with stone mixed in. The species grows to 60 cm high and has an open branched habit. The attractive small flowers are brilliant white and contrast with the small dark green leaves. This plant is not common in cultivation. However the specimen shown growing in a well-drained rockery bed at the Burrendong Arboretum near Wellington, N.S.W., shows the potential for use as a garden specimen.

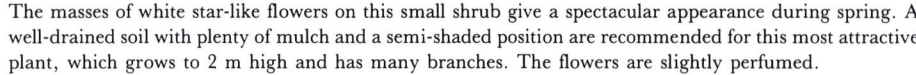

Ricinocarpos pinifolius   N.S.W., Qld, Vic., Tas.
Wedding Bush   Spring

The masses of white star-like flowers on this small shrub give a spectacular appearance during spring. A well-drained soil with plenty of mulch and a semi-shaded position are recommended for this most attractive plant, which grows to 2 m high and has many branches. The flowers are slightly perfumed.

Rulingia hermanniifolia   N.S.W. Spring
Wrinkled Kerrawang

The deep green, wrinkled leaves of this groundcover make an interesting contrast in a rockery, where the branches will grow gracefully over the rocks. In early spring, the plant is covered with pink-tinged buds followed by small straw-like flowers which open white and fade to pink with a red centre. Plants rarely grow taller than about 100 mm, but can spread up to 1 m across over a period of 2 years. This species has adapted well to cultivation and prefers a well-drained sunny position.

Scaevola albida (see also p. 60)   N.S.W., Qld, Tas., Vic., S.A., N.T. Spring and summer

Another spreading groundcover, *S. albida* is an excellent rockery plant, hardy in most locations where reasonable drainage is available. It can also make a handsome specimen for a hanging pot with the foliage cascading over the edge. The white or lilac flowers are fan-shaped and the leaves add a touch of bright green. Pruning will maintain a bushy appearance.

Sollya heterophylla   W.A. Spring and summer
Bluebell Creeper

The common name is somewhat misleading, since several colour forms of this vigorous climber or small shrub exist. In addition to the blue form, white and pink flowers are common. The dainty bell-shaped flowers hang on short stems, either singly or in groups, from the oval, pointed green leaves. The flowers are followed by sprays of berries which turn blue as they ripen. This plant is very hardy and suitable in most soils where drainage is reasonable. It is useful for climbing over fences or banks, and can also be grown as a small garden specimen to 1 m in height, or in a hanging basket.

Spyridium parvifolium   N.S.W., Vic., Tas., S.A.
Dusty Miller   Spring and early summer

This beautiful specimen of the Dusty Miller has attractive grey rounded leaves which are strongly veined. The terminal flowerheads are surrounded by white leafy bracts and almost completely cover the foliage. This species grows as a rounded shrub to around 1.5 m with a similar spread. It can be a most attractive specimen and is generally hardy in well-drained soils with almost any aspect in the garden.

Telopea speciosissima 'Wirrimbirra White' Cultivar. (see also p. 54)   N.S.W. Spring

In contrast to the more familiar red form of the N.S.W. Waratah, this white form found in the Wirrimbirra Nature Reserve near Bargo N.S.W., has been grown very successfully, as illustrated by this specimen at the Australian National Botanic Gardens in Canberra.

Westringia fruticosa (see also p. 80)   N.S.W. November
Coastal Rosemary

Probably one of the most widely grown natives on the east coast, this shrub is an excellent choice for a simple and neat feature in any garden. It is easily grown in a wide range of soils including clays, reaching a height of 1.8 m. It is a good choice for a seaside garden as it is resistant to salt spray and is often seen growing right on coastal headlands. The lower branches provide effective cover right down to the ground and can extend up to 4 m across. Young tip growth and leaf undersides have a silvery tint that adds to the overall attractiveness of the shrub. The small white flowers resemble other flowers of the mint family but are conspicuous against the dark foliage and seen most months of the year except in extreme heat or cold. They are generally abundant in November. The stiff straight sprays are surprisingly handsome, especially in a large arrangement. They live well in water and continue to open for weeks.

6 Colour Without Flowers

Flowers that smell like sweet honey,
Flowers like puffs of snow,
Fruits like wooden goblets,
Buds a dark red glow—
Darling of the summer-time,
Wherever it may grow.

Nuri Mass
Australian Wildflower Magic
(The Writer's Press, 1967)

Although a flush of flowering is likely to occur in most gardens in spring and summer, an attempt should be made when planning the garden and selecting plants to have some colour throughout the whole year.

Colour in autumn and winter should be carefully planned. Species of *Banksia, Crowea, Correa* and *Grevillea* can provide flowers in these periods.

However many attractive colours and shades are evident in the foliage, fruits, and bark of many shrubs and trees. These colours can complement those of the flowers or give colour to the garden at times when flowers are limited or absent.

Fruits and Nuts

Fruits, or nuts, are the products of fertilisation of flowers and contain the seeds for reproduction. After fertilisation, the fruit develops as a woody capsule with valves which open on drying to release the seeds.

Many fruits are also a source of food for native birds and mammals, who disperse the seeds, and these fruits may have an attractive scent. Fruits have an interesting range of colours and give character to a garden. The operculum or bud cap of the eucalypts is also quite colourful.

The fruits are an important consideration in choosing plants and are one of the most commonly used means of identifying species of some genera.

The following plates show plants which produce attractive fruits and nuts and are generally available for use in the home garden. Details of the individual species are presented in chapters 1 to 5.

The eucalypts are often quite distinctive in the size, shape and colour of the flower buds and fruit. A characteristic of the species known as the yate gums are the long horn-shaped operculums or bud caps. The large fruits which follow the flowers of the Bushy Yate (*Eucalyptus lehmanni*) show up against the green-yellow flowers and narrow, dark green leaves at the end of the flowering season.

The bright red, biretta-like operculums of the Red Cap Gum or Illyarrie (*Eucalyptus erythrocorys*) make it one of the most spectacular gum trees during the flowering season. This species is commonly grown as a street tree in various parts of Adelaide.

The graceful weeping foliage of one of the most beautiful ornamental eucalypts, *Eucalyptus caesia* 'Silver Princess', is enhanced by the attractive grey bell-shaped fruits which remain on the tree for several months after flowering finishes. They can be dried and used for indoor arrangements with other fruits or dried flowers.

The Tasmanian Blue Gum (*Eucalyptus globulus*), floral emblem of Tasmania but also found in southern Victoria, is a rapid-growing forest tree, often reaching a height of 30 m. The attractive blue-grey juvenile foliage is suitable for floral arrangements. The grey-green bud caps shown here with the cream-yellow flowers contrast with the dark green adult foliage.

The yellow-white bud caps of the Swamp Mahogany (*Eucalyptus robusta*) add to its value as a medium-size, fast-growing tree. It is valuable for use in heavy wet soils since it naturally inhabits wet swampy areas. However, it adapts to drier conditions and tolerates coastal areas. The dark green leaves are also attractive.

The Swamp Banksia (*Banksia robur*) is a handsome garden specimen with large rumpled leaves and metallic green flower spikes which turn yellowish green as the flowers open and finally darken to a bronze-brown cone with age. The velvety new foliage is quite striking and adds an attractive touch of colour to the dark green leaves. Like many of the banksias, the seed follicles usually open only after a fire. The flowers attract honeyeaters and the cones are excellent for dried floral arrangements.

Many *Banksia* and *Dryandra* species produce remarkable fruiting cones which add colour and interest to the garden. *Banksia coccinea* and *Banksia speciosa* were painted by Ferdinand Bauer who visited Australia from 1801 to 1805 on the *Investigator*. These exquisite paintings include details of the flowers and fruit.

The Coastal Banksia (*Banksia integrifolia*) is generally prolific in producing attractive cones. The seed follicles open when mature to release the seeds and remain on the trees often for years. This species is common to many parts of the east coast and adapts to a wide range of soils and conditions as a garden specimen.

The narrow cones of *Banksia ericifolia* can often be as long as 25 cm and are generally tapered slightly toward the tip. This specimen has several opened follicles at the end, with the majority remaining unopened. This shrub is one of the most popular *Banksia* species cultivated in gardens and reserves.

The *Hakea* genus is renowned for its attractive and often unusual fruits which vary extensively in colour, shape and size. One of the largest is that of *Hakea bakerana*, shown here with several flowers, which originate from the old wood. These fruits grow up to 5 cm in diameter.

The flowers of the grass trees or black boys which are common along roadsides, are white, star-shaped and crowded at the top of a long, cylindrical flower spike. After the flowers die, the blackened fruit remain on the spike for many months and are an attractive feature. This specimen of *Xanthorrhoea preissii*, from W.A., is growing in the Terrace Garden at the Mount Annan Botanic Garden near Campletown, N.S.W. Grass trees are very slow growing and many years pass before a trunk is formed.

The *Syzygium* genus contains some 50 species which are mostly found in the rainforests of the eastern states. They generally have glossy foliage with colourful new growth and fluffy flowers followed by a variety of fruits which are attractive to many birds. The Riberry or Small-Leaved Lillypilly (*Syzygium luehmanni*) is one of the best lillypillies for cultivation. The dense weeping foliage often reaches the ground and the new growth changes through a range of bright to pastel pinks over a period of several weeks at least twice a year. The cream flowers are followed by masses of small pink to red fruits.

The larger, rounded red fruits of the Magenta Cherry (*Syzygium paniculatum*) make a very showy display during autumn. They follow the fluffy white flowers and generally appear in clusters. The glossy aromatic leaves are enhanced by new dark red growth after the fruits have matured.

Pittosporums are very hardy and make attractive and decorative garden or street specimens. The foliage is glossy and the fragrant flowers are followed by attractive long-lasting colourful fruits. *Pittosporum undulatum*, often referred to as Mock Orange, is the most popular species. In springtime it has a mass of creamy white, very fragrant flowers which last for about three weeks. Its foliage is quite attractive with the light green new foliage making an interesting contrast with the older dark green leaves. The flowers are followed by masses of yellow seed capsules which split open to display ruby-coloured seeds.

Pittosporum rhombifolium (Hollywood, Queensland Pittosporum, Diamond-Leaved Pittosporum or White Holly) is another native which has occasionally been used as a street tree. The cream coloured flowers in late spring are followed by a very dense cover of yellow capsules, each with two black seeds. These are quite showy and last until almost mid-winter.

The fruits of some species of the *Dodonaea* genus, commonly known as the hop-bushes, were used by the early settlers as a substitute for hops in beer making. Although the flowers are generally small and insignificant the colourful inflated fruits are attractive. The fruits of some species remain on the plant for long periods, making these plants useful ornamental specimens. Fruits vary in colour from green to bronze-red and are a favoured food for many birds. The bronze-red winged fruits of this species are typical of the genus.

Although a native of the warmer rainforest of the east coast, the Plum Pine (*Podocarpus elatus*) is popular as a specimen or street tree. The bluish-black, plum-like fruits, 25 mm in diameter, occur on female plants and are an attractive feature of the tree in autumn. Although sweet, the fruits are not as delectable as a plum. The fresh growth of the narrow leaves is also colourful and noticeable, varying in colour from pinkish-red to shiny pale green.

Although not common in cultivation, the Woody Pear (*Xylomelum pyriforme*) is well worth considering as a garden specimen, having similar requirements to the Waratah. A native of N.S.W., this species has long sprays of yellowish-brown flowers followed by large pear-shaped fruit covered by grey felty hairs. The new leaf growth is reddish-brown and very attractive. These unusual plants make good features in any garden. The fruits are also sought after for dried arrangements.

Known throughout the world for its delicious nuts, the *Macadamia* genus has only about 8 nut-producing species native to Queensland and N.S.W. rainforest. As well as producing nuts, these woody trees can make attractive garden specimens. The long sprays of creamy flowers are followed by rounded, extremely hard, green fruits which encase the nuts, dropping from the tree when dry. The species and associated hybrids used for commercial nut production, are propagated vegetatively. Some of the natural species produce toxic fruits. These trees are readily grown and prefer a rich soil in a sunny location.

Another of the Queensland rainforest plants, *Mackinlaya macrosciadia*, is not widely grown but can make an interesting garden plant for shady places or indoors as a pot specimen. The unusual symmetrical flowerhead, which lasts for up to 2 months, gradually changes into a cluster of dark-fleshed, blue-grey berries lasting for another 2 months. The leaves are similar to those of the Umbrella Tree (*Schefflera actinophylla*), however this plant is much smaller, sometimes growing several stems with a sprawling habit to a height of 2 m.

The *Casuarina* genus contains some 30 species which are endemic to Australia. The attractive foliage of these trees makes them most suitable for garden specimens, provided sufficient space is available. They can also be used for street trees. The foliage consists of graceful fine branchlets with inconspicuous leaves. Red or reddish-brown male or female flowers may be produced on the same or a different plant depending on the particular species. The fruits of the River Oak (*Casuarina cunninghamiana*), produced on the female plant, are an attractive feature of this species. The woody cones attract birds and open to release many seeds when mature.

The Tulipwood (*Harpullia pendula*) has also been called the Black Tulip on account of its beautiful timber which is highly figured with contrasting dark and light bands. A native of the drier rainforests of Qld and N.S.W., it is often grown as an ornamental street tree around Brisbane. It has a dense rounded canopy of light green foliage and somewhat insignificant small yellowish-green flowers. The orange seed cases with their shiny black seeds which mature between early winter and late spring are very attractive.

The Blueberry Ash (*Elaeocarpus reticulatus*) is one of the toughest rainforest plants of the east coast, adapting to almost any conditions as a garden tree. In winter the brilliant blue fruits hang on the tree for months, attracting large numbers of native birds. The dark green shiny leaves and dainty aniseed-scented flowers make this native tree well worth a spot in any garden.

The Turquoise Berry (*Drymophila cyanocarpa*) is a very dainty small perennial plant with small white flowers which hang beneath the branches. The globular blue or occasionally white, berries are produced mainly in late autumn and winter.

Growing in or around the rainforest of N.S.W. and Qld, the Orange Thorn (*Citriobatus pauciflorus*) produces attractive, small, edible, orange berries in spring and summer, sometimes extending to autumn. This small, much-branched, spiny shrub is very hardy and is best grown in a well-shaded position. The orange fruits are preceded by small white tubular flowers.

The N.S.W. Christmas Bush (*Ceratopetalum gummiferum*) is very common in the bush and as a garden tree in many parts of N.S.W. It is an outstanding ornamental tree, bearing masses of small starry white flowers in spring, but is best known for its calyx which enlarges and turns red, giving the impression of red flowers in summer. The flowers and calyces make excellent indoor specimens and have long been used by nurserymen as a Christmas cut flower.

The pale green succulent fruits of the Pine-Leaf Geebung (*Persoonia pinifolia*) are attractive against the dark green pine-like leaves. This graceful large shrub from N.S.W. will grow easily where good drainage is available and also under fairly dry conditions. Geebung is an Aboriginal word for the edible fruits. The foliage and bright yellow flowers are good for indoor floral arrangements.

The terminal flower spikes of *Rhagodia baccata*, commonly known as the Coastal Saltbush, are followed by attractive red berries which persist for most of the year. This plant is common along the sand dunes of N.S.W., Victoria, Tasmania, S.A. and W.A. It is very hardy and makes a good screen plant.

Colour in Foliage

Casuarina

The last, the long-haired casuarina
stands upon the hillside where,
against the turquoise night of those first
yellow stars, she shakes her hair.

Roland Robinson
Selected Poems
© The Estate of Roland Robinson 1989
Reprinted with permission, Collins/Angus &
Robertson Publishers

When we think of the foliage colour of our native plants and trees, our thoughts automatically turn to the majority of these which are evergreen. There are of course many shades of green and some botanical colour charts list at least 100 different shades to assist in plant identification.

The new growth on many species is often a much lighter green than the mature foliage and can make a very attractive contrast. With some species, for example, the Tasmanian Blue Gum (*Eucalyptus globulus*), the grey juvenile foliage of the tree in its early years of growth is distinctively different from the dark green adult foliage of the mature tree. It is therefore possible to create a range of foliage greens by choosing species which offer the desired variations.

However in addition to shades of green, there are also many other foliage colours (both of mature foliage and new growth) which can add colour to the garden outside the flowering seasons. These include the blue-greens, greys, reds, reddish-browns and copper.

Some Australian native species also have variegated forms as well as the normal green leaves. These are not easy to propagate or to cultivate and may be difficult to procure in most nurseries. Propagation by cutting or grafting is the only certain way of duplicating the variegations as plants grown from seed often revert to the original green colour.

Apart from adding colour to the garden, colourful foliage is very useful in floral arrangements and many florists make extensive use of native foliage as backing because of the range of colours and leaf shapes available. Foliage can also be used in dried arrangements where the colour is usually retained for many months.

Foliage is therefore very important in the garden and it is well worthwhile considering the options available when planning a garden. Since it is difficult to judge foliage colours from small plants in nurseries it is helpful to observe mature specimens in established gardens to choose desirable species. It is hoped that the illustrations in this chapter will help you to appreciate the variations which are possible and encourage a wider interest in discovering new species.

Our many native ferns offer a wide choice of shades of green. Since some of these are only relatively small, they can easily be grown in containers or hanging baskets, allowing them to be moved around as desired. Often ferns can be left indoors for short periods and make an attractive touch, especially when the new light green fresh growth is present. This rather large patch of Coral Fern (*Gleichenia dicarpa*), with its beautiful long creeping rhizomes, is ideal in a spacious moist position in the garden.

The maidenhairs are a group of delicate-looking ferns which grow in moist areas along stream banks or in rainforest. Most are quite hardy and can readily be grown in the home garden. The ever popular Common Maidenhair (*Adiantum aethiopicum*) with its delicate light green fronds has been grown for many years as a pot or basket plant.

The Bird's Nest Fern (*Asplenium australasicum*) is a very widespread and familiar fern that mainly grows on rocks or in trees in rainforest or protected situations in open forest. The attractive tussock of radiating fronds makes this fern very popular in cultivation. The light green colour of the new fronds is especially attractive. This specimen has been grown in a pot in the authors' garden in a shady damp corner.

One of the hardiest of all native ferns is the Prickly Rasp Fern (*Doodia aspera*) normally seen growing along creek banks and around rocks in cool areas. It is extremely easy to grow and adapts to most locations in a garden as long as it has an ample supply of water. The soft immature fronds shown here on a clump in the authors' garden have an attractive rosy-pink tinge which shows up the darker green, rough textured, mature fronds.

The Hare's Foot Fern (*Davallia pyxidata*) is an excellent fern for a hanging basket or on large boulders in a cool spot in a rockery. The outstanding, fresh, light green, creeping stems or rhizomes covered in hair-like scales turn to an attractive glossy dark green as the fronds mature. This specimen in the authors' garden is growing in a basket hanging from a tree in a cool semi-rainforest area at the side of the house and is a year-round feature.

The tree ferns come from rainforest areas of several states and are ideally suited for gardens where a damp, protected area free from frost is available. The Soft Tree Fern (*Dicksonia antarctica*) is popular with many home gardeners and grows to several metres over many years. The new light green foliage is attractive as the fronds unfold from the apex. These leaves can grow up to 3 m long.

The epiphytic or lithophytic ferns which grow on trees or rocks in the cooler rainforest areas of N.S.W. and Qld include two magnificent species, the Staghorn (*Platycerium superbum*) and Elkhorn (*Platycerium bifurcatum*). The two outstanding specimens seen growing here on trees show that these species can readily be grown in the home garden in a cool position. They can also be grown on large hardwood slabs. An adequate supply of water is essential in the warmer months and they must be protected from strong winds and frosts. As with many other ferns, the immature fronds are a beautiful light green.

This group of shrubs and trees in a built-up area in the authors' garden shows the pleasing effect which can be achieved from the contrasting greens of different species. The grey-green foliage of the *Homoranthus flavescens* at the front contrasts with the deep green leaves of the *Eriostemon myoporoides* on the left at the front. The fresh light-green foliage (and pink-red calyces) of the *Ceratopetalum gummiferum* and darker green leaves of the *Melaleuca armillaris* add both height and colour to the group. The tall leaves of the *Anigosanthos flavidus* plant next to the *Eriostemon myoporoides* complete the overall picture.

Many native plants and trees lend themselves to planting together either as a group of one species or as different species; as a windbreak, dividing fence or hedge. This group of *Acacia howittii* has been used to separate a garden from the road. The attractive, weeping, light green foliage of this species makes it most suitable for this application. It adapts readily to a range of conditions and is frost resistant. The phyllodes have a spicy aroma and masses of lemon flowers are an added bonus in spring.

Several specimens of the Willow Hakea (*Hakea salicifolia*) have been planted along the inside of this fence to provide privacy from the busy road in front. The attractive red colour of the tips of the new foliage make an interesting contrast with the dark green mature leaves.

The Coastal Rosemary (*Westringia fruticosa*) is one of the hardiest of all native shrubs. The narrow dark green leaves with silky grey undersurface give an overall greyish appearance. Several of these plants have been used in this attractive hedge. This shrub can be grown with little difficulty under any conditions.

This common, light green, tufted, perennial herb occurs in alpine parts of the country but adapts readily to the home garden and makes a somewhat unique specimen for rockery landscaping. The Cushion Bush (*Scleranthus biflorus*) forms a tight mat with the appearance of moss. The plants will shape themselves in and around rocks quickly to give a soft green background to more colourful neighbours. Regular watering is essential in dry periods.

In contrast to the green foliage which is common to the majority of native species, there are quite a number which have grey foliage either as immature or juvenile leaves or as mature growth. Several *Acacia* species have outstanding grey foliage which is very attractive in its own right or against the yellow flowers. The Cootamundra Wattle (*Acacia baileyana*), one of the most popular of all wattles, has ferny blue-green foliage and large clusters of brilliant yellow flowers.

The rounded silver-grey phyllodes of the Queensland Silver Wattle (*Acacia podalyriifolia*) are typical of the attractive foliage of some wattles. Like most wattles, this species is fast growing and adapts to a wide range of conditions, although it is often subject to disease in some areas. The seed pods are flat and crinkly and add to the character of this species.

Several species of eucalypt have grey or grey-green foliage, this feature often compensating for the somewhat inconspicuous flowers. This large specimen of the Argyle Apple (*Eucalyptus cinerea*) is a superb example of the species. The juvenile leaves are rounded and of an attractive blue-grey colour. The mature leaves are also blue-grey but elongated. This tree, with its decorative appearance, is excellent as a specimen street tree. It is suited to areas of low rainfall and is frost hardy.

The grey foliage of this group of *Eucalyptus cinerea* growing along the entrance to the Australian National Botanic Gardens in Canberra makes a most attractive contrast to the green foliage on many of the surrounding shrubs. This species normally grows into a very large tree with dark green leaves unless kept pruned to retain the juvenile growth.

The small, ovate, silver-blue leaves of the Silver-Leaved Mountain Gum (*Eucalyptus pulverulenta*) retain their attractive colour to full maturity. Its natural occurrence is restricted to two areas in the Blue Mountains and the southern highlands of N.S.W., but it adapts well to cultivation and is commonly planted in home gardens and commercial landscaping projects, as a result of its attractive features. It is also used extensively as an ornamental tree in California. The small white flowers are most attractive to bees, as shown here.

The new growth on many *Banksia* species is red or bronze-red. This specimen of *Banksia conferta* var. *penicillata* is most attractive with its masses of hairy, rusty-brown, new foliage. The mature leaves are deep green. Although this particular species is common in the bush around the Blue Mountains in N.S.W., it is not very common in cultivation as the flowers are usually somewhat hidden and not as attractive as those of some other species. Nevertheless the new foliage is typical of many banksias.

Several of the everlasting daisies have grey foliage and are well suited to rockery beds as an added source of colour when not in flower. The Common Everlasting (*Helichrysum apiculatum*) is a very hardy species that will grow easily in most soils provided drainage is good. The foliage is silver-grey with a cottony appearance. This plant is a vigorous grower and benefits from regular pruning. Clusters of small golden flowerheads appear from spring to autumn. These flowers are very useful in dried arrangements.

One of the most attractive melaleucas, as far as foliage is concerned, is the Grey Honey-Myrtle (*Melaleuca incana*). This graceful shrub has weeping branches with feathery grey leaves, and the new growth has delicate red tips which add to the effect. Many small pastel yellow flower brushes are produced in spring.

Red or orange tips are common on many of our native plants. The red gum tips which appear on many eucalypt species are a common sight along roadsides and in home gardens. While these red tips are attractive on the trees, they do not last in indoor arrangements and are best left on the trees. The orange-red tips on this roadside specimen are typical of many eucalypts.

In addition to its weeping habit, this paperbark or Willow Bottlebrush (*Callistemon salignus*) has distinctive copper-pink new foliage once or twice a year. Provided the tree is pruned after flowering each year it can yield an excellent well-shaped specimen or be used to cover a fence or as part of a screen.

Growing as a twisted shrub or small tree, the Dwarf Apple (*Angophora hispida*) is well worth cultivating in the home garden where sufficient space is available. In addition to the broad stem-clasping leaves which are rough and hairy and a profusion of white flowers in summer, this tree has beautiful young branches and flower buds covered in velvety rust-red hairs. The seed capsules which follow the flowers are attractively ribbed.

This *Baeckea* cultivar, known as *Baeckea virgata* 'Howies Feathertips', originated from a seedling grown at S.A. and J.M. Howie's nursery in Coopers Plains, Queensland. It has beautiful, fine, red-brown, new foliage which makes it an outstanding species for home gardens. It is a very adaptable shrub growing to around 1 m with a weeping habit. Brilliant white flowers which occur in small clusters at the ends of branchlets are a prominent feature from November to March.

This group of small shrubs along one of the paths in the rockery area at the Australian National Botanic Gardens in Canberra, shows the manner in which variation in foliage colour can be used to advantage when flowers are not present. The cream-yellow foliage of *Hypocalymma cordifolium* 'Golden Veil' in the centre contrasts most effectively with the red-tipped new growth of *Baeckea virgata* 'Howies Feathertips' in the foreground and *Crowea* 'Festival' in the background.

Originating in the Blue Mountains area of N.S.W., *Persoonia chamaepitys* is a most attractive prostrate plant with light green foliage resembling pine needles. The new growth has beautiful red tips which almost cover the plant in late winter and early spring. It likes a well-drained soil in a sunny position.

Another of the many plants which have attractive red tips on the new growth is *Woollsia pungens*. The mature leaves are dark green and quite prickly. This species has fine roots, prefers a well-drained sandy soil, and makes an ideal rockery subject.

The she-oaks or casuarinas are generally most attractive for their foliage and are well worth considering for use as street trees or garden specimens in large gardens. They are quick growing and adapt to almost all soil conditions. The Forest Oak (*Allocasuarina torulosa*) has the most attractive foliage of all of the casuarinas, with slender drooping branchlets showing a lovely copper-brown colour for many months of the year. As an added attraction, the trunk has rough corky bark.

Some of the native grasses can be quite attractive, both in foliage and flowers, when grown as rockery specimens or as part of a much larger garden plan. This specimen of *Pennisetum alopecuroides*, or Swamp Foxtail, growing in a rockery at the Narla Retirement Village in Newcastle, N.S.W., makes an unusual and attractive addition to the rockery. This grass clump is fast growing and flowers all year round in the garden. It is the only species of the genus which occurs naturally in Australia. The roundish, bluish-green leaves curve back to the ground, while the purple flower spikes, produced continually, grow to 1 m high, with the whole clump eventually spreading to 1 to 1.5 m across. It will grow with minimal attention in a wide variety of soils, but prefers some moisture.

The contrasting colours of juvenile and mature leaves, a feature relatively common in some eucalypts, can make an interesting display. This specimen of *Eucalyptus globulus*, or Tasmanian Blue Gum, shows a striking contrast between the somewhat rounded, grey-green, juvenile leaves and the long, dark green, mature ones.

Tree Trunks and Barks

Scribbly-Gum

The cold spring falls from the stone
I passed and heard
The mountain, palm and fern
spoken in one strange word.
The gum-tree stands by the spring.
I peeled its splitting bark
and found the written track
of a life I could not read.

Judith Wright
Collected Poems
® Judith Wright 1971
Reprinted with permission,
Collins/Angus & Robertson Publishers

Carnivorous plants are to be found on all continents and are not uncommon in Australia. It is thought that their unusual appetite for living creatures arises from a need to supplement certain deficiencies in the soil. Some of these unusual plants are quite colourful and are of interest as garden or pot specimens. The sundews or *Drosera* employ 'flypaper' traps to attract their prey. The leaves of these plants are covered on the upper surface with long sticky-tipped hairs or tentacles. These are sensitive and when a tentacle catches an insect it will bend over to begin enfolding it. In the meantime an impulse is conveyed to its neighbouring tentacles causing them to bend over to complete the capture. The digestion and absorption of the prey are also the function of these sticky hairs. The two rosetted *Drosera* species shown are quite attractive with their red leaves. These plants require plenty of water, so if grown in a pot they should be placed in a saucer or tray of water. They generally like a sunny spot away from strong breezes. A pot on a window sill can make an attractive conversation piece as well as giving an opportunity to observe the plants feeding on flies and other insects. Part of the charm of these plants is in the glistening appearance of the sticky glands.

Trunks and bark are a beautiful and distinctive feature of many native trees. This is particularly so with species which are deciduous, producing textures and colour patterns which change with the seasons. In general the most attractive barks are associated with large shrubs and trees since the trunks of smaller trees and shrubs are often covered by branches and foliage. A well chosen tree with attractive bark can make one of the most attractive features of any garden. Eucalypts show great variety in the texture and colour of their barks and very often the choice of a particular species is based on the characteristics of the trunk as the flowers of some species are insignificant.

The rough, almost black bark of the Mugga or Red Ironbark (*Eucalyptus sideroxylon*) is characteristic of ironbarks from N.S.W. and Victoria. The trunk is deeply furrowed and the colour of the bark on the trunk continues onto the lower branches. The soft grey-green new foliage and pendant flower clusters also add to the beauty of these trees. The flowers, in autumn and spring, are generally pink to bright red but sometimes white. This small to medium-size tree is extremely hardy and will grow under a wide range of conditions.

The irregular markings or 'scribbles' on the smooth pale-coloured bark of this Scribbly Gum (*Eucalyptus haemastoma*) are typical of a group of eucalypts with this common name. The irregular markings are caused by the larvae of insects. *E. haemastoma* is a small to medium tree with small creamy flowers in spring.

Growing in a rather restricted area around the border between N.S.W. and Qld, the Wallangarra White Gum (*Eucalyptus scoparia*) has slender white powdery bark, sometimes with light grey blotches. It is a graceful tree and is generally well branched, resulting in an open crown with plenty of shade. This species is tolerant of dry conditions and is frost resistant.

A medium to tall forest tree, the large-fruited Grey Gum (*Eucalyptus canaliculata*) has dark brown flaky bark which makes way in spring for newly emerging grey-brown bark. This tree is endemic to a restricted area in the Dungog-Gloucester district of the coastal ranges of northern N.S.W.

Probably one of the most popular of all eucalypts for home gardens and street trees, where sufficient space is available, the Narrow-Leaf Black Peppermint (*Eucalyptus nicholii*) has an attractive fibrous brown bark. It does not usually grow to more than 12 m and has rather irregular branches with a tendency to weep. It is frost resistant and moderately drought resistant.

The Sydney Blue Gum (*Eucalyptus saligna*) is a common tall tree of the coast and nearby ranges of N.S.W. and adjacent parts of Qld. It usually has smooth white bark except for a short stocking of persistent rough bark at the base of its trunk. As the old bark is shed to make way for new growth, the long curly strips hang down from the new bluish-white bark. This is an attractive tree for parks, avenues and large spaces.

The *Casuarina* genus is well known for its range of fast growing species with graceful branchlets and colourful flowers and cones. Some species also have most attractive bark. The Forest Oak (*Allocasuarina torulosa*), in particular, is renowned for its interesting rough corky bark.

Multi-stemmed eucalypts have a different character from the usual single-trunked type. The Brittle Gum (*Eucalyptus mannifera* subsp. *mannifera*) is a medium-sized tree which is often naturally multi-stemmed or responds well to coppicing to obtain a multi-stemmed specimen. The white bark, often mottled with patches of grey and pink, is most striking. This tree needs good drainage and has a tendency to drop branches, as the name suggests.

Often mistaken for eucalypts, the angophoras are closely related but differ in that the leaves are usually opposite and the buds do not have the operculum or bud cover of the eucalypts. The Smooth-Barked Apple (*Angophora costata*) grows to a height of 20 m and is renowned for its gnarled and twisted branches with pitted salmon-pink bark. This handsome tree is fast growing and suited to most well-drained soils. Large clusters of white flowers are produced in spring.

Often seen growing with roots in salt water lakes or creeks, the Swamp Oak (*Casuarina glauca*) grows into a large tree 20 m high. The branchlets are much stiffer than those of some other species, but the tree often has a slightly drooping habit. Although it thrives in very wet soils, this species adapts to most conditions and is frost resistant. The rough grey bark often has patches of a grey-green fungus which add to its appearance.

Some species of *Melaleuca* are often referred to as paperbarks since they have papery, white or grey-textured bark which can be peeled off in thin layers. The Broad-Leaved Paperbark (*Melaleuca quinquenervia*) is typical of these. The dull green leaves and cream bottlebrush-type flowers in late autumn complement the beauty of the bark.

In contrast to the rough furrowed barks of some casuarinas, the Coastal She-Oak or Horsetail She-Oak (*Casuarina equisetifolia*) has rather smooth grey-brown bark as a young tree. This species is salt and wind tolerant and has been used extensively for seaside plantings along the Queensland coast. It generally has an open habit with soft weeping silver-grey foliage.

One of the largest of the banksias, the Saw Banksia (*Banksia serrata*) has a gnarled appearance with large, rough, oblong, saw-toothed leaves. This species is salt tolerant and excellent in a seaside garden. As well as large, beautiful, silver-grey to yellow flowers and pale red or brown new growth, it has unusual grey-green bark with a slightly furrowed appearance.

Fungi in the Garden

Fungi are separated from other members of the plant kingdom by the fact that they lack chlorophyll, the compound that gives plants their green colour. Light is essential for green plants, but has no effect on the growth of fungi as they are unable to manufacture their own food and have to grow on dead or living organic matter. Reproduction is from spores rather than seeds. Though fungi lack chlorophyll some species have different green and other coloured compounds which contrast with the foliage of surrounding plants.

Grass trees are a common sight in many parts of the Australian bushland. They are very slow growing and ones like this specimen of *Xanthorrhoea glauca* subsp. *angustifolia* growing at the Australian National Botanic Gardens in Canberra are often many hundreds of years old. Although they usually have a single stem, some plants branch out to form multiple heads. The blackened trunks make an attractive feature and specimens of this genus can often be used to advantage in a home garden.

The papery bark of the Willow Bottlebrush (*Callistemon salignus*) is somewhat similar to that of some *Melaleuca* species, although it is not nearly as thick. The pinkish colour of this bark, on a mature specimen, adds to its attractive appearance. The coppery-pink new tip growth on the leaves is also outstanding.

This distinctive and colourful specimen is typical of many of the saprophytic fungi which can often be found growing on dead organic matter in the garden. Saprophites can be very efficient at digesting organic material of all kinds, destroying stored products and even structural timbers where very damp conditions exist.

7 Plant Selection, Care and Maintenance

Though poor and in trouble I wander alone
   With a rebel cockade in my hat;
Though friends may desert me, and kindred disown,
   My country will never do that!
You may sing of the Shamrock, the Thistle and Rose
   Or the three in a bunch if you will:
But I know of a country that gathered all those,
And I love the great land where the Waratah grows,
   And the Wattle-bough blooms on the hill.

Henry Lawson
Waratah and Wattle

Australia has a wide range of soils and climates and an extensive variety of plants, many of which can make attractive garden specimens. However, it is only in relatively recent years that attention has focussed on cultivation of many of these plants in home gardens. Although some are extremely adaptable to variations in soil type and climatic conditions, others can only be grown under very restricted and specialised conditions.

Careful attention to the selection, planting and maintenance of native plants is advisable when planning or expanding a native garden.

When selecting a particular species it is important to ensure that it is suitable for the location, soil condition and climate. Some of the larger trees have extensive root systems and can cause damage to drainage pipes, sewers and concrete footpaths if planted too close to these fixtures. Details of individual plant requirements have been given in the descriptions of specific plants in the earlier chapters of this book, and provide a guide for their selection.

This chapter presents some comments on various aspects related to obtaining, selecting, propagating, planting and maintaining native plants in home gardens and other areas. Detailed listings of plants for special soils and locations are included in several of the references given in the Further Reading section.

Selecting Plants

A reasonable range of native plants is available from local nurseries, although a more extensive range can be obtained from nurseries specialising in Australian plants. Plants are also available at several locations from Forestry Commission nurseries. A list of native plant nurseries has not been included here as these change from time to time. However details of nurseries specialising in native plants in the various states are included in the regular editions of *Australian Plants* published by The Society for Growing Australian Plants (SGAP). Local groups of this society exist in many areas and can generally be located through the telephone directory.

In some cases, especially for the more unusual species, it may not be possible to obtain plants from these sources and it is necessary to resort to propagation, either from seeds or cuttings. Some guidelines on propagating your own plants are included later in this chapter.

In the initial planning of a garden, or in selecting a particular plant for a specific purpose or location, it is usually best to confine your choice to plants which have been observed growing in your local area under similar conditions, or to seek advice from friends or your local nursery or SGAP group. As your garden and interests develop, you may wish to become more adventurous and try some of the more unusual species to complement your original plantings.

Since the majority of plants are likely to be purchased from nurseries, it is important to know what to look for when selecting individual plants. Most species grow better if planted into their permanent position when quite young, since many develop extensive or long tap roots at an early stage.

It is preferable, therefore, to choose a reasonably small vigorous plant, not too tall or leggy. The sooner the plant is in position the sooner it will adapt to the conditions existing there. As many of our plants are fast growing, a small vigorous plant will soon outgrow a taller leggy plant with root problems. The majority of nurseries use artificial fertilisers to stimulate root growth, and if too much is used to force growth, this can result in poorly developed root systems and very soft, weak tip growth.

Plants which have been left in a pot or container for too long can become root bound, with the roots coiling around the bottom of the container. These plants are not likely to grow well since the tap root may not be able to straighten out and penetrate deeply into the soil. The end result is usually a rather weak plant, which can easily be blown out of the ground by strong winds.

Plants come in a variety of containers, including plastic pots or bags and, in some cases, steel or plastic tubes. Root coiling is more common in tapered plastic pots. Smaller plants require a little more attention than larger ones when removing them from the container, since the root systems are generally not as well established and the soil can easily break away from them. When choosing plants in larger pots or bags, an ideal height for trees is about 50 cm, and for shrubs about 25 to 30 cm.

Plants should be chosen to suit the purpose in mind. If the plant is to be a specimen tree, a well-shaped upright plant with a strong main growing shoot should be chosen. For windbreaks, choose bushy plants with a lot of low branches. Do not buy plants which show signs of yellowing. Healthy plants will be green. Ensure that plants are free from disease and make sure there are no weeds in the pot as this can cause trouble for a long time if undesirable weeds are introduced into the garden in this way. Plants which have been tightly staked should be avoided, since it

is unlikely that they will have developed a strong root system. Ties around the tree and stake can also injure the bark.

Soil and Garden Preparation

While some species of plants can readily tolerate poor soil and drainage conditions, for example, *Melaleuca*, *Callistemon* and *Casuarina* spp., most plants will benefit from some form of soil preparation prior to planting. Plants often die because of inadequate soil preparation, especially in heavy soils where they become waterlogged. It is important to realise that many plants, especially smaller-growing species, require relatively small quantities of soil, and so it is not essential to prepare very large areas unless a complete garden is being planted. Weeds are a real cause for concern and should be removed. Creeping weeds such as couch and kikuyu can be particularly hard to control once plants become established, as the runners become entangled around the roots of the plant, restricting growth and using up valuable nutrients from the soil.

Where the plant is to be grown, the ground should be dug to a depth of about 30 cm to break up large clods. Drainage in heavy clay-type soils can be improved by uniformly digging in gypsum (at a rate of approximately 1.5 kg per square metre). Clay soils are also improved by digging in mulch and well-rotted organic compost. When using compost, it is best to make sure that it is free of weeds or seeds to avoid later weed growth.

Perhaps one of the most important aspects of soil preparation for many native plants is ensuring good drainage. Poor drainage can most easily be improved by raising the level of the growing area, since this will stop water from accumulating around the base of the root system. Where plenty of space is available, mounds of soil can be located where desired prior to planting.

Where space is limited or where garden beds are desired, the level can be built up with logs, sleepers, rocks, cut timber or other suitable materials. Local soil should be used wherever possible to backfill built-up beds. If insufficient local soil is available, imported soils should be well blended with the local material. Imported soils can often introduce unwanted weeds and fungal diseases which can attack the root systems of many Australian plants. Once new beds have been prepared it is advisable to leave the soil for a few weeks before planting, to allow any weeds to germinate and be removed.

An alternative to raising the level of the soil to improve drainage is to construct surface and underground drains to remove excess water. Earthenware or plastic drainage or agricultural pipes can be used for this purpose, either with or without gravel or coarse sand. Even with drainage pipes and drains of this nature, difficulties can still be experienced if there is insufficient slope for the water to drain away readily.

In seaside areas where soils may be saline, it is desirable to plant salt-tolerant species, or alternatively to improve drainage so that built-up salts can be flushed away by rain. Well-drained sandy soils are often lacking in nutrients and organic material, and these components need to be regularly replenished to promote healthy growth.

Pots or containers offer another alternative to creating well-drained conditions. With pots, the soil mixture most suitable for the particular species can be provided. In most cases, a free-draining mixture consisting of equal parts of coarse river sand, well-rotted leaf mould or peat moss, and weed-free sandy loam will provide adequate drainage.

The acidity or alkalinity of the soil is referred to as the pH and can be a significant factor when assessing the suitability of soils for various native plant species. The pH (hydrogen potential) is measured on a scale from 1 to 14. Soils with a pH of 4–4.5 are considered to be strongly acidic; those of pH 5.5–6

are moderately acid; while those with a pH of 6.5–7 are neutral. Alkaline soils have a pH of 7.5–8, and strongly alkaline a pH of 8–10.

Some plants grow happily over a wide range of pH, while others are very sensitive to acid or alkaline soils. The majority of plants prefer a neutral to slightly

acidic soil. Species from dry or arid areas are generally tolerant of alkaline conditions. Yellowing of foliage resulting from alkaline soils may be overcome by spraying with a solution of ferrous sulphate. The pH of strongly acidic soils can be increased by adding lime or dolomite.

These built-up beds at the Australian National Botanic Gardens in Canberra provide ideal conditions for a range of native plants requiring very well-drained conditions. In this case, treated logs have been used to form the beds.

In this new garden at the authors' home, small built-up pockets have been provided for unusual plants by inserting large concrete circular containers (open at the bottom) at different levels to achieve the desired drainage. These individual containers also allow separate soil mixes to be used for each container if desired. Some of the plants include *Lechenaultia formosa*, *Dampiera diversifolia*, *Thomasia pygmaea* and *Pimelea ferruginea*.

Planting

Correct planting procedures are important in ensuring that your plants have the best chance of establishing themselves in your garden. Planting time is important and should be based on local conditions and on the time when the plant is likely to achieve maximum development.

In higher areas where frosts can occur over several months, it is essential to wait until they are over before planting. In coastal areas, plants can be grown at almost any time, except during very hot periods. Generally the period from July to September is an ideal time.

In inland areas, it is probably best to plant after a period of rain when the soil is relatively wet. This is not always possible and regular watering after planting becomes important in these areas.

Frosts can create problems with some plants, and result in freezing of plant tissue. If thawing does not take place quickly leaf tissue can be damaged. Exposure of frozen tissue to direct sunlight can also result in damage, but this effect can be lessened by spraying the surfaces with water to promote more even thawing.

Plants are more likely to be damaged at the lower levels, where temperatures are lowest. Ground level temperatures are generally several degrees lower than at heights above 2 metres. Many species are able to cope with frosty conditions once they have reached a reasonable height. These plants are best protected with a cover during frost periods until they become established.

Smaller plants can be protected by planting them

under larger trees with spreading branches. Planting on the top of hills where temperatures are higher than at lower levels is recommended. Where some form of protection is necessary, a hessian cover around a frame can be effective. It is best to remove this cover during the day so that the plant does not become straggly and weak. Plastic is not recommended as a cover since the space inside can become quite hot and result in rapid thawing and damage to plant tissue. Inorganic mulch such as gravel or coarse sand is preferred to organic material, since it is less likely to retain moisture which can freeze. Weeds should also be removed from around the base of plants.

After the plant has been watered, by soaking thoroughly in the container, it should be allowed to drain while a suitable hole is dug. This soaking procedure is especially important in dry areas. The hole should be approximately 50 cm diameter (or at least twice the diameter of the container) and twice the depth of the pot. The hole should be filled with water, unless the ground is quite damp, and allowed to drain. If the water only subsides slowly, it is an indication that the soil is poorly drained and plants suitable for these conditions should be chosen.

Soil preparation, as discussed above, is important. If the soil removed from the hole is not reasonably open and friable, some of it should be mixed with loam or coarse river sand and well-rotted humus such as peat moss, leaves or cow manure. Fowl manure must not be used since it is too strong for most native plants. Addition of humus is especially important in very sandy soils to assist in the retention of water. Clay is usually reasonably rich in nutrients and a large variety of plants will thrive in it, provided it is prepared in the above way. Gypsum is valuable in breaking up the clay, but must be dug well in.

The plant should be removed from the container by inverting and tapping the edge of the pot while supporting the soil with the fingers. If the plant has been grown in a plastic bag, it should be removed by carefully cutting the bag down two sides and folding the plastic down to allow removal of the contents. Plants are sometimes supplied in steel tubes and care should be exercised in opening the container along the edge to avoid disturbing the roots.

After removal from the container, the root system should be inspected, and pruned where necessary with sharp secateurs. Care needs to be exercised in not disturbing the root ball to any great extent. Old and damaged roots should be removed. If coiling of the roots is evident, an attempt should be made to straighten them or selectively remove the worst sections, so long as their removal will not greatly affect the plant's growth.

It is generally advisable to add about 50 grams of blood and bone or one of the slow-release fertilisers manufactured specifically for native plants to some of the soil and return this to the hole, so that the remaining depth is about the same as the depth of the pot.

The plant should then be placed in the hole without disturbing the roots to within about 5 cm of the top of the hole and lightly tamped down. When the soil is relatively dry, the remaining hole is again filled with water and allowed to drain. Further soil should then be added to almost completely fill the hole and lightly tamped down as before. During very dry weather, it is useful to leave a small space between the top of the hole and the plant to aid watering. Regular watering is necessary for the first few weeks until the plant is established.

Care and Maintenance of Plants

Mulching

Although often neglected, mulching is most important, especially in dry areas. Mulching can help plant survival and growth by assisting in the retention of moisture in the soil, by reducing soil temperatures around the roots, and by reducing the growth of weeds.

A range of materials is suitable for use as mulches. These include: wood chips, shavings, bark, coarse river sand, gravel, bush litter and compost. Several layers of newspaper or plastic sheeting will help to eliminate the germination of weed seeds. Mulches of sand and gravel are preferred in frost-prone areas, where organic mulches which can retain large amounts of water are readily frozen and can cause additional damage to plants.

Care must be taken in ensuring that mulches are not placed too close to tree trunks. This is a common practice and unfortunately can damage the bark and provide conditions for attack by fungi and disease entry.

Fresh grass clippings are especially harmful if heaped around the trunk, since the decaying material generates heat which can damage or even kill the bark.

Once a plant has been planted and watered, it is beneficial to mulch it immediately. If this is done, it adjusts to conditions much more easily than if it is constantly watered during the early stages of growth.

Mulch can also improve the appearance of the garden as well as providing a good cover.

These mounds around the new Chancellery at the University of Newcastle provide excellent conditions for a range of native plants. Pine bark mulch has been applied generously to retain moisture and give an attractive appearance.

Staking

Stakes should only be used where severe wind damage is likely to occur, since a less robust plant may result. Too often stakes are left beyond their useful time and cause damage to the trunk. If a stake must be used, it should be as short as possible and be driven well into the ground so that it provides good support for the tree. Stakes should be put in at the time of planting to avoid damage to roots.

Good quality hardwood or steel stakes are preferable so that they do not easily decay. It is better to insert the stake on the windward side of the tree, where there is less chance of damage to it.

A relatively loose tie should be used to allow some movement. For larger trees it may be desirable to use more than one stake to avoid rubbing. Pieces of water hose enclosing the tie material may also be used to avoid cutting the bark. The stake should be checked regularly to ensure that the bark is not being damaged and stakes should be removed as soon as the tree is strong enough to support itself. Trimming the boughs as the tree grows can improve its balance.

The stake in this *Eucalyptus nicholii* tree is an example of the damage that can result if the stake is not removed when its job has been done.

Pruning

The primary purpose of pruning is to promote healthy growth, to preserve or enhance the shape of a tree or shrub, and to increase flowering. Pruning can also extend the life of plants, especially fast-growing species, and allow removal of dead or diseased material which could result in further damage if left unattended.

Almost all native plants will respond well to pruning. Regular pruning is essential if an attractive shape with healthy growth is to be retained. Superfluous growth should be cut away. Plants that have too much growth will suffer from poor flowering. Judicious pruning during the early stages of growth can eliminate the need for staking.

Tip pruning can be done at almost any time. However general pruning is normally best carried out after flowering has finished, so that subsequent flowering is not affected to any great extent. This time also usually coincides with the period of maximum new growth. Many native plants provide excellent cut flowers, and removal of flowers can be used as a means of pruning. Some species, such as *Grevillea* 'Robyn Gordon', flower almost continually in some areas and pruning can be done at any time.

A sharp pair of secateurs should be used to expose the smallest area, thereby minimising the possibility of disease. A slanting cut is preferable as the sap which is released covers the cut and allows it to heal quickly. If it is necessary to remove a large branch, the exposed area should be covered with creosote or an appropriate material.

This attractive hedge of *Westringia fruticosa* clearly shows the benefits of pruning to maintain a compact appearance. Many native plants can be used as hedges, provided they are pruned regularly to develop the desired shape.

Watering

It is often stated that Australian natives do not require watering. This idea probably arises from observing some plants growing in bushland areas under very dry conditions. Indeed there are many species which are drought resistant and plants which naturally grow in, or can adapt to, dry conditions should be selected for areas where water is in short supply. In addition, many of these species will also grow under a wide range of conditions and require a minimum of attention, as well as helping to conserve water.

In general most plants do not require regular watering, but there are some species which grow naturally in constantly wet conditions, and this requirement needs to be recognised when selecting species for garden cultivation. Because we often try to grow a much wider range of plants in our gardens than would occur naturally together, it is sometimes necessary to provide additional water.

Shallow-rooted plants require more watering than deep-rooted ones, because water applied on the surface will migrate to the lower roots before it is absorbed in the shallow roots. A single thorough soaking of the whole root area is preferable to a large number of brief waterings which can easily evaporate before penetrating the upper soil layers. Trickle irrigation systems are ideal for native plants, since they supply controlled amounts of water over a long period and minimise the quantity of water used. Light soils require more frequent watering than heavy soils, which retain the water more easily. Too much water can produce soft growth and result in wilting during dry periods. It is always best to water during a cool period.

Fertilising

In their natural state, Australian native plants generally rely on decaying organic material for their supply of nutrients, with those species found in rainforest areas generally receiving more nutrients than those from drier areas, where soils have a lower nutrient level.

In the garden, mulch and organic material can supply some nutrients. However, as a general rule, some additional fertiliser will generally be beneficial, especially in sandy soils where watering tends to leach out nutrients. Organic fertilisers (such as blood and bone or well-composted animal manures) or slow-release inorganic fertilisers are the safest to use, since they release nutrients at a controlled rate over relatively long periods. Fresh animal manures should be avoided, since they can easily burn the roots of native plants.

Fertilisers should be used relatively sparingly and are best applied when the soil is moist. Soluble inorganic fertilisers can be useful for pot plants and hanging baskets, but should only be applied sparingly.

Weeding

Weeds provide competition for water and nutrients and should be kept under control at all times. They are best removed when they are small and before they have an opportunity to spread. Mulching can be an effective way of reducing weed growth, by minimising the germination of seeds. Annual weeds are relatively easy to remove, provided regular attention is given. However perennial weeds, which include the creeping varieties such as kikuyu and couch, are extremely difficult to remove once established, and should be completely removed before planting.

A range of chemical sprays is available for eradicating and controlling a variety of weeds. These should be used with caution, since some types can sterilise the soil and render it unsuitable for native plants. Information on the use and handling requirements of specific chemicals should be sought from the supplier prior to use.

Pests

Plants should be inspected regularly for the presence of pests or diseases which can eat the flower buds and foliage, or in some cases destroy the whole plant or tree. It is not unusual to see some minor pest damage to native plants growing in their natural environment, and so it is expecting a little too much to hope that we can have a garden free from pests. Nevertheless it is disappointing to wait for several months for that special flower to open, and discover that the bud has been devoured by a borer or some other unwanted pest.

Regular observation can help to find pests which can often be picked off the plant and destroyed. Native gardens having a variety of flowers year round can attract a range of birds which can assist in control of insects. Chemical sprays should only be used as a last resort, since they can be dangerous and can affect birds and other beneficial insects and bees. Pesticides can also upset the natural balance of pests and predators, leading in some case to the introduction of a new range of pests which are not normally encountered. In some cases it may be essential to make use of a chemical pesticide to achieve pest control. In this case, advice should be sought on the safest and most effective pesticide for the particular problem.

Propagating Plants

A large number of Australian native plants can be propagated either from seeds or cuttings with little difficulty provided a few simple basic directions are followed. It is not always possible to purchase a full range of plants from local nurseries. Propagation not only makes it possible to grow a wide variety of plants, but also saves money and provides an added interest in gardening with Australian plants. Although many native plants are protected by law, most gardeners are more than happy to provide seeds or cuttings for propagation.

Cuttings are generally preferable to seeds since plants grown from cuttings are true to type and in general flower more quickly than those grown from seed. In addition, material suitable for cuttings can be found almost all year round. Plants grown from cuttings taken soon after the flowering season will, with some species, produce a flowering plant up to 30 cm tall the following spring. Seeds are also generally available from SGAP members, from native reserve seed banks and also from various nurseries.

Cuttings

Most trees, shrubs and smaller plants can be grown from cuttings. Exceptions include: *Eucalyptus, Casuarina,* some *Acacia* species and some of the lesser known genera. Some progress has been made in striking eucalypts from cuttings taken from small seedling material.

Cuttings should be taken from healthy plants and preferably in the shade or on a cool day. If the cuttings cannot be planted soon after taking they should be moistened with cool water and stored in a sealed plastic bag in an ice box or refrigerator. The cuttings should be taken with a clean sharp razor blade or knife. If the cuttings are kept for any length of time, they should be wrapped between sheets of damp newspaper in preference to leaving them in the plastic bag. Cuttings kept in this way will last for several days.

Two basic types of cuttings are usually taken: tip cuttings and lateral cuttings. Lateral cuttings generally contain a small heel (or portion of hard wood) to which the softer wood is attached. The base of the heel should be trimmed to remove any loose fibres and give a clean cut. Although it is difficult to generalise, the most suitable material for cuttings will generally consist of the current year's growth and some of the previous year's growth. With some species, however, the growth following the flowering provides a better material. In general more rapid growth is achieved with newer wood than with older wood.

Since in most cases the home gardener only requires one or two plants of a particular species or variety, it is possible to take several cuttings from different parts of the plant to enhance the chances of producing the preferred root growth. It should be emphasised that there is no substitute for experiment when growing cuttings. The size of the cutting will vary for each plant. For small plants such as *Thryptomene, Bauera* and *Prostanthera,* a typical cutting would be 35 to 60 mm long; whereas for large species such as *Callistemon* and *Grevillea,* a suitable cutting would be 60 to 80 mm.

After trimming the cutting, all leaves must be removed from the part of the stem that will be inserted into the rooting mix, otherwise the leaves will rot and could cause disease. Flower buds and flowers need to be removed as these deprive the young growth of nourishment and may also cause disease. Hormone powders are beneficial in stimulating root formation and can be obtained from most gardening stores and nurseries.

The Cutting Medium

Although many types of mixture are used for propagation of cuttings, personal experience has shown that a general mixture containing 4 parts coarse sharp sand and 1 part peat moss or vermiculite is suitable. The components should be spread out in layers, moistened with a fine spray of water, then thoroughly mixed.

It is important to use sharp (angular) coarse sand rather than fine beach sand to achieve rapid and well-developed root growth. The above mixture has the advantage that sterilisation is not normally necessary because the individual components are themselves sterile.

Planting the Cuttings

Cuttings are preferably planted in individual plastic containers (about 30 mm diameter by 75 mm long) to avoid disturbing the roots when transplanting. The moist soil medium should be transferred to the containers leaving the surface raised slightly above the rim. A hole is then made (to within about 4 mm of the base) using a pointed stick about 3 mm in diameter. The cutting is moistened by dipping into water and shaking off the excess. It is then dipped in hormone powder, shaken to remove the excess and inserted to the correct depth in the hole. The medium is pressed firmly around the cutting and the container watered freely with a fine mist spray.

Propagation Box

An inexpensive propagating box can be constructed from a polystyrene foam fruit or vegetable container. A moistened layer of coarse sand (about 30 mm deep) provides a suitable base for the tubes. A sheet of glass painted with white paint is placed on top of the box which is placed in a semi-shaded frost-free position. Any holes in the bottom of the box need to be covered and the top should be trimmed to provide a level base for the glass to fit. A deep box is best to allow sufficient space between the cuttings and the glass.

If only a small number of cuttings are to be grown, a 4-litre plastic ice-cream container covered with a plastic bag supported on a wire frame and secured at the top end is satisfactory. It is most important that the container not be placed in direct sunlight or overheating can easily occur and the cuttings will be burnt. Regular watering using a fine mist spray is necessary to maintain a high humidity inside the box. The plastic bag requires less watering since it is better sealed. A weekly spraying of the foliage with a complete nutrient is beneficial.

Transplanting Cuttings

Once an adequate root system has developed (usually from 4 to 10 weeks), the cuttings should be transplanted to larger pots to allow unhindered growth. First moisten the cuttings, then remove them from the container by turning it upside-down and tapping the rim on a solid surface (with the fingers supporting the cutting and contents of the tube). The contents are then transferred without disturbing the roots to a pot filled to within 75 mm of the top (or the depth of the propagating tube). Additional soil is then firmed around the cutting to almost fill the pot. A suitable potting mixture is: 1 part coarse sand; 1 part leaf mould, peat moss or fine pine bark; 1 part sandy loam. Plant growth can be considerably enhanced by the addition of 20 to 30 grams of a slow-release fertiliser to the pot before planting the cutting.

Plants can be left in the pots for extended periods if desired. However they should be transplanted progressively into larger pots to avoid the plant becoming pot-bound. The newly potted plant should be thoroughly watered and kept in a well protected shady area for several weeks prior to being hardened off in partial sun, and transplanted into the garden.

Seeds

Some native plants can be more readily propagated from seeds than cuttings. Typical examples include *Acacia*, *Eucalyptus*, *Anigosanthos* and some *Melaleuca* species. Although seeds can be readily collected from individual plants, it is probably best in the initial stages to purchase seed from a nursery, seed supplier or from your local SGAP seed bank.

Some seeds require pre-treatment prior to sowing to ensure ready germination and to speed up the process of germination. One of the simplest forms of pre-treatment involves pouring almost boiling water over the seeds and allowing them to soak for several hours. The main purpose is to swell the embryo and soften the outer shell. This procedure is particularly recommended for large hard seeds such as *Acacia*, *Chorizema*, *Hardenbergia* and *Kennedia*. The majority of small fine seeds such as *Melaleuca*, *Eucalyptus*, *Anigosanthos* and *Callistemon* can be successfully raised without any form of pre-treatment. It is important that seeds be sown when they are still fresh since many species deteriorate rapidly.

The Sowing Medium

As with the mixture for cuttings, the seed-raising medium should be sufficiently open to allow drainage but capable of retaining sufficient moisture to prevent rapid drying out of the surface, especially for fine seeds. A suitable mixture contains 1 part coarse sand and 1 part sifted peat moss or leaf mould. The mixture should be watered thoroughly (preferably with a weak fungicide) and allowed to drain prior to sowing.

Sowing Seed

Larger seeds can be sown in individual propagation tubes if desired. However it is generally more convenient to use a single container for several seeds. A convenient arrangement consists of a polystyrene carton filled with sowing medium to within approximately 75 mm of the top.

Larger seeds should be planted individually with the heavier end pointing downwards and covered with a layer of dry sifted sand to approximately the same depth as the seed. Fine seeds should be spread evenly over the surface of the medium (a pre-mix with fine dry sand permits a more even distribution to be achieved) and covered lightly with sifted dry sand. The surface is then patted down lightly and watered with a fine spray.

The seed box should be covered with a sheet of glass (painted white) and placed in a draught-free shaded position. The glass should be raised from time to time and removed as soon as the seedlings appear.

Transplanting

Plants should be transplanted (using a mixture similar to that recommended for transplanting cuttings) as soon as the first leaves appear. Some young seedlings (such as eucalypts) very quickly develop a long tap root and should be repotted early into tall pots to ensure that the tap root continues to grow steadily without curling around the base of the pot. Once the seedling has become established it should be repotted into a larger pot.

The plant should be removed from the propagation box by loosening the soil around it (with a pointed stick) to avoid damaging the roots. It should then be placed in a hole in the pot. Further soil is added while the plant is supporting, and then pressed gently around the seedling. The freshly potted plant should be watered with a fine spray and protected in a box or frame covered with glass or shadecloth for 2 to 3 weeks. The seedling can then be transferred to a shaded position to allow hardening before being planted into larger containers or the garden.

Propagation by Division

A limited number of native plants can be readily propagated by the division of established clumps. Perhaps the genus most suited to this form of propagation is *Anigosanthos*.

Clumps should be carefully lifted from the ground with a garden fork or spade without disturbing the roots. The larger clumps should then be separated into smaller ones and replanted. Separated clumps can be planted in pots to allow them to become established prior to planting in the garden if desired.

Other Methods of Propagation

Some genera such as *Dampiera*, *Scaevola* and *Helichrysum* produce suckers which grow from the root or stem of the plant under the ground. New plants can be established by cutting this sucker from the main plant and transplanting it into a pot until established. Violas produce vegetative shoots called stolons at the leaf nodes which run along the surface of the ground. New plants of this genus can be established by cutting the shoots from the parent plant and transferring them to a pot or directly into the garden.

Ferns are reproduced from spores which develop on the underside of the fronds. This primitive form of reproduction evolved well before that of the flowering plants.

The technique of grafting to establish new plants dates back to ancient times. It has been in use since 1000 BC and was used in Europe to introduce many species into cultivation in the 16–17th centuries. Grafting involves the union of two different plants by allowing the cambium region (actively growing tissue layer between the bark and wood) of the stock plant to come in intimate contact with a piece of the plant to be propagated (scion). This technique allows some of the more difficult plants to be grafted on to hardy easy-to-grow stock plants. In recent years several native plant genera and species have been cultivated successfully in this way. Notable examples include the grafting of *Prostanthera* species on to *Westringia fruticosa* and *Hakea* species on to *Grevillea robusta*.

A relatively new technique, tissue culture was originally developed to produce virus-free strains of commercial crops. In this technique, the tissue is dissected under sterile conditions and placed in a nutrient medium. The technique is being used with success to propagate some of the more difficult and endangered native plants. Examples include some species of *Anigosanthos* and *Platycerium*.

These latter methods are perhaps beyond the reach of the average gardener. However they do offer the prospect of producing more reliable garden plants and reproducing some of the rare and endangered species for widespead cultivation in the future.

8 Guide to Native Gardens

We stand in awe and wonder at the beauty
of a single tree. Tall and graceful it stands,
yet robust and sinewy with spreading arms
decked with foliage that changes through the
seasons, hour by hour, moment by moment as
shadows pass or sunshine dapples the leaves.

Richard St Barbe Baker
My Life My Trees

Botanic Gardens, Arboreta and Wildflower Gardens

LOCATION MAP

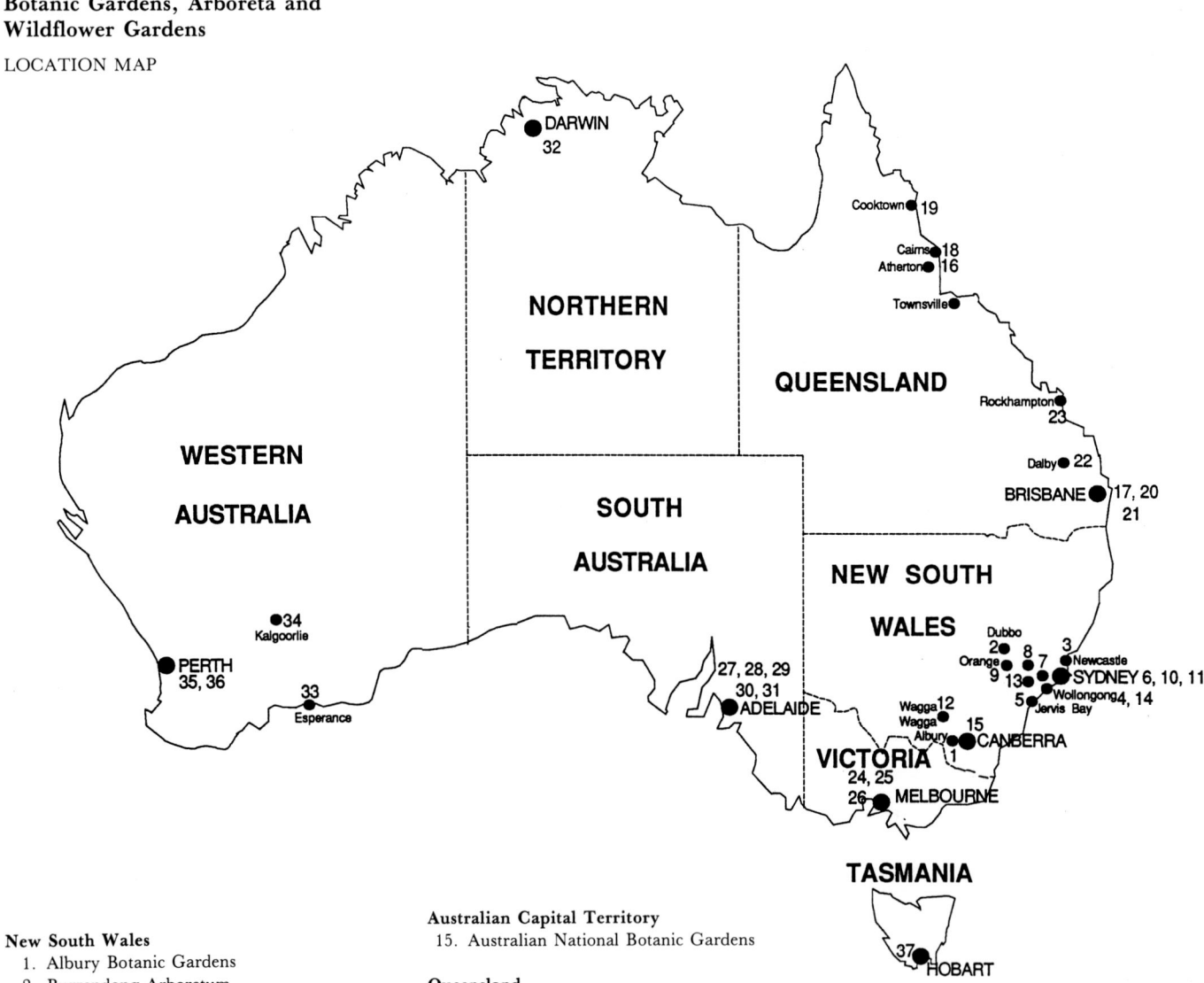

New South Wales
1. Albury Botanic Gardens
2. Burrendong Arboretum
3. Hunter Region Botanic Gardens
4. Illawarra Grevillea Park
5. Jervis Bay Annexe, Australian National Botanic Gardens
6. Kuring-gai Wildflower Garden
7. Mount Annan Botanic Garden
8. Mount Tomah Botanic Garden
9. Orange Botanic Gardens
10. Royal Sydney Botanic Gardens
11. Stony Range Flora Reserve
12. Wagga Wagga Botanic Gardens
13. Wirrimbirra Sanctuary
14. Wollongong Botanic Garden

Australian Capital Territory
15. Australian National Botanic Gardens

Queensland
16. Atherton Arboretum
17. Brisbane City Botanic Gardens
18. Cairns Flecker Botanic Gardens
19. Cooktown Gallop Botanic Gardens
20. Indooroopilly Long Pocket Rainforest
21. Mt Coot-tha Botanic Gardens
22. Myall Park Botanic Garden
23. Rockhampton and Kershaw Botanic Gardens

Victoria
24. Ballarat Botanic Gardens
25. Cranbourne Botanic Gardens
26. Royal Melbourne Botanic Gardens

South Australia
27. Adelaide Botanic Gardens
28. Black Hill Conservation Park and Native Flora Park
29. Mount Lofty Botanic Garden
30. Waite Arboretum
31. Wittunga Botanic Garden

Northern Territory
32. Darwin Botanic Gardens

Western Australia
33. Esperence Helms Arboretum
34. Kalgoorlie Arboretum
35. Kings Park Botanic Gardens
36. Western Australian Herbarium

Tasmania
37. Hobart Royal Tasmanian Botanic Gardens

Many botanic gardens and arboreta devoted entirely to native plants or with native plant sections have been developed throughout Australia. These gardens provide an excellent opportunity to see plants growing in the local environment and to observe the growing habits and cultural requirements. Some gardens have established extensive collections of plants from various parts of Australia. Specimen plants are often labelled, making identification easy.

The Society for Growing Australian Plants (SGAP) is an Australia-wide organisation aimed at encouraging interest in Australian native plants.

Some relevant details of this society, together with the location and a brief history and description of the features of the various botanic gardens, wildflower gardens and arboreta are included here. Details of native gardens and other wildflower areas under development are also included in the SGAP magazine *Australian Plants*.

The Society for Growing Australian Plants

In the 1950s, a group of gardeners who were interested in native plants founded the Society for Growing Australian Plants (SGAP). The main aims of the Society include:

encouraging the study, growing and propagation of Australian native plants
encouraging the preservation and conservation of Australian native plants
encouraging the use of Australian native plants as garden and other landscaping subjects.

The SGAP is an Australia-wide organisation with self-managing societies in each state. Each state society has a number of local groups which cater for the interests of members in the local areas.

These groups organise local meetings involving specialist and local speakers, local garden and field visits, propagation days, landscaping and garden advice, libraries of native plant publications, seed banks and other services concerned with the above aims.

Many of the groups hold an annual wildflower exhibition early in spring where native plants and flowers from the local area and other parts of Australia are displayed.

The Society publishes a beautifully produced magazine, *Australian Plants*, as well as local newsletters and other publications of general and specialist interest.

The SGAP has several study groups who take an active interest in paticular specialist plant genera or

groups and undertake experimental propagation and cultivation trials to determine specific requirements and means of propagating some of these plants in home gardens.

Members of the SGAP are pleased to assist new gardeners in selecting garden plants, obtaining cuttings, developing propagation skills or in any other aspect of native plant gardening. Visitors are always welcome at group meetings.

Details of local group activities can be easily obtained by contacting any SGAP member or the local group secretary (usually listed in the local telephone directory).

New South Wales

Albury Botanic Gardens

The Albury Botanic Gardens have been established for over 100 years and contain many mature tree species and varied plant life, some of which are of historical significance as well.

Formation of the botanic gardens first began in 1871 with the original government grant of 20 ha of land, now occupied by the sportsground, Hovell Tree Park, Noreuil Park, the Albury Base Hospital and the botanic gardens.

The gardens are situated on the Murray River alluvial flood plain, sheltered by the hills on the western side from the cold air flow in winter and the hot drying winds of summer. These conditions have allowed the establishment of a wide range of plant material.

The gardens have many magnificent specimens of various Australian native plants. These include *Eucalyptus citriodora* (Lemon-Scented Gum), *Stenocarpus sinuatus* (Queensland Firewheel Tree), *Flindersia australis* (Australian Teak or Crows Ash), *Castanospermum australe* (Black Bean or Moreton Bay Chestnut), *Brachychiton acerifolium* (Illawarra Flame Tree), *Toona australis* (Australian Red Cedar), *Agathis robusta* (Queensland Karri), *Backhousia citriodora* (Lemon-Scented Myrtle), *Araucaria bidwilli* (Bunya Bunya Pine), *Podocarpus elatus* (Brown Pine) and *Macadamia ternifolia* (Queensland Nut). One additional interesting and unusual specimen is the variegated Queensland Brush Box (*Tristaniopsis conferta* 'Aurea Variegata') which has beautiful golden yellow leaves with a broad irregular margin of green.

A guided walk brochure which gives details of the various trees in the garden as well as other points of interest is available from the gardens office.

The Albury Botanic Gardens are located in Wodonga Place, Albury.

Burrendong Arboretum (near Wellington)

An arboretum is a place where trees, shrubs and other plants are grown for scientific and educational purposes and for the conservation and propagation of plant species. Burrendong Arboretum conforms to this purpose, but unlike most arboreta around the world it contains a collection comprising only plants native to Australia.

Mr George Althofer, of Dripstone, N.S.W., who owned the first nursery in Australia for the propagation and sale of native plants, established the Burrendong Arboretum in 1964. This step was the

realisation of a dream which had been developed over many years as a result of his concern for the devastating effect on Australian native plants of the clearing of land for pastoral, agricultural and sylvicultural purposes.

With the aid of a small group of voluntary helpers, Mr Althofer planted 4000 plants during the first year. Now after 25 years of existence, the Arboretum, which comprises some 16 ha of rough, rocky hills ranging through gentle gravel and loam slopes to flat swampy land, now contains some 50 000 plants of more than 1600 species. These range from the ghost gums of Central Australia, royal hakeas of W.A., bloodwoods of Queensland and mallee of Victoria to the wattles of S.A. and mint bushes of N.S.W.; from the poverty bushes of the arid inland to the she-oaks and banksias of the coast; and the giant eucalypts to tiny prostrate cover plants.

Within its boundaries are more than 20 miles of roads and numerous walking paths. It also contains an artificial shade area in which ferns and subtropical plants are grown.

When it was first established it was hoped that of the 25 000 different species of Australian plants, 10 000 species would ultimately be grown at the arboretum. Annual plantings amount to some 5000 plants.

The Burrendong Arboretum is adjacent to the Burrendong Dam and State Recreation Area and is approximately 30 km south-east of Wellington. Access is via Dripstone. The Dripstone road leaves the Mitchell Highway approximately 5 km south of Wellington. The arboretum can also be reached from Orange via Stuart Town and Mumbil.

One of the built-up garden areas which have been used very successfully at the Burrendong Arboretum to grow a wide range of plants from all states of Australia, including many W.A. species. The rolling hills in the background add to the natural beauty of this area.

Hunter Region Botanic Gardens (Motto Farm, near Raymond Terrace)

The Hunter Region Botanic Gardens are being developed in an area of 140 ha of the much larger Tomago Sandbeds Water Catchment Area. This land is owned by the Hunter Water Board, and the gardens have been established under a lease arrangement with the Board formally signed in February 1988. The design, development and management of the gardens are under the control of the Hunter Region Botanic Gardens Ltd, which was established in November 1985.

The establishment of the gardens was entirely a community initiative. A grant was obtained from the local government initiatives program to assist in the construction of a visitor centre. A 'Friends' group has been established to assist in ongoing development and improve public awareness of the gardens. The overall gardens development plan is being implemented using voluntary community effort.

Several walking trails have been established in the gardens. These include the Cunningham Track and other tracks, named in honour of botanists prominent in Australian history. These tracks pass through the natural vegetation of the area. Information sheets available from the visitor centre give details of the flora and other points of interest along the tracks. Group plantings of prominent Australian genera, such as *Acacia*, *Banksia* and *Grevillea*, have been established. There is a large variety of birdlife in the gardens.

The Hunter Region Botanic Gardens are adjacent to the Pacific Highway at Motto Farm, about 4 km north of the Hexham Bridge (the junction of the New England and Pacific Highways). The township of Raymond Terrace lies about 4 km north of the gardens.

Illawarra Grevillea Park (Wollongong)

In 1978, a Special Interest Study Group was formed by members of the Society for Growing Australian Plants. This group had the aim of studying and collecting the various forms of the genus *Grevillea*.

In the decade following the formation of this group, it has been extremely active and a vast amount of plant study material has been collected. The largest collection of living *Grevillea* plants ever grown has been established. This collection contains almost 300 species, and subspecies, most of which have been grown from plants in the wild.

This represents the first time that many of these species have been grown outside their native habitat. The collection includes 20 species from the N.T. The study group has collected 113 of the 126 species listed by the CSIRO as endangered species.

In 1987, the Illawarra Grevillea Park Society, which grew out of the study group, was formed to establish a grevillea park to house this collection and to develop plants in a botanic garden situation for the purposes of study and public display.

A 10 ha area of land has been leased by the Wollongong Council to the Society to develop this park. During 1989, fences have been erected, garden areas have been prepared and some plantings have commenced. Once established, the park will be open to the public and educational groups.

The site is located on the lower part of the escarpment directly west of the township of Bulli, 15 km north of Wollongong.

Jervis Bay Annexe (Australian National Botanic Gardens, Canberra)

The Jervis Bay Annexe to the Australian National Botanic Gardens in Canberra was established in 1951. The site allows the cultivation of frost-sensitive native plants in conditions more favourable than those of Canberra. The Annexe covers approximately 80 ha and has an extensive collection of native plants for display and study. About 25 ha have been planted with native plants from around Australia. The remaining 55 ha are bushland. There are walking trails to guide visitors around the garden and attractive areas for picnicking.

Three trails, the Nature Trail, the Lake Trail and the Aboriginal Trail, provide well-marked paths through various parts of the gardens. The Rainforest Gully has a boardwalk to give a view of the many rainforest plants being grown. A booklet containing details of these walks and other garden features is available from the gardens.

The Green Hut contains displays featuring aspects of the botany and horticulture of Australian native plants.

Several trial plots have been established to grow some of the increasing number of native plants under threat in the wild. This area is not open to the public, but may be viewed from outside the fence.

The entrance to the Jervis Bay Annexe is off Cave Beach Road, south of Jervis Bay. The Annexe is closed on Saturdays and public holidays except on special occasions.

Kuring-gai Wildflower Garden (Near St Ives)

The Ku-ring-gai Wildflower Garden was established in 1963 by the Ku-ring-gai Municipal Council in conjunction with the North Shore Group of the Society for Growing Australian Plants with the aim of 'growing plants from all parts of Australia for preservation and public display, and by these means to attract tourists and visitors to the Ku-ring-gai Municipality.'

The total area of the garden is about 123 ha and it has been notified as a Reserve for the 'Promotion of the Study and Preservation of Native Flora and Fauna'. It is located on the northern side of Mona Vale Road, 5.5 km from the Pacific Highway and 19 km from Mona Vale.

To help visitors enjoy the garden, a number of walks have been made, passing through deep moist valleys and over windswept hilltops, through tall-treed forests and among massive rock formations, to open hillsides with shrubs which display flowers at almost all seasons of the year.

A booklet outlining these walks and including details of many of the plants in the garden is available from the pavilion in the garden.

Mount Annan Botanic Garden (Narellan)

Development of the first stage of the 400 ha Mount Annan Garden began in 1986 and is a Bicentennial project of the N.S.W. government undertaken by the Royal Botanic Gardens, Sydney. It is designed to display the diversity of the Australian flora, and representatives of many of the 25 000 known native plant species are already established there.

Mount Annan has theme gardens featuring bottlebrushes, wattles and banksias. The Western Garden also features major groups of Australian plants and the conservation areas contain valuable remnants of the original vegetation. The 4-5 ha Terrace Garden is a major part of the development; more than 30 000 plants demonstrate the nature of the Australian flora.

Twenty kilometres of walking track give visitors opportunities for recreation and exercise while enjoying close contact with the plantings, including the arboretum plantings which feature species of *Acacia* and *Eucalyptus*.

Mount Annan Botanic gardens are off Narellan Road, Narellan near Campbelltown.

One of the several callistemon gardens at Mount Annan Botanic Garden. The magnificent collection of callistemons in these gardens provides an almost endless range of colours during spring.

Mount Tomah Botanic Garden (near Bilpin)

Mount Tomah Botanic Garden is a 31 ha site of which 18 ha are being developed as one of the world's finest collections of cool climate plants of the Southern Hemisphere.

Late last century the land was a dairy farm, then used to rear horses. In 1935, French-born hoticulturalist Alfred Louis Brunet and his wife Effie started producing flowers there for the Sydney market. They offered their property to the Royal Botanic Gardens and in 1972 it was handed over and planting of the botanic garden commenced. In 1983, development of the garden was declared a joint commonwealth/state Bicentenary project. The garden was officially opened on 1 November 1987.

Collection expeditions overseas and in Australia began in 1983 to gather plants demonstrating the evolution of plant groups from cool climate areas of the Southern Hemisphere. The cool, moist climate and rich basaltic soil provide Mount Tomah Botanic Garden with an ideal environment for plants that would be difficult to grow on the surrounding sandstone-derived soils.

Huge forest giants, the eucalypts Blaxland's Stringybark (*Eucalyptus blaxlandii*) and Brown Barrel (*Eucalyptus fastigata*) are the dominant trees of the hilltops. Additional stands have been planted as windbreaks.

'Tomah' meant tree-fern to the Aboriginals of the district. Two tree-ferns, the Black or Rough Tree-Fern (*Cyathea australis*) and the Brown or Soft Tree-fern (*Dicksonia antarctica*) grow on the protected hillsides and sheltered gullies.

As well as the original native species of *Eucalyptus*, *Cyathea* and *Dicksonia*, several other genera, including *Sassafras*, *Indigophora* and *Prostanthera*, can be seen growing along the nature trail through the remnant sclerophyll forest. Hedges of native species are being established in the formal garden to give protection from wind and fire. The rhododendron collection includes *Rhododendron lochae*, the only specimen of this genus native to Australia. Other regional collections of flowering trees, shrubs and conifers from cool climate areas of the world are being established.

Spectacular views of the deep valley which separates Mount Tomah from the neighbouring ridge on which Mount Wilson (NW), Mount Irvine (NNE) and Mount Tootie (NE) stand can be seen from the deck of the visitor centre.

Mount Tomah Botanic Garden is located 12 km west of Bilpin, on the Bells Line of Road in the Blue Mountains area.

A view of one of the large rockery areas which contain a range of Australian native plants at Mount Tomah Botanic Garden. As well as many native plants, spectacular views of the Blue Mountains from several vantage points make this garden a most worthwhile stop when in the area.

Orange Botanic Gardens

The Orange Botanic Gardens Project developed from a suggestion of community representatives on Council's Parks and Street Trees Advisory Committee in 1979. In 1981, a 9 ha site was dedicated by the Bathurst-Orange Development Corporation, and a plan was adopted by Council in 1982. In September, Miss Betty Cuthbert launched the gardens as a Bicentennial project.

Preliminary works were commenced in 1982-83 and continued through 1985 with the construction of a dam, viewing decks and ancillary trails. 1986 was a cornerstone, as during this year the Bicentennial Authority approved a grant to assist with development works during 1987-88.

In addition, the Outreach Division of the Orange College of TAFE was successful in obtaining a Bicentennial grant for the construction of a horticultural therapy centre. 1988 also saw the acquisition of two additional parcels of land. The smaller parcel, 0.5 ha, has been used for historic school and church buildings, and the larger parcel, 1.57 ha, is being developed as a repository for native species which are both common in and unique to the areas surrounding Orange. This latter area will be known as the Indigenous Montane Area and will ultimately contain an extensive and unique collection of Australian flora.

The first stage of the development included the Orchard and the Alpine and Homestead Gardens. Fine views of the Orange district can be had from the pathways that wind through these areas. Further development plans for the gardens include a 'forest' of European, North American and Asian trees, together with additional native woodland. Proposed specific interest points will include alpine plants, Australian conifers and a shade garden of rhododendrons and azaleas.

The Orange Botanic Gardens are located off Kearneys Drive, north of Orange Civic Centre.

Royal Botanic Gardens, Sydney

The traditional foundation date of the botanic gardens is taken as the date of completion of Mrs Macquaries Road on 13 June 1816, and is recorded above the Chair, which was carved from a rock ledge in part of the original Government Domain used by Mrs Macquarie for recreation. Mrs Macquarie's Chair remains a notable Sydney landmark.

In 1816, Governor Macquarie appointed Charles Fraser, a soldier of the 46th regiment, as 'Superintendent of the Botanic Gardens', and by 1817 his title had been changed to Colonial Botanist. This ranks the Sydney Botanic Gardens among the oldest of the important gardens in the world.

Charles Fraser applied himself to his new job with talent and zeal, and the botanic gardens were well established in 1820. He travelled extensively, accompanying the explorer Oxley on his three expeditions.

He visited Tasmania, New Zealand, Norfolk Island, W.A. and Queensland.

As a consequence of the Australian visit of Queen Elizabeth in 1954, the official title became the Royal Botanic Gardens, Sydney in 1959.

Today the gardens contain close to 7000 different living species, varieties, hybrids and cultivars, collected in the wild or exchanged with botanic gardens and arboreta throughout the world. The gardens also house the National Herbarium of N.S.W. which has a reference collection of almost one million specimens, used by botanists to help them classify the many thousands of plant species and study their features.

The numerous Australian species in the gardens are easily picked out by their blue labels, but these are world gardens and the living collection contains a wide range of exotics, or specimens from outside the country.

Many well-established specimens of various species of *Araucaria*, *Podocarpus*, *Eucalyptus*, *Ficus*, *Brachychiton*, *Adansonia*, *Syzygium*, *Toona*, *Flindersia*, *Buckinghamia*, *Macadamia*, *Ceratopetalum*, *Acacia*, *Casuarina* and other genera can be seen in various parts of the gardens.

Plantings of some of the smaller and more colourful flowering varieties are concentrated in smaller garden beds. One particular area, bed 13, contains plants which commemorate the Swedish botanist, Daniel Solander, who with Joseph Banks accompanied James Cook on his voyage of discovery to eastern Australia in 1770. Plants in this area are representative of those collected during that trip.

An excellent booklet outlining the history of the gardens and containing details of the various plantings, including the Australian native species, is available from the gardens.

The Royal Botanic Gardens, in their superb location beside Sydney Harbour at Farm Cove, are a wonderful scenic attraction and well worth several visits at different times of the year to see the range of native plants growing in the various locations.

Stony Range Flora Reserve (Near Dee Why)

The Stony Range Flora Reserve is a public reserve administered by Warringah Shire Council and covers an area of approximately 3.5 ha of typical sandstone formation. In addition to the particular vegetation which grows naturally on such sandstone formation, a wide variety of native plants from different parts of Australia have been added. The reserve was first dedicated in 1956 and development began in 1957.

The extensive system of paths is designed to allow the visitor to fully appreciate the different characters of the reserve. One of the main objectives of the reserve is to provide education in Australian plants, so that they may become more readily known and cultivated, thus helping to preserve the Australian flora. An attractive booklet providing information on native plants is available from the reserve office. The booklet contains information on the plants of the reserve and the various techniques used in the propagation and cultivation of plants.

Entering Dee Why from the direction of Sydney, Stony Range is on the right, soon after the intersection with Warringah Road.

Wagga Wagga Botanic Gardens

The present botanic gardens have been established on an area at the base of Willans Hill, which until development was a holding and grazing paddock. Many years were spent in establishing the basic layout and advance planting of the existing tree cover.

The gardens were officially opened to the public on 24 August 1969, by the then Director of Botanic Gardens Adelaide, Mr T.R.N. Lothian. During this opening, trees were planted in the Australian native flora section by representatives of each of the states of Australia. These trees have since matured, and form the basic framework of this portion of the gardens.

Wagga's Botanic Gardens have continued to develop over the years with the latest addition being the Commemorative Gardens established for the 1988 Bicentenary Year celebrations.

In the Australian native flora section, collections of a range of native trees, shrubs and groundcovers can be found in the pleasantly secluded area. Many of the existing shrubs have been allowed to grow unchecked, to provide the home gardener with an insight into ultimate growth forms if judicious pruning is not practised.

The best time to view this part of the garden is during late winter to mid-spring, when many wattles, grevilleas and callistemons are to be found in flower. In the lower section of the garden, beds of Australian annual everlasting flowers are to be found in bloom into the mid-summer period.

The rainforest gully is accessed by redgum steps and board walks and has displays of assorted ferns, orchids and rainforest trees.

A picnic table is provided by the small ponding area for use on hot days. The gardens also have a model railway, a camellia garden, a Shakespearian garden, a cactus and succulent garden and an exotic section. A playground cooled by thick groves of trees and a bird and animal enclosure are very popular with visitors.

The Wagga Wagga Botanic Gardens are located at the corner of Macley Street and Baden Powell Drive.

Wirrimbirra Sanctuary (Bargo)

Carmen Coleman, a Sydney accountant, discovered an area of interesting bushland at a reasonable distance from Sydney near Bargo on the Hume Highway, where the lyrebird and koala were first discovered by Europeans. In 1962 he purchased a portion of this land, which initiated the establishment of Wirrimbirra Sanctuary. Unfortunately Carmen died soon afterwards. The name 'Wirrimbirra' is believed to mean 'to preserve' in the local Aboriginal dialect.

The David G. Stead Memorial Wildlife Research Foundation of Australia is located at the Wirrimbirra Sanctuary and was founded to expand and manage the sanctuary and to honour the memory of David G. Stead who died in 1957. He was a pioneer of the conservation movement and founded the Wildlife Preservation Society of Australia in 1909 which is still functioning. The first president of the Foundation was Mrs David Stead who, as Thistle Y. Harris, has written many books on Australian wildflowers.

In 1973 the Wirrimbirra Field Studies Centre, the second of its kind in N.S.W, was established. It is managed and staffed by the Department of Education. Excursions for school children are arranged, often over several days, to develop a better understanding of the natural environment.

A wide variety of native plants is for sale in the native plant nursery and expert advice is available on selection, propagation and cultivation of Australian plants. The nature trails have been designed to arouse an interest and appreciation of the local environment and wildlife. A wide range of native plants can be seen along these trails.

Accommodation cabins are provided for overnight accommodation at the study courses. These are available for hire by the general public when not in use by the Field Studies Centre. A variety of booklets, posters, cards and stickers is available in the bookshop. The exhibition area has a series of displays which illustrate wildlife and conservation aspects of the area.

Wirrimbirra Sanctuary is located on the National Trust property, 5 km south of Tahmoor on the eastern side of the Hume Highway.

Wollongong Botanic Garden

The history of the Wollongong Botanic Garden site extends back to the early days of white settlement in Wollongong. In 1825, James Spearing was promised two one thousand acre grants near Wollongong. By 1828 his 'Paulsgrove' estate was the largest centre of population in the Illawarra, with 43 people. Spearing and his property are remembered in street names near the garden.

In 1842, this large estate, then known as 'Mount Keera Estate', was subdivided into farm and house lots. Higher on the slope of Mount Keira the Illawarra's first coal mine was opened in 1849. The rich coal seams thus exploited were to lead to the development of Wollongong as a major city and directly to the foundation of the botanic garden.

When it was decided to relocate the Hoskins Steelworks from Lithgow to Port Kembla, Mr Sidney Hoskins, a foundation director of Australian Iron and Steel Pty Ltd, purchased several farms in 1928, planning to build his home there; it is part of this land that has become the botanic garden. The land was generally cleared, except for a few trees along the creek and the turpentines on the north-eastern hill, and where the Woodland Garden is today.

In 1938, construction and planning of the garden commenced. To give a sense of maturity to the garden, large coral trees were brought in by truck from as far as Gerringong. The terraces around the house were made, together with a rockery and the ornamental pool on the west side of the house.

Mr A.S. Hoskins resigned from Australian Iron and Steel in 1949 and 18.6 ha of his property was donated to the Wollongong City Council for a war memorial or botanic garden. Subsequently 8 ha of this land was transferred to the Sydney Church of England Girls' Grammar School, and in 1954, Council took possession of 10.5 ha of land extending from Murphys Avenue to Northfields Avenue for the future botanic garden.

On 12 November 1963, the gardens were officially named the Wollongong Botanic Gardens. However it was not until 1964 that the first site activity began, and planting of the Asiatic zone commenced in March. Several trees were also planted in other parts of the garden. By March 1969, 4000 plants had been planted out and 2000 were growing in the nursery.

The Captain Cook Bicentenary in 1970 gave an important impetus to the gardens and plans were made to develop them to a stage where they could be opened to the public. On 26 September 1970, Mrs A.S. Hoskins officially opened the gardens as 'Hoskins Park-Wollongong Botanic Gardens' and the gardens

were opened to the public early in 1971. Additional grounds were acquired, and by 1978 the total area of the gardens was 27.41 ha.

The layout was changed from the original design to provide various habitats. These include Illawarra rainforest, wet sclerophyll forest, dry sclerophyll forest, bog garden, arid zone and moraine, woodland garden, conifers, flowering trees and shrubs, economic plants and special collections in the plant houses. Further development of the gardens is continuing.

The main entrance to the Wollongong Botanic Garden is off Murphys Avenue. Leaflets containing details of the various areas and walks are available from the education centre in the gardens.

Australian Capital Territory

Australian National Botanic Gardens (Canberra)

The national collection of Australian native plants is being grown at the Australian National Botanic Gardens, Canberra and its annexe at Jervis Bay on the N.S.W. coast.

Mr J.G. Gorton, then Prime Minister of Australia, officially opened the gardens on 20 October 1970. During the preceeding years, however, many plants had been introduced to the site which occupies 90 ha on the lower slopes of Black Mountain. Forty ha are planted, and 50 ha on steeper slopes south of Black Mountain Drive await development.

The gardens were developed to display the Australian flora and encourage the study of its horticulture and botany. They are a place for passive recreation and a place to enjoy.

The collection is based on plant material gathered on field trips to all states and territories. The material is sent back to Canberra from the field trips for propagation in the gardens' nursery and preservation in the gardens' herbarium.

Plants are arranged in several ways. Taxonomic sections contain species belonging to the same plant group, ecological sections contain plants that grow in similar environments, and in some sections plants requiring similar soil conditions are grouped together in specially prepared beds.

Scientific names are used on all plant labels in the gardens. No widely accepted common names exist for many Australian plants and some frequently-used common names apply to different plants in different regions.

A rainforest gully has been developed from a once dry gully by hundreds of misting sprays controlled by a time switch. Plantings in various parts of the gully represent rainforest communities found at different latitudes along eastern Australia. A board walk in the floor of the gully is a special attraction.

The rockery area, completed in 1980, provides a range of modified soils for plants with differing moisture and drainage needs. The raised soil pockets between the rocks provide better opportunities for visitors to view small plants which would otherwise be lost in a larger garden bed.

The Hawkesbury sandstone section has been planted with a very rich range of flora from the sandstone areas of the Sydney Basin.

In the mallee shrubland area, the multi-stemmed species of *Eucalyptus* (popularly known as mallees)

which dominate the vegetation over large areas of arid southern Australia are planted in specially prepared soil. Trees from four different mallee communities are included.

The Eucalyptus Lawn displays a selection of eucalypt species in a large grassed area in the centre of the gardens. Many other eucalypt species are planted throughout the gardens.

In the Banksia Centre, a selection of plants which can be easily identified by the disabled has been included. This area has been especially designed to make gardening easier for the disabled. Scented and textured plants are featured.

Three well identified walks which cover various sections of the gardens have been prepared. One of these leads visitors past plants which are labelled to explain how Aborigines used them.

A series of leaflets outlining the many facets of the gardens, together with details of the walks, are available from the information centre.

The herbarium houses the gardens' collection of pressed dried plant specimens which are used for botanical research and to identify the living plants in the gardens. The herbarium is closed to the public.

The entrance to the Australian National Botanic Gardens is off Clunies-Ross Street at the bottom of Black Mountain.

Part of the rainforest gully at the Australian National Botanic Garden in Canberra.

Queensland

Atherton Arboretum (CSIRO Division of Wildlife and Ecology, Tropical Forest Research Centre)

The planting of the arboretum at CSIRO Atherton, was begun in 1971 when the station was set up. It was conceived as a living complement to the preserved species being collected in the Queensland Herbarium's Atherton branch, also on the same site.

There are approximately 15 500 trees planted so far and changes are constantly taking place as the arboretum is a dynamic living environment. In recent years, planting has been done more closely in an attempt to create a living biome rather than a live museum.

The arboretum has been essentially divided into 4 main areas: two of these are planted mainly with northern Queensland rainforest species (other than those from Cape York Peninsula); another, is planted with rainforest species from Cape York Peninsula; and the fourth area is planted with open forest species.

The Arboretum also harbours a variety of wildlife, notably the family of curlews which is often to be found on plots in front of the front carpark. Around the back flocks of masked plovers are often seen, and snipe frequent the banana patch. Some rainforest species have also been spied in the arboretum, for example the grey-headed robin, which has probably moved in from nearby Halloran's Hill nature reserve.

The Atherton Arboretum is not generally open to the public. However visitors are welcome and should contact the CSIRO Division of Wildlife and Ecology, Tropical Forest Research Centre in Atherton. A leaflet containing further details of the arboretum, together with a list of various plants and locations, is also available.

Brisbane City Botanic Gardens

The area now known as the City Botanic Gardens had its origin as a fruit and vegetable garden, supplying food for the infant Moreton Bay penal settlement. The site of the garden was selected in 1828 by Charles Fraser, N.S.W. Colonial Botanist and Sydney Botanic Garden superintendent. Apart from supplying food for convicts and soldiers, the government garden supplied new cuttings and seeds free to the local people.

In 1842, the N.S.W. government gave the 17 ha site to the settlers of Moreton Bay and a board of trustees was established to administer the garden. By 1881, an impressive collection of both indigenous and imported trees and shrubs had been established. The first bunya pines (*Araucaria bidwillii*), along what is now known as Bidwill Walk, were planted as early as 1858. Three other significant specimens in the gardens—macadamia, litchi and tamarind trees— were planted in the same year.

The botanic gardens suffered a period of decline, and a series of major floods during the 1890s resulted in a deterioration in the gardens. Following the creation of the Greater Brisbane City Council in 1925, the gardens passed to Council control, and in 1956 significant collections of native palms were introduced.

A shortage of land and damage from the devastating flood of 1974 precipitated the development of new botanic gardens at Mt Coot-tha in the late 1970s. Since that time, the City Botanic Gardens have continued as an attractive inner city recreational facility and this role, combined with their obvious historical significance, makes their preservation essential. A new native rainforest area has been established between the mixed rainforest area and the natural mangroves.

The Brisbane City Botanic Gardens are located in the area between the Brisbane River and George and Alice Streets.

Cairns Flecker Botanic Gardens

Established as a recreational reserve in 1886, the Flecker Botanic Gardens are today the only such gardens in the wet tropics of Australia.

In about 1888, Mr Eugene Fitzalan, a botanical collector, moved to Cairns from Bowen where he later arranged with the Cairns City Council to establish a small nursery near the present garden site. He grew and sold native plants and orchids to local residents, under an agreement that he opened his gardens to the public. The resulting 'Fitzalan Gardens' effectively established the location of the city's present botanic gardens. Mr Fitzalan also collected extensively and a small tree, *Randia fitzalani*, and the orchid, *Eria fitzalani* were named in his honour.

The garden took on a broader meaning with the arrival of Dr Hugo Flecker in Cairns in 1923. Although he conducted a radiology practice, Dr Flecker's interests included natural history. He founded the North Queensland Naturalists Club, and during his term as president formed the Flecker Herbarium, which is today incorporated with the CSIRO Herbarium in Atherton. He also conducted valuable work on the Queensland Finger Cherry and Tar Trees. His energies were then directed to marine stingers, and one species he collected was subsequently named *Chironex fleckeri*.

In 1958, the Naturalists Club formed a Botanical Preservation Society to construct botanic gardens, which the Council named the Flecker Botanic Gardens in 1971. Today the gardens cover an area of 319 ha at Edge Hill and contain some 150 different species of palms, a collection of fruit trees, both native and exotic rainforest trees, and a selection of gingers and aroids.

The Flecker Botanic Gardens consist of three areas: the main botanic gardens in Collins Avenue, and the saltwater and freshwater lakes which make up the area known as Centenary Lakes in Greenslopes Street. Opened in 1976, Centenary Lakes contains 28 ha of wetlands, providing an ideal habitat for an abundance of birdlife.

The tall forest between Centenary Lakes and the botanic gardens, consisting predominantly of Alexandria and Lawyer Palms and large paperbark trees, is a fair representation of the flora which once covered large swampy areas within the Cairns District.

Along Collins Avenue is the main botanic gardens, more formal in landscape design. The Munroe Martin fernery displays rare plants and orchids.

The hills to the north of the gardens, which are dominated by the peaks of Lumley Hill and Mt Whitfield, are also a part of the gardens complex. A series of walking tracks has been organised, including walks up to 4 hours long.

Seed exchanges with other cities, both nationally and overseas, ensure a continued variety of indigenous and exotic flora.

The garden also displays useful plants in sections: edible food plants, medicinal plants, fibre and miscellaneous plants, weapons, utensils, shelter and watersource plants. A brochure containing details of the excellent collection of plants, together with other items of interest is available from the gardens office.

The main entrance to the Flecker Botanic Gardens is in Collins Avenue, Cairns.

Cooktown Gallop Botanic Gardens

Cooktown, along with many newly established towns in Queensland during the last quarter of the 19th century, was endowed with 60 ha of land to be set aside as a botanic reserve. In October 1885, the Council commenced development of the gardens and planting of young trees and shrubs began. In 1892, a cottage was built on the reserve and lawns, shrub and garden beds were established. The area was named Queens Park.

Although a wide range of trees and shrubs of both decorative and economic value were planted in the gardens, they gradually fell into disrepair; by the mid 1970s, only 18 plant species had survived. Some restoration of the rock pools was undertaken in the early 1970s.

In October 1980, the Cook Shire Council resolved to name the gardens the Gallop Botanic Gardens to commemorate the contributions of Mr R.D. Gallop and Mr G.D. Gallop, previous administrators of the shire. In 1984, Council commenced reconstruction of the gardens with the assistance of commonwealth employment funding. The original gardens area was cleared, stonework rebuilt and trees removed. A walking track has been cleared to Finch Bay along the old dray track.

Continuing works will include a 'Palmetum', a section of native plants and a Banks garden. A list of trees identified by attached number tags in the cleared area is available from the gardens. The list includes 82 surviving original and descendent specimens of the gardens of 1886.

Nineteen specimens of plants collected by Banks and Solander between April and August 1770 are included in the collection and so a large proportion of the trees are indigenous to the Cooktown area. This unique collection of trees includes several species with edible fruits used by the Aborigines for food and fish poisons.

Indooroopilly Long Pocket Rainforest (CSIRO Division of Tropical Animal Science)

The Long Pocket Laboratories Rainforest was planned as part of the original landscaping through the interest of the CSIRO Rainforest Ecology Section which was located at the laboratories until 1980.

The site was a gravelly clay gully which originally supported Spotted Gum, Ironbark, Grey Gum and Stringybark woodland, but few of the original trees remained. Planting of rainforest seedlings commenced in October 1969 with the site selection based on knowledge of natural conditions in which the species were found.

Seedlings were grown by the Rainforest Ecology Section from material collected in rainforests, mainly from north Queensland. Frequently, staff of the section encountered undescribed and little-known plants. By collecting seeds and cuttings from these and establishing them in the gully, they were often able to monitor closely the growth of these plants and correlate the often significantly different immature and advanced stages. These plants were available close at hand for taxonomic study not only by CSIRO staff but also by scientists from the Queensland Herbarium. Seedlings from other sources were bought from time to time to build up the collection. Understorey species including orchids and ferns were added in niches as the canopy developed.

The synthesis of this rainforest made full use of cover plants of early successional species such as Wild Tobacco (*Solanum mauritianum*). These plants grow quickly and shade out grass which competes with the young rainforest seedlings, and they mobilise nutrients, encourage fruit-eating birds and wildlife, and provide a natural bush house for protection of future canopy trees.

Since 1980, care of the rainforest has been left to the gardener under supervision of the site committee. Maps and records of many of the plants have been made, as a baseline for future censuses, measurement of growth rates, etc. More than 300 species still survive in the rainforest.

Much public interest has been aroused and the project has prompted the development of rainforests at James Cook University and in the grounds of St Peter's Lutheran College, Indooroopilly, Nudgee Junior and Xavier Christian Brothers College, Indooroopilly, and the Teachers Training College, Kelvin Grove.

The use of succession species and other experience gained at the Long Pocket Rainforest has been applied in the development of the rainforest in the Mt Coot-tha Botanic Gardens.

The CSIRO Long Pocket Rainforest is located

within the 7 ha site of the laboratories off Meiers Road, Indooroopilly. Contact should be made with the CSIRO laboratories for further details of the rainforest.

Mt Coot-tha Botanic Gardens (near Toowong)

The Mt Coot-tha Botanic Gardens offer visitors relaxation and learning amid a profusion of Australian and exotic plants.

The Brisbane City Council founded the gardens in 1976 and since then more than 10 000 plant species have been acquired from local and overseas sources.

Of particular interest in stage one of the gardens is the Australian Rainforest Garden. This section was commenced in the mid 1970s as the only native Australian plant section and has thrived on generous applications of water and mulch to the extent that plants are now becoming self-mulching and a canopy effect is developing. Some of the pioneer plants used to start the area included members of the *Euodia*, *Eucalyptus* (in addition to the existing Ironbark and Tallowwood trees) and *Macaranga* genera.

Tropical and subtropical species are not separated, with emphasis being placed on developing a long-term collection of a wide range of species in an aesthetic and interesting garden.

Some species in this area have been documented in a brochure as being useful to Aborigines and Torres Strait Islanders. The circular walking track is suitable for wheel chairs.

Stage two of the gardens, under development in the south-western section, features 25 ha of Australian native plants in a bushland setting. The native flora is arranged in geographic regions around a large central lake system and can be enjoyed by all; as well, both vehicular and walking tracks are provided.

The Mt Coot-tha Botanic Gardens are located off Mt Coot-tha Road which runs off the Western Freeway at Toowong.

Myall Park Botanic Garden (Glenmorgan, near Dalby)

The Myall Park Botanic Garden was established by David Gordon, who in 1926 acquired 18 000 ha of land at Glenmorgan, and by 1942 had begun to preserve endangered Australian native plants by growing them on his property.

Since this time he has planted many hundreds of species, many of which are now extinct in the wild. Wherever possible, particular species have been planted closely in groups to encourage the establishment of natural hybrids. Two of the most beautiful *Grevillea* hybrids, now widely grown throughout Australia, *Grevillea* 'Robyn Gordon' and *Grevillea* 'Sandra Gordon', originated from this property.

David Gordon has travelled extensively through Australia to collect material for propagation and to discover the natural growing habits and requirements of the various species. He has established an extensive herbarium from much of the material collected during his travels.

Myall Park was declared a botanic garden in 1985 and now occupies some 130 ha. Visitors are welcome during open days which are held each year in September and at other times by arrangement. Myall Park is located at Glenmorgan, 450 km west of Brisbane and is a two-hour drive from Dalby.

Rockhampton and Kershaw Botanic Gardens

The Rockhampton Botanic Gardens, established in 1869, were developed by the colonial government as one of the regional gardens throughout the state. These gardens initially experimented with economic food crops and were under the guidance of the Queensland Acclimatisation Society.

In the period from 1869 to 1932, one of the finest collections of plant material in Australia was established. The large Hugo Lassen Fernery, which houses a fine collection of tropical plants, was completed by 1957. Further development and planting of the gardens continued from 1957 to 1972 and a grove of Queensland Kauris, now one of the features of the gardens, was planted.

One of the more recent additions is the Japanese garden which has been developed as part of a cultural exchange between Rockhampton and its sister city, Ibusuki.

The most significant group of plants displayed at the Rockhampton Botanic Gardens is the palms which are found throughout the grounds. The collection now includes some 200 species. Some of the most spectacular trees include the avenue of gigantic Bunya Pines and mahoganies near the entrance, the groves of Hoop Pines and Kauri Pines and the colossal spreading Bombax.

The botanic gardens zoo has been dramatically expanded in recent years and is really a major tourist attraction on its own. The botanic gardens and the adjacent Murray Lagoon provide a home for many native animals and are a popular place for bird-watchers.

The Rockhampton Botanic Gardens are administered by the Rockhampton City Council and are located on the western slopes of the Athelstone Ranges and on the edge of the Murray and Yeppen Lagoons.

A major additional attraction of the botanic gardens, and in particular for those interested in native plants, are the Kershaw Botanic Gardens. This 50 ha development was commenced in 1974 and is solely devoted to the display of Australian native plants. This exciting bicentennial project includes some 3000 different species.

Many of the garden areas in the first stage of the project have reached a mature stage of growth and numerous types of wattles, grevilleas and bottlebrushes can be seen in full colour at various times of the year. Strong growth can also be seen in the trees of the rainforest and sclerophyll forest areas. Water features, including a large melaleuca swamp, are a prominent part of the natural landscape being created. Plans for further development include the addition of display houses for native plants requiring special attention.

It is intended that the Kershaw Botanic Gardens become an educational centre, promoting the intelligent use of Australian plants and an appreciation of our natural heritage.

The Kershaw Botanic Gardens are located adjacent to the Bruce Highway in North Rockhampton.

Victoria

Ballarat Botanical Gardens

In 1858, two years after the municipality of Ballarat was formed, a decision was made to convert the Ballarat police horse paddock into a botanical garden. George Longley, trained in horticulture at Lowther Castle, England, was appointed to develop the garden. It was gradually improved over the years and has become widely known for its glorious displays of tuberous begonias.

One of the most recent additions to the gardens is the rock and alpine garden, funded by the state government as part of the 150th celebrations of Victoria and the Cuthbert Bequest.

The gardens are noted for the many specimens of mature trees ranging in age to over 120 years, some 46 of which have been registered on the National Trust Register of significant trees. The Bunya Pines (*Araucaria bidwillii*) from Queensland are excellent specimens of this Australian native tree which produces large cones containing edible nuts. A fernery is located at the north end of the gardens.

The Ballarat Botanical Gardens are located off Wendouree Parade in Ballarat.

Cranbourne Botanic Gardens

The Cranbourne Garden of the Royal Botanic Gardens, Melbourne comprises 340 ha of natural vegetation, pasture and land disturbed by sand mining. The natural vegetation consists of sandy heathland and woodland on clay soil.

The land was selected as a result of study, initiated by the Maud Gibson trust, of areas with the potential for the conservation and cultivation of native plants. In 1970, the Victorian government helped to purchase 174 ha just south of the town of Cranbourne as an annexe to the Royal Botanic Gardens. The area was designated as a botanic garden and research institute devoted to the growing, display and study of Australian plants for the people of Victoria.

In 1976, an additional 22 ha were purchased on the western edge to control an erosion risk caused by earlier sand extraction activity. Then in 1980, 68 ha on the north-western edge was purchased by the Maud Gibson Trust. This land contained woodland on the Narre clay soils and some agricultural land. Another 60 ha of agricultural land to the south were purchased in 1981 by the Maud Gibson Trust to act as a buffer in the event of developments to the south that would adversely affect the garden. In 1987 a buffer zone and access to the South Gippsland Highway was added to the northern boundary.

The garden has been divided into several zones. The heathland zone supports heathland vegetation on old sand dunes and will be conserved in its natural state with a series of walking tracks. The woodland, to the west, is on relatively fertile clay soil and is an important remnant of the vegetation which once covered the agricultural land to the south. It will be a conservation area with a limited number of walking tracks. The arboretum will be a collection of some 2000 trees in an attractive landscaped valley to the south and west of the heathland zone. Eucalypts and acacias will predominate, but representatives of all Australian groups of trees suited to the climate will be planted.

In the special collections area, set on a sand-mined area between the arboretum and the heathland, attention will be given to experimentation on the domestication of Australian plants and the conservation of endangered species. It will also house research collections of native plants. The Society for Growing Australian Plants has already established extensive collections of *Banksia, Dryandra* and related plants.

The major development is on the sand-mined north-west corner of the annexe. A landscaped native botanic garden will blend with the surrounding heathland and woodland. When fully planted, the botanic garden will contain in excess of 5000 species of small plants, shrubs and selected trees. An extensive collection of monocotyledons (rushes, grasses, sedges and lilies) will surround the main lake, while the two natural lagoons and their indigenous vegetation will be enhanced with plants from similar wetland habitats throughout Australia.

An access road and picnic area have opened the natural heathland and arboretum to visitors. The native botanic garden area was opened in 1991.

The Cranbourne Garden is located off Ballarto Road, slightly west of the South Gippsland Highway, near Cranbourne.

Royal Melbourne Botanic Gardens

Established in 1846, the Royal Botanic Gardens are world renowned for their beautiful 19th century landscape. The gardens cover approximately 36 ha and contain more than 10 000 species and cultivated varieties of plants from all over the world.

The plant collections are used for horticultural and botanical research, and for conservation and educational purposes. Plant labels include botanical and common names as well as the plant family and distribution.

The herbarium houses more than one million preserved plant specimens and is the state government's major centre for botanical studies in plant classification. The collection includes examples of most Australian flowering plants and is particularly rich in those that occur in Victoria. There are also numerous specimens of cultivated plants and weeds from most countries. Other plant groups such as algae, mosses, lichens and ferns are also well represented.

The new extension adjacent to the herbarium will house the herbarium's priceless plant collections as well as the botanical library.

The Royal Botanic Gardens contains some 700 species of Australian plants. Most are planted in the Australian Border and Queensland section, although many native trees, particularly eucalypts, figs, palms and araucarias, feature prominantly throughout the gardens. A selection of smaller species may be seen in the rock garden at the southern end of the nymphaea lily lake.

The Australian Border is dominated by trees from the rainforests of eastern Australia. These trees cast heavy shade and make it difficult to grow the shrubs of heathland and open woodland that are popular in suburban gardens. The gardens' new annexe at Cranbourne is in sandy heathland and will enable the display of plants from a wider range of habitats. The annexe will also have a role in the introduction of new species into cultivation and the conservation of endangered species.

A booklet containing details of a self-guided tour is available and shows a representative selection of the Australian plants in the gardens. Additional booklets containing details of plants and attractions in the gardens at different times of the year are also available

from the visitor centre. The visitor centre houses a unique display exploring the history of the gardens and the herbarium and the diversity of plants which form the gardens' landscape. Free guided walks hosted by the voluntary guides group are available and feature seasonal highlights.

The Royal Botanic Gardens in Melbourne are located on the southern bank of the Yarra River, 1.5 km from the centre of Melbourne.

South Australia

Adelaide Botanic Gardens

In 1854, the agricultural and horticultural society recommended the establishment of a 16 ha botanic garden on the present site. In April 1855, George Francis was appointed superintendent of the garden which opened to the public in 1857. The garden now covers an area of 19.4 ha, and to its north lies the 30 ha botanic park.

Between 1855-1856, Francis developed an area adjacent to the North Terrace and it is here that the oldest plantings can be seen. Later, under the guidance of the second director, Richard Schomburgk, an area, which included the botanic park, was developed between where the Simpson Kiosk now stands and the River Torrens. The youngest plantings are to be found in the eastern side of the garden, an area which has only been developed since 1940.

The gardens can be explored along two main well-marked walks.

In the arboretum, a canopy of *Eucalyptus* species provides shade for a range of Australian shrubs and small trees. The most spectacular eucalypts are the smooth-barked Sydney Blue Gum (*Eucalyptus saligna*), Lemon-Scented Gum (*Eucalyptus citriodora*) and spotted Gum (*Eucalyptus maculata*). A well-grown specimen of Bottle Tree (*Brachychiton rupestre*) can be seen east of the walking trail. Several other impressive native specimens, including the Umbrella Tree (*Schefflera actinophylla*), Illawarra Flame Tree (*Brachychiton acerifolius*), Black Bean (*Castanospermum australe*), River Red Gum (*Eucalyptus camaldulensis*) and *Casuarina torulosa* can be seen.

The new Bicentennial Glass Conservatory, funded jointly by the state and federal governments, shelters a very young rainforest. The conservatory, standing 27 m tall, is the world's third largest tropical greenhouse (after Kew and Berlin) and has fine misting nozzles set along the arching spars to maintain the relative humidity at 85 per cent and the temperature between 16 and 33 degrees centigrade. Eventually the collection of 4000 plants will be sited to present a varying display of shape and colour. Orchids will cover the trunks of the tall palms.

A deliberate decision has been made to plant only species from the South-East Asian region. Many endangered species will eventually be introduced to provide a reserve collection for these plant specimens.

The Adelaide Botanic Gardens are located at the eastern end of North Terrace, Adelaide.

A magnificent specimen of *Eucalyptus camaldulensis*, or River Red Gum, at the Adelaide Botanic Gardens.

Black Hill Conservation Park and Native Flora Park, Athelstone

In 1974, to establish the Black Hill Conservation Park and Native Flora Park, the state government acquired the Athelstone Wildflower Garden and Nursery from the Corporation of the City of Campbelltown. In January 1977 a director was appointed and in the following year a trust was formed to develop the area.

In the same year, laboratories and a nursery were established to provide facilities for research into the Australian flora, and these were officially opened in 1986. Since then these facilities have been administered by the Botanic Gardens of Adelaide. The National Parks and Wildlife Service administer the park.

The objectives of the park are to assist in the conservation of the Australian flora, to research and develop methods of plant breeding and propagation, to identify and develop the potential of the Australian flora, and to promote horticultural science and research.

Black Hill Flora Centre has a modern nursery complex where plant propagation is carried out for the Adelaide Botanic Garden. The area is not open to the public because of strict hygiene controls. Rare and uncommon native plants are made available to the public through plant sales held annually at the Flora Centre. The public is also invited to view the displays in the administration building which is open through the week. Picnic tables are provided under attractive gum trees in adjacent grounds.

The Black Hill Conservation Park and Native Flora Park (now commonly known as the Black Hill Flora Centre) is located off Maryvale Road in Athelstone.

Mount Lofty Botanic Garden (Crafters)

The Mount Lofty Botanic Garden has displays of plants from both hemispheres brought together in a dramatic landscape setting. Spring and autumn are both good seasons, but a fern gully, woodland garden, bog garden and tranquil lake make any time of the year worth a visit. The native stringybark forest provides an effective backdrop for many of the exotic species in the garden.

The garden is reached only by car from Summit Road or Piccadilly Road, Crafters.

Waite Arboretum (The University of Adelaide, Agricultural Research Institute)

The Waite Arboretum was established under the provisions of a bequest to the University of Adelaide by Mr Peter Waite. The gift included an endowment and his Urrbrae Estate, a mansion house set in 53 ha of agricultural and grazing land in the foothills of Adelaide.

Under the terms of the deed of gift, the eastern half of the property was to be used for teaching and research, while the remaining 27 ha were to be held in perpetuity as a park or garden for the recreation and enjoyment of the public. It was decided that the park should take the form of an arboretum in which trees and shrubs from all parts of the world would be grown as specimen trees to demonstrate their value for shelter and ornament.

The arboretum is virtually frost free with a winter rainfall of 625 mm followed by a warm, dry summer.

Planting of the arboretum began in 1928. The original vegetation was open savannah woodland of River Red gum (*Eucalyptus camaldulensis*), Blue Gum (*E. leucoxylon*) and Grey Box (*E. microcarpa*). Several of these original trees remain together with Sugar Gums (*E. cladocalyx*) planted by Waite in 1877.

Initially, two main areas were envisaged, with hardier indigenous trees on the higher areas where the soil is shallow and the subsoil of a gravelly nature, and exotic trees on the lower areas with deeper soil. A third area of mixed native and exotic species planted for aesthetic effect was intended, but this objective was never really achieved and has since lapsed.

Each tree in the arboretum is labelled, with its number, botanical name, common name, family, general area of origin, and date of planting.

Every year 15 to 20 new trees are planted as spaces become available due to losses from storm damage or natural senescence, or to removal of duplicate specimens whose commonness or lack of vigour do not justify retention.

The early plantings contained few eucalyts, but due to the personal interest of Mr F.A. Couzens who was associated with the arboretum for nearly forty years, it now has one of the most comprehensive collections of eucalypts anywhere, about 260 species and subspecies. There are two special areas planted with eucalypts, one of more than 70 large species established in 1949, the other an enclosed area which is mown, where 160 mallees were planted in 1955. On any one day of the year, there are at least 20 species of eucalypt in flower, and in spring as many as 40 species. The flowers attract many birds and a total of 86 species has been recorded in the arboretum.

In addition to the extensive collection of eucalypts, there is a very fine collection of 30 species of oaks (*Quercus*), particularly evergreen Californian oaks. Other smaller special collections include honey-myrtles (*Melaleuca*), pine (*Pinus*), pears (*Pyrus*), she-oaks (*Casuarina* and *Allocasuarina*), junipers (*Juniperus*), and pistachios (*Pistacia*).

Future plantings will expand the eucalypt collection with the aim that eventually all species which are suitable to this climate and soil will be represented.

The arboretum also includes many other excellent specimens of Australian native trees, including Native Frangipani (*Hymenosporum flavum*), Crow's Ash (*Flindersia australis*), Wilga (*Geijera parvifolia*), Broad-Leaved Apple-Myrtle (*Angophora subvelutina*), Cigar Cassia (*Cassia brewsteri*), Mudgee Wattle (*Acacia spectabilis*) and Queensland Silver Wattle (*Acacia podalyriifolia*). The arboretum contains a total of about 1500 trees, representing 770 species in 202 genera.

The arboretum is open to the public, without charge, every day of the year during daylight hours. A marked trail is in place with an explanatory pamphlet available, and guided tours are conducted.

The Waite Arboretum is located in Glen Osmond, at the University of Adelaide Agricultural Research Institute.

Wittunga Botanic Garden (Blackwood)

This garden is of interest all year round but its displays of Australian and southern African plants are especially dazzling in spring.

In the collection of Australian natives, species of the *Banksia* and *Hakea* genera are noteworthy.

Two lakes and a sandplain garden make a visit memorable.

The Wittunga Botanic Garden is in Shepherds Hill Road in Blackwood.

Northern Territory

Darwin Botanic Gardens

In 1870, Captain Douglas Bloomfield, the first government resident reported that bananas, sugar cane and pineapples were thriving at the settlement of Palmerston (later Darwin). In any garden developments, emphasis was placed on experimentation with potentially important economic plants, since agriculture was seen as a means of attracting industry, trade and population. Several early 'experimental gardens' were established and failed.

In 1879, the government resident, Edward Price, appointed a German-born and Russian-educated settler, Dr Maurice Holtze, to be the first curator of the Darwin Botanic Gardens. By 1883, the soil in the Fannie Bay area was exhausted and the trees were transplanted to the present site during 1884/85. Of the 237 trees transplanted, only 14 were lost. In 1887, Holtze listed more than 400 plant species of economic importance as having been successfully established.

The commercial plants programme continued to be pursued over the years by subsequent curators and, despite destructive cyclones in 1897 and 1937 and a huge fire in 1902, attempts were made to include other values normally associated with 'true' botanic gardens. Plant identification labels, seed exchange and distribution of plants to settlers was part of this development.

Following the bombing of Darwin in February 1942, the army took control of the whole town until 1945 when Mr Jack Agostini became curator. He had the unenviable task of restoration. Nevertheless his labours were successful, so much so that when care of the gardens was given to the city council in 1957,

they were described as being Darwin's most attractive feature.

In 1957, the experimental farm was established outside the city at Berrimah. The gardens, under the control of the city council, have become the city's major park and nursery, the source of street, park and forshore beautification plants.

On 24 December 1974, Cyclone Tracy struck Darwin. The botanic gardens lost 78 per cent of its trees, the fern house, the nursery and finally, having survived two cyclones and a war, the original Holtze Cottage succumbed.

Since Tracy, the opportunity has been taken to begin a program of establishing collections of plant families and a start has been made on a collection of *Ficus* (fig) species, *Terminalia* and *Arecaceae*.

Local interested citizens see the Darwin Botanic Gardens, in its second hundred-year period, taking its place in the national system of botanic gardens as a major local and tourist recreation park and as a scientific and educational botanic garden of national and international importance.

The latest developments to be completed include a rainforest gully with ponds and a waterfall, and a coastal development with sand dunes and tidal creek with associate wetlands.

The recent Cyclone Max claimed about 10 large trees and a few shallow-rooted local eucalypts and acacias.

The garden celebrated its first centenary on 1 October 1986.

The entrance to the garden is in Gardens Road, Darwin.

Western Australia

Esperence Helms Arboretum

The Helms Arboretum commemorates the name of Andy Helms who was well and affectionally known by generations of forestry students at the Australian Forestry School, Canberra, where he lectured in forest management and mensuration during the 1940s and 1950s.

Born in Denmark, he had a varied forestry career which included periods with the N.S.W. Forestry Commission, the W.A. Forests Department, as a private consultant at Esperence and with the Tasmanian Forestry Commissioner, before becoming a well respected academic in Canberra.

He was manager of Esperence Pine Forests Limited when planting began in 1928. The experience with pines led to nutritional trials that became the starting point for further research and eventual development of the Esperence plains.

The arboretum is really in two parts: a small pine plantation planted in 1956-1969 and the arboretum, created in 1973 to ascertain if there were other types of trees which would flourish in Esperence, with plantings in 1973-1980.

The soil type ranges from deep Gibson sands in the north-east section to varying depths of shallow sand in the western section. The arboretum lies in the 500 to 550 mm rainfall area. The majority of species are in 0.5 ha blocks at a spacing of 4 m. As the trees mature, inferior trees will gradually be removed to make way for the full development of better trees. The arboretum contains some 150 species. A large proportion of these are Australian native species.

A guide containing details of the types and location of trees in the arboretum, as well as planting requirements, is available from the Department of Agriculture in Esperence.

The Helms Arboretum is located along Brockway Road, off the Coolgardie-Esperence Highway, 18 km from Esperence.

Kalgoorlie Arboretum

The Kalgoorlie Arboretum was established in 1954 to evaluate Goldfields' trees for use in the Kalgoorlie area.

The area provides passive recreational activities such as picnics, walks and short drives. Picnic tables are supplied in a shaded grassed area. A short drive takes the visitor around the arboretum, where trial plots are clearly marked with species' names for identification. A shady walking trail meandering through the arboretum allows visitors to identify trees from marked signs. The bird life is extensive, probably because of the permanent water and different flowering times of tree species.

The Kalgoorlie Arboretum is located off Hawkins Street, alongside Hammond Park in Kalgoorlie.

Kings Park Botanic Gardens (Perth)

When the Swan River colony was founded in 1829, the surveyor-general, John Septimus Roe, evidently intended that Mount Eliza should be reserved as a public park. In 1872 the first part was gazetted and most of the present park was added in 1890. The name Kings Park marks the accession of King Edward VII in 1901 and the visit of his son, the Duke of Cornwall and York (later King George V) to Australia, including Perth and Kings Park.

The government of W.A. decided to make the state botanic garden in Kings Park and work began in 1962. A largely informal layout was adopted. Many of the original trees of Jarrah, Marri and Tuart were retained to maintain the landscape, to provide shade and to form part, in some cases, of the flora displayed. Good specimens of the blackboy and Zamia Palm were retained also, because of their slow rate of growth and distinctive appearance. Some W.A. Red-Flowering Gums, Ilyarrie and W.A. Peppermints had been planted earlier and were retained.

Apart from plants retained from the natural vegetation and former plantings, each section has been planted with species characteristic of a particular area or group of plants. The greater part of the botanic garden (but not the whole of Kings Park) is devoted to the flora of W.A., especially that of the South-West, in which botanical province Perth is situated. There are estimated to be about 7000 species of flowering plants occurring naturally in W.A., with 3600 in the South-West of which 2400 are endemic, that is, they do not occur naturally anywhere else in the world. The botanic garden has specialised in the cultivation and display of the native flora because of its unique nature and comparative previous neglect.

Small sections also display the flora of eastern Australia, especially South Australia, the Mediterranean basin, South Africa and California.

Opening on the last Friday in September, the wildflower exhibition and native plant display is staged annually at the exhibition ground within Kings Park. Cut wildflowers from throughout W.A., native plants in cultivation and other exhibits of botanical and horticultural interest are shown.

The administrative centre is approximately 400 m from the main entrance on the west side of Fraser Avenue, Perth.

This row of *Eucalyptus citriodora*, or Lemon-Scented Gums, lines the entrance to Kings Park Botanic Gardens in Perth.

Western Australian Herbarium (Como, near Perth)

In the 1890s official herbaria were established in W.A., in the newly formed museum and in the Department of Agriculture. In 1916, the Forests Department established a herbarium for species from South-West forests.

In 1928, the decision was made to merge the three herbaria into a single State Herbarium and this amalgamation was finally completed in 1959 when the museum collection was transferred on permanent loan to the herbarium in the Department of Agriculture. The whole herbarium was transferred in 1988 to the Department of Conservation and Land Management to form a vital arm of its Research Division.

The herbarium aims to provide a system of internationally accepted names for the estimated 11 000 plant species found in W.A. Of these, about 8000 species are currently recognised and a further 3000 are recognised but do not yet have scientific names. The herbarium maintains a collection of over 300 000 named plant specimens and an associated library of over 6500 titles.

The work of the herbarium is concentrated mainly on the taxonomy of native and naturalised flora of W.A. Botanical information is disseminated by means of technical articles in scientific journals, flora manuals, checklists, distribution maps and leaflets.

The herbarium also provides plant identification and advisory services to government, other scientists and the general public.

Members of the public who wish to identify their own specimens can use the Community Reference Herbarium. A reference library located there has many useful botanical works to assist users in identification of specimens.

Plant collections are acquired in the course of the herbarium's activities. A range of plants, shrubs and trees has been planted in the grounds of the herbarium. This display is open for general inspection.

The Western Australian Herbarium is located in Hayman Road, Como.

Tasmania

Hobart Royal Tasmanian Botanic Gardens

The land now occupied by the botanical gardens, together with other land at Pavilion Point, afterwards laid out as the grounds of Government House and totalling 20 ha in all, was presented as a grant of land by Governor Collins in 1806 to John Hangan, after whom the locality was called Hangan's Farm.

The farm was purchased in 1813 by R.W. Loane who, in 1818, was dispossessed by Governor Sorell as having no title, with the result that the area was developed as a government garden with an overseer in charge.

In 1826, Governor Arthur commenced the erection of a new government house on a section of the area which had been Hangan's farm. This was to be a much more suitable residence than the original incommodious brick building built in 1807. However, with plans prepared, stone quaried on the site, and foundations laid, the undertaking was abandoned because of the great expense involved.

Governor Arthur, although disappointed, directed that more labour should be supplied from the penitentiary in order that a botanical garden should be 'proceeded with in the Domain'.

In 1828, Mr William Davidson was appointed as the first superintendent. He came out to Australia from Northumberland and brought with him about 2000 vines and fruit trees. In his first year of office, 1829, Davidson caused a large quantity of trees and seed to be ordered from England. He also gathered the seed of 150 native plants from the slopes and summit of Mt Wellington.

A great impetus to the garden's future was given by the formation, on 14 October 1843, of the Botanical and Horticultural Society of Van Diemen's Land, now the Royal Society of Tasmania, the oldest society of its kind in the Commonwealth outside the British Isles. The gardens were handed over to the Royal Society in January 1844.

During the next few years, much new material was presented to the gardens, including a valuable herbarium consisting of Tasmanian native plants collected by Ronald Campbell Gunn, a famous Tasmanian botanist.

At the end of 1885, the Royal Society gave the gardens back to the Crown and a body of trustees was appointed. The next major change came in 1950 when by a new Act of Parliament, the management of the botanical gardens was vested in a board of trustees, consisting of four government representatives and a representative from each of Hobart City Council, the Royal Society and the University of Tasmania. Since 1950, constant improvements have been made to the gardens, including the addition of 2.2 ha previously included in the government house grounds.

The gardens contain a native plant and fern rockery which features many Tasmanian plants and ferns attractively planted alongside a series of small rock pools and waterfalls. This area was established in 1982. The gardens also feature the rare indigenous Huon Pine.

The Royal Tasmanian Botanic Gardens are situated on the Queen's Domain adjacent to Government House and are approximately 2 km along the Tasman Highway from the city.

Glossary

Alternate   Arranged at different levels, not opposite each other (leaves on a stem)

Anther   The pollen-bearing part of the stamen

Axil   Angle between the leaf and stem

Axis   Main stem or part of a plant

Bract   Leaf-like structure which surrounds or encloses a flower or group of flowers

Calyx   Outer or lower ring of floral leaves, each called a sepal

Capsule   Dry fruit which opens to release seeds when mature

Cone   Woody fruit

Coppicing   Cutting to encourage numerous slender trunks to regenerate from the root stock

Cordate   Heart-shaped

Corolla   Inner series of floral leaves, each known as a petal

Corymb   Inflorescence where the branches start at different points reaching about the same height, giving a flat-top appearance

Cultivar   Cultivated variety of a plant

Deciduous   Falling off (loss of leaves on a tree)

Decumbent   Refers to a plant with prostrate stems for most of its length but ascending or erect at the tip

Elliptical   Narrow, oval, tapering at both ends

Epiphyte   Plant growing on the outer surface of another plant or object

Follicle   Dry fruit, opening when mature to release seeds and spilling along one side only

Fruit   Mature ovary with part of flower attached when the seed is ripe

Genus   Taxonomic group of closely related species

Gland   Liquid-secreting organ, usually on the leaves

Glaucous   Greyish

Head   Compact cluster of flowers

Herbaceous   Perennial (plant) without a woody stem

Hybrid   Result of cross-fertilisation of plants of different genetic composition or offspring of two different species

Inflorescence   Arrangement of flowers on a plant

Lanceolate   Lance-shaped

Lignotuber   Swelling at base of stem or below soil level, often bearing dormant buds

Linear   Long, narrow with parallel sides

Lobed   Rounded division of leaf, petal or plant organ

Mallee   Shrub-type eucalypt with several slender stems appearing from base

Nut   One-celled dry fruit with one seed. Does not open when ripe

Oblong   Roughly rectangular

Obovate   Ovate with the broadest part above the middle

Opposite   At the same level but on opposite sides (leaves)

Ovate   Egg-shaped

Panicle   Much branched racemose inflorescence

Pedicel   Stalk of a flower in a compound inflorescence

Pendulous   Hanging downwards

Peduncle   Main axis of a compound inflorescence or stalk of a solitary flower

Perennial   Plant living for more than one year

Petal   One part of the corolla of a flower

Phyllode   Flattened leaf stalk serving the function of a leaf

Pilose   With scattered long simple hairs

Pinnate   Compound (leaf) with leaflets arranged in a feather-like manner along each side of a common leaf stalk

Procumbent   Trailing or lying flat without rooting

Pseudobulb   Bulb-like stem of some plants (orchid)

Raceme   Inflorescence of stalked flowers arranged along an unbranched stem

Racemose   In the form of a raceme

Rhizome   Stem below ground level

Rosette   Arrangement of leaves coming from the centre of the plant

Scape   Leafless peduncle originating near the ground

Sepal   Leaf-like segment of the calyx

Serrated   Saw-toothed leaf margin with teeth pointing outwards

Species (sp.)   A group of closely related plants which naturally interbreed

Spike   Arrangement of flowers without stalks

Spore   Reproductive body without an embryo (fern)

Stamen   Male part of the flower which produces the pollen, usually consists of an anther and a filament

Stigma   Part of the flower which receives the pollen

Tendril   Plant organ modified to support stems used in climbing

Terminal   At the end or tip

Trifoliate   (Leaf) having three leaflets

Trunk   Main stem of a tree

Tuber   Swollen underground stem or shoot, which acts as a food reservoir. Often has buds capable of producing flowers

Valve   Capsule segment which lifts to release the seed

Whorl   Ring of flower petals or leaves around a stem

Further Reading

Adams, G.M. (1980) *Birdscaping Your Garden*, Rigby, Adelaide.

Armitage, Z.I. (1977) *Acacias of New South Wales*, The Society for Growing Australian Plants, N.S.W. Region, Sydney.

Australian National Botanic Gardens (1971-1899) *Growing Native Plants*, Vols. 1 to 14, Canberra.

Australian Plant Study Group (1979) *Grow What Where*, Thomas Nelson (Australia) Ltd, Melbourne.

Beadle, N.C.W., Evans, O.D. and Carolin, R.C. (1972) *Flora of the Sydney Region*, A.H. & A.W. Reed, Sydney.

Blomberry, A.M. (1972) *What Wildflower is That?*, Paul Hamlyn, Sydney.

Blomberry, A.M. (1975) *Wildflowers to Cultivate*, Paul Hamlyn, Sydney.

Blomberry, A.M. (1977) *A Guide to Native Australian Plants*, Angus & Robertson, Sydney.

Brooker, M.H. and Kleinig, D.A. (1983) *A Field Guide to Eucalypts*, Vol.1, Inkata Press, Sydney.

Brooks, A.E. (1973) *Australian Native Plants for Home Gardens*, Lothian Publishing Co., Melbourne.

Chadwick, D. (1985) *Australian Native Gardening Made Easy*, Little Hills Press, Sydney.

Clyne, D. (1972) *Australian Rock and Tree Orchids*, Lansdowne Press, Melbourne.

Conabere, B. and Garnet. Ros (1974) *Wildflowers of South-Eastern Australia*, Vols 1 & 2, Thomas Nelson (Australia) Ltd, Melbourne.

Costermans, K.A.W. (1984) *Native Trees and Shrubs of South Eastern Australia*, Rigby, Sydney.

Elliot, W.R. and Jones, D.C. (1980-1986) *Encyclopaedia of Australian Plants Suitable for Cultivation*, Vols 1 to 4, Lothian Publishing Co.Pty Ltd, Sydney

Erickson, R., George, A.S., Marchant, N.G. and Morcombe, M.K. (1973) *Flowers and Plants of Western Australia*, A.H. & A.W. Reed, Sydney.

Galbraith, J. (1977) *Collins Field Guide to the Wildflowers of South-East Australia*, Collins, Sydney.

George, A.S. (1983) *The Banksia Book*, Kangaroo Press in association with the Society for Growing Australian Plants, Sydney.

George, A.S. (1984) *An Introduction to the Proteaceae of Western Australia*, Kangaroo Press, Sydney.

Greig, D. (1987) *The Australian Gardener's Wildflower Catalogue*, Angus & Robertson, Sydney.

Harris, Thistle (1973) *Wildflowers of Australia*, Angus & Robertson, Sydney.

Harris, Thistle (1977) *Gardening with Australian Plants*, Nelson, Melbourne.

Harris, Thistle (1980) *Gardening with Australian Plants*, Three Vols, Shrubs, Small Plants and Climbers, Trees, Nelson, Melbourne.

Hodgson, M. and Paine, R. (1971) *A Field Guide to Australian Wildflowers*, Rigby, Melbourne.

Holliday, I. (1973) *Australian Shrubs*, Rigby, Adelaide.

Hosell, J. (1969) *Wildflowers of South Eastern Australia*, Lansdowne, Melbourne.

Jones, L. and Clemesha, S.C. (1976) *Australian Ferns and Allies*, A.H. & A.W. Reed, Sydney.

Kelly, S. (1969) *Eucalypts*, Nelson, Melbourne.

Macdonalds, R. and Westerman, J. (1979) *A Field Guide to Fungi of South-Eastern Australia*, Nelson, Melbourne.

Millett, M. (1971) *Native Trees of Australia*, Lansdowne, Melbourne.

Newby, I.K. (1968) *West Australian Plants for Horticulture*, The Society for Growing Australian Plants, Sydney.

Rigby, Geoff (1985), *The Australian Gardener's Guide to Native Plants*, Reed Books, Sydney.

Rigby, Geoff and Lightfoot, Paddy. (1985) *Australian Native Trees and Large Shrubs Suitable for Planting in the Lower Hunter*, The Society for Growing Australian Plants, Newcastle Group, Newcastle.

Rogers, F.J.C. (1971) *Growing Australian Native Plants*, Nelson, Melbourne.

Rotherham, E.R., Briggs, B., Blaxwell, D.F. and Carolin, R.C. (1975) *Flowers and Plants of New South Wales and Southern Queensland*, A.H. & A.W. Reed, Sydney.

Stead, David, Memorial Wildlife Research Foundation of Australia, Bargo, N,S.W. (1974) *Your Australian Garden, No.1, Propagation*, (1977) *Your Australian Garden, No.4, Grevilleas*, (1980) *Two Hundred Wattles for Gardens*, edited by Chandler, B., (1981) Ferns and Clubmosses.

The Society for Growing Australian Plants (1959 to date) Australian Plants, Sydney

Williams, K.A.W. (1979,1984) *Native Plants of Queensland*, Vols 1 & 2, Keith A Williams, North Ipswich.

Willis, J.H, Fuhrer, B.A. and Rotherham, E.R.(1975) *Field Guide to the Flowers and Plants of Victoria*, A.H. & A.W. Reed, Sydney.

Reds and Pinks — Summary of plants and flowering times

Botanical name	Common name	Flowering period
Allocasuarina rigida		Summer
Aloygyne huegelii	Lilac Hibiscus	Spring–summer
Anigosanthos 'Dwarf Delight'	Kangaroo Paw	Summer
Anigosanthos flavidus	Yellow Kangaroo Paw	Summer
Anigosanthos 'Regal Claw'	Kangaroo Paw	Spring–summer
Bauera rubioides	Dog Rose	Spring–summer
Blandfordia grandiflora	Christmas Bell	Summer
Boronia ledifolia	Ledum Boronia, Sydney Boronia	Spring
Boronia mollis	Soft Boronia	Winter–Spring
Boronia pinnata		Spring–summer
Boronia serrulata	Native Rose, Sydney Rock Rose	Spring
Boronia 'Telopea Valley Star'		Spring
Brachychiton acerifolius	Illawarra Flame Tree	Autumn–winter
Brachysema lanceolatum	Swan River Pea	Spring
Callistemon brachyandrus		Summer
Callistemon chisholmii		May–August
Callistemon citrinus	Crimson Bottlebrush	Spring–September
Callistemon citrinus 'Briar Hill'		September–December
Callistemon cintrinus 'Harkness', 'Gawler Hybrid'		September–December
Callistemon citrinus 'Reeves Pink'		September–December
Callistemon linearis	Narrow-Leaf Bottlebrush	Spring–summer
Callistemon pachyphyllus	Wallum Bottlebrush	Spring–autumn
Callistemon phoeniceus	Fiery, Lesser Bottlebrush	Summer
Callistemon polandii		Summer
Callistemon subulatus		Summer
Callistemon viminalis	Weeping Bottlebrush	Spring
Callistemon viminalis 'Bob Bailey'		August–October
Callistemon viminalis 'Captain Cook'		Spring
Callistemon viminalis 'Hanna Ray'		Spring
Callistemon viminalis 'Little John'		Spring
Calothamnus quadrifidus	One-Sided Bottlebrush, Net Bush	Spring–summer
Calothamnus villosus	Silky Net Bush	Spring–summer
Ceratopetalum gummiferum	N.S.W. Christmas Bush	Summer
Chamelaucium uncinatum	Geraldton Wax	Spring
Chorizema cordatum		Spring
Clianthus formosus	Sturt's Desert Pea	Spring–summer
Correa decumbens		Summer
Correa 'Dusky Bells'		March–September
Correa reflexa	Native Fuchsia	Autumn–spring
Correa reflexa var. *reflexa*		Autumn–spring
Crowea 'Festival'		Most of the year
Crowea saligna	Lance-Leaf Crowea	Summer–autumn
Darwinia citriodora	Lemon-Scented Myrtle	Winter–summer
Dendrobium tetragonium	Tree Spider Flower	September–October
Diplolaena angustifolia	Yanchep Rose, Native Rose	Winter–spring
Epacris impressa	Common Heath	Most of the year
Epacris longiflora	Native Fuchsia	Most of the year
Eremophila glabra	Common Emu Bush, Fuchsia Bush, Tar Bush	August–March
Eremophila longifolia	Berrigan, Emu Bush	July–December
Eremophila maculata	Spotted Emu Bush	Spring–summer
Eriostemon australasius	Pink Wax Flower	Late winter–spring
Eucalyptus caesia 'Silver Princess'		Winter–spring
Eucalyptus ficifolia	Red Flowering Gum	Summer
Eucalyptus lansdowneana		Winter
Eucalyptus leucoxylon 'Rosea'		May–September
Eucalyptus macrocarpa	Mottlecah, Rose of the West	Winter
Eucalyptus ptychocarpa		Winter
Eucalyptus sideroxylon	Mugga, Red Ironbark	Winter–summer
Graptophyllum excelsum		Summer
Grevillea alpina	Mountain Grevillea	Winter–summer
Grevillea aquifolium	Variable Prickly Grevillea	Winter–spring
Grevillea aspera		Spring
Grevillea aspleniifolia		Most of the year

Botanical name	Common name	Flowering period
Grevillea 'Austraflora McDonald Park'		Spring
Grevillea banksii	Red Silky Oak	Most of the year
Grevillea barklyana		Spring-summer
Grevillea baueri		Winter-spring
Grevillea bipinnatifida	Grape Grevillea	Winter-spring
Grevillea 'Bonnie Prince Charlie'		Spring-summer
Grevillea 'Boongala Spinebill'		Spring-summer
Grevillea brachystylis		Spring-summer
Grevillea caleyi	Caley's Grevillea	Winter-summer
Grevillea confertifolia		Spring
Grevillea dimorpha	Flame Grevillea	Winter-spring
Grevillea dryandri	Dryander's Grevillea	Autumn-winter
Grevillea 'Frampton's Hybrid'		Spring-summer
Grevillea gaudichaudii		Spring-summer
Grevillea hookerana	Toothbrush Grevillea	Spring-summer
Grevillea ilicifolia	Holly Grevillea	Spring-summer
Grevillea 'Ivanhoe'		July-November
Grevillea johnsonii		Spring
Grevillea juniperina	Prickly Spider Flower	Most of the year
Grevillea lanigera		Spring
Grevillea lavandulacea		Most of the year
Grevillea longistyla		Winter-summer
Grevillea 'Misty Pink'		Most of the year
Grevillea 'Ned Kelly', Mason's Hybrid		Most of the year
Grevillea pilosa		
Grevillea 'Pink Surprise'		Most of the year
Grevillea 'Poorinda Peter'		Spring-summer
Grevillea 'Poorinda Royal Mantle'		Spring-summer
Grevillea rivularis	Carrington Falls Grevillea	Most of the year
Grevillea 'Robyn Gordon'		Most of the year
Grevillea rosmarinifolia	Rosemary Grevillea	August-December
Grevillea sericea	Pink Spider Flower	Most of the year
Grevillea 'Shirley Howie'		Winter-spring
Grevillea 'Sid Cadwell'		Most of the year
Grevillea speciosa	Red Spider Flower	Spring
Grevillea steiglitziana		Winter-spring
Grevillea thelemanniana		Winter-spring
Grevillea tripartita		Winter-spring
Grevillea victoriae	Royal Grevillea	Winter-spring
Hakea bakerana		Winter-spring
Hakea bucculenta	Red Pokers	Winter-spring
Hakea crassinervia		Winter
Hakea laurina	Pincushion Hakea	Autumn-winter
Hakea multilineata	Grass-Leaf Hakea	Winter-spring
Hakea purpurea	Crimson Hakea	Winter-spring
Hakea trineura		Winter-spring
Helichrysum bracteatum	Golden Everlasting	Spring-summer
Helichrysum cassinianum	Pink Cluster Everlasting, Pink Everlasting, Cassini's Everlasting	Spring
Helipterum roseum		Spring
Indigofera australis	Austral Indigo	Winter-spring
Kennedia prostrata	Running Postman	Winter-spring
Kennedia rubicunda	Dusky Coral pea	Spring-summer
Kunzea ambigua	White Kunzea, Tick Bush	Spring
Kunzea baxteri	Scarlet Kunzea	Winter-spring
Lambertia formosa	Mountain Devil, Honey Flower	Most of the year
Lechenaultia formosa	Red Lechenaultia	Winter-spring
Leptospermum lanigerum var. macrocarpum		Summer-autumn
Melaleuca fulgens	Scarlet Honey-Myrtle	Spring-summer
Melaleuca hypericifolia	Hillock Bush	Summer
Melaleuca lateritia	Robin Redbreast Bush	Spring-summer
Melaleuca 'Payne's Hybrid'		Spring-summer
Melaleuca radula	Graceful Honey-Myrtle	Spring-summer
Nematolepis phebalioides		Autumn-summer
Oreocallis wickhamii	Tree Waratah, Red Silky Oak	Spring
Passiflora aurantica	Golden Passionflower	All year
Pelargonium rodneyanum	Magenta Storksbill	Spring-summer
Pimelea ferruginea	Pink Rice-Flower	Winter-spring

Botanical name	Common name	Flowering period
Pimelea ferruginea 'Magenta Mist'		Winter-spring
Rhododendron lochae	Australian Rhododendron	Spring-summer
Schefflera actinophylla	Umbrella Tree	Summer-winter
Schoenia cassiniana	Pink Cluster Everlasting, Pink Everlasting, Cassini's Everlasting	Spring
Stenocarpus sinuatus	Firewheel Tree	Autumn-winter
Stylidium graminifolium	Grass Trigger Plant	Spring-summer
Syzygium wilsonii	Powder-puff Lilypilly	Spring-summer
Tecomanthe hilli	Pink Trumpet Vine	Winter
Telopea oreades	Gippsland Waratah	Spring
Telopea speciosissima	N.S.W. Waratah	Spring
Telopea speciosissima × Telopea mongaensis,	Telopea 'Braidwood Brilliant'	Spring
Templetonia retusa	Cocky's Tongues	Winter-spring
Tetratheca stenocarpa		Spring
Thryptomene saxicola	Rock Thryptomene	Most of the year
Woolsia pungens		Most of the year
Zieria smithii		Spring

Oranges, golds and browns — Summary of plants and flowering periods

Botanical name	Common name	Flowering period
Anigosanthos 'Regal Claw'		Spring-summer
Banksia ericifolia	Heath Banksia	April-October
Banksia 'Giant Candles'		Winter-spring
Banksia media	Southern Plains Banksia	February-October
Banksia robur	Swamp Banksia	Winter-spring
Banksia spinulosa	Hairpin Banksia	Autumn-October
Grevillea alpina	Mountain Grevillea	Winter-summer
Grevillea buxifolia	Grey Spider Flower	Most of the year
Grevillea floribunda		Winter-spring
Grevillea 'Honey Gem'		Most of the year
Grevillea pteridifolia	Fern-Leafed Grevillea	May-September
Grevillea robusta	Silky Oak	Summer
Hibbertia stellaris		Spring-Autumn
Lechenaultia formosa	Red Lechenaultia	Winter-spring
Prostanthera magnifica	Splendid Mintbush	Spring

Yellows and greens — Summary of plants and flowering periods

Botanical name	Common name	Flowering period
Acacia amblygona		Late winter-spring
Acacia amblygona 'Australflora Winter Gold'		Late winter-spring
Acacia baileyana	Cootamundra Wattle	Winter-spring
Acacia decurrens	Black Wattle	Spring
Acacia drummondii	Drummond's Wattle	Summer
Acacia fimbriata	Fringed Wattle	Spring
Acacia flexifolia	Bent-Leaf Wattle	Winter
Acacia floribunda	White Sallow Wattle	Spring
Acacia glaucescens	Coastal Myall	Late spring
Acacia iteaphylla	Port Lincoln Wattle	Autumn to winter
Acacia longifolia	Sydney Golden Wattle, Sallow Wattle	Winter-spring
Acacia podalyriifolia	Queensland Silver Wattle	Winter
Acacia prominens	Golden Rain Wattle, Gosford Wattle	Spring
Acacia rigens	Nealie, Needlebush	Winter-spring
Acacia saligna	Golden Wreath Wattle, Orange Wattle	Spring-summer
Acacia vestita	Hairy Wattle, Weeping Boree	Spring-summer
Anigosanthos flavidus	Yellow Kangaroo Paw	Summer
Anigosanthos viridis	Green Kangaroo Paw	Spring-summer
Banksia integrifolia	Coast Banksia, White Honeysuckle	All year

Banksia integrifolia var. *compar*		April–September
Banksia marginata	Silver Banksia	March–October
Banksia oblongifolia		March–June
Banksia robur	Swamp Banksia	Autumn–winter
Banksia serrata	Saw Banksia	March–June
Boronia megastigma	Brown Boronia	Spring
Bossiaea foliosa	Leafy Bossiaea	November–February
Bulbine bulbosa	Bulbine Lily, Wild Onion, Native Leak	September–December
Callistemon pachyphyllus	Wallum Bottlebrush	Spring–autumn
Callistemon pallidus	Lemon Bottlebrush	Summer–autumn
Callistemon pinifolius		Spring
Callistemon pityoides (sieberi)	Alpine Bottlebrush	Summer
Carpobrotus spp.	Coastal Pig Face	Spring–summer
Cassia artemisioides	Silver Cassia	Winter–spring
Conostylis aculeata		Spring–summer
Conostylis seorsiflora		Spring
Correa bauerlenii	Chef's Cap Correa	Autumn–winter
Correa glabra	Rock Correa	May–August
Correa reflexa	Native Fuchsia	Autumn–spring
Correa reflexa var. *nummularifolia*		March–September
Craspedia glauca	Billy Buttons	Spring–summer
Cymbidium suave		August–October
Dendrobium gracilicaule		July–August
Dendrobium speciosum	Rock Lily, King Orchid	Spring
Eremophila maculata	Spotted Emu Bush	Winter–spring
Eucalyptus dwyeri	Dwyer's Gum	July–November
Eucalyptus erythrocorys	Illyarie, Red Cap gum	Winter
Eucalyptus kruseana	Kruse's Mallee	Autumn–winter
Eucalyptus lehmanni	Lehmann's Mallee, Bushy Yate	July–December
Eucalyptus robusta	Swamp Mahogany	Winter
Goodenia ovata	Hop Goodenia	Spring–summer
Grevillea 'Coochin Hills'		Spring
Grevillea dielsiana		Spring–autumn
Grevillea 'Honeycomb'		Spring
Grevillea ilicifolia	Holly Grevillea	Spring
Grevillea 'Sandra Gordon'		April–October
Grevillea sessilis		Winter–spring
Grevillea venusta	Byfield Spider Flower	Autumn–spring
Hakea cinerea		September–October
Hakea leucoptera		
Hakea petiolaris	Sea Urchin Hakea	Autumn–winter
Hakea suaveolens	Sweet-Scented Hakea	Autumn–winter
Hakea sulcata		Spring
Helichrysum apiculatum	Common Everlating	Spring–autumn
Helichrysum bracteatum 'Cockatoo'		Winter–spring
Helichrysum bracteatum 'Dargan Hill Monarch'		Spring–summer
Helichrysum bracteatum 'Diamond Head'		Summer–winter
Helichrysum bracteatum 'Montrosa Nana'		Spring–summer
Helichrysum ramosissimum	Yellow Buttons	Spring–summer
Helichrysum rutidolepis		Summer–autumn
Hibbertia aspera		Most of the year
Hibbertia cuneiformis	Cut-Leaf Hibbertia	Spring–summer
Hibbertia dentata		Spring–summer
Hibbertia empetrifolia		Spring–summer
Hibbertia obtusifolia	Showy Guinea Flower	Spring
Hibbertia pedunculata		Most of the year
Hibbertia scandens	Climbing Guinea Flower	Spring–winter
Hibbertia vestita		December
Homoranthus darwinioides		Most of the year
Homoranthus flavescens		Spring–summer
Hymenosporum flavum	Native Frangipani	Spring
Isopogon anemonifolius	Broad-Leaf Drumsticks	Spring–summer
Isopogon dawsonii	Nepean Cone Bush	Spring
Kennedia nigricans	Black Coral Pea	Spring
Melaleuca diosmifolia		Summer
Melaleuca incana	Grey Honey-Myrtle	Spring
Melaleuca quinquenervia	Broad-Leaved Paperbark	Summer–autumn
Oxylobium robustum		Spring–summer

Botanical name	Common name	Flowering period
Persoonia chamaepitys		Summer
Phebalium ambiens		Spring–summer
Phebalium squamulosum	Scaly Phebalium	Spring
Phebalium whitei		Spring
Pomaderris elliptica		Spring–summer
Pultenaea daphnoides	Large-Leaf Bush Pea	Spring
Ranunculus lappaceus	Common Buttercup	
Senecio linearifolium		Spring–summer
Synaphea polymorpha	Albany Synaphea	July–September
Telopea speciosissima 'Wirrimbirra White'		Spring
Tristaniopsis laurina	Kanooka, Water Gum	Summer
Xyris spp.		

Blues, purples and mauves — Summary of plants and flowering times

Botanical name	Common name	Flowering period
Alyogyne huegelii	Lilac Hibiscus	Spring–summer
Brachycome multifida		Most of the year
Calectasia cyanea	Blue Tinsel Lily	August–December
Callistemon citrinus 'Mauve Mist'		November–January
Callistemon 'Purple Splendour'		November–January
Carpobrotus glaucescens	Coastal Noonflower	Spring–summer
Dampiera diversifolia		Spring–summer
Dampiera purpurea		Spring
Eremophila nivea		Spring
Halgania cyanea	Rough Halgania	Most of the year
Hardenbergia violacea	False Sarsaparilla, Purple Coral Pea	August–November
Hemiandra pungens	Snake Bush	Spring–summer
Hibiscus huegeli	Lilac Hibiscus	Spring–summer
Kunzea parvifolia		Summer
Lasiopetalum baueri		Spring and summer
Lechenaultia biloba	Blue Lechenaultia	Winter–summer
Lechenaultia biloba 'White Flash'		Winter–summer
Lobelia membranacea		Spring–summer
Melaleuca armillaris	Bracelet Honey-Myrtle	Spring–summer
Melaleuca decussata		Spring–summer
Melaleuca nesophila		Spring
Melaleuca squamea		Spring–summer
Melaleuca thymifolia	Thyme-Leaf Honey-Myrtle	Spring–summer
Orthrosanthus laxus	Morning Iris	Spring
Pratia pedunculata	Trailing Pratia	Spring–summer
Prostanthera hirtula	Hairy Mint Bush	Spring–summer
Prostanthera incana	Hoary Mint Bush	Spring
Prostanthera ovalifolia	Purple Mint Bush	Spring
Prostanthera rotundifolia	Round-Leaf Mint Bush	Spring
Scaevola albida		Spring–summer
Scaevola aemula	Fairy Fan Flower	Spring–summer
Solanum brownii		Spring–summer
Thomasia macrocarpa	Large-Fruited Thomasia	Spring
Thomasia petalocalyx	Paper Flower	Spring–summer
Thomasia pygmaea		Spring
Thomasia rhynchocarpa		Spring
Thomasia sarotes		Spring
Thysantus patersonii	Fringed Lily	Spring–summer
Viola betonicifolia	Wild Violet, Purple Violet	Spring–summer
Viola hederacea	Ivy-Leaf Violet	Spring–summer
Wahlenbergia communis	Grass-Leaf Bluebell	Spring–summer
Westringia eremicola		Spring–summer
Westringia longifolia		Spring–summer

Creams and whites — Summary of plants and flowering periods

Botanical name	Common name	Flowering period
Actinotus helianthi	Flannel Flower	September–December
Ammobium alatum		Summer
Baeckea virgata	Twiggy Heath–Myrtle	Summer
Bauera rubioides	Dog Rose	Spring–summer
Burchardia umbellata	Milk Maids	September–December

Botanical name	Common name	Flowering period
Callistemon citrinus	Crimson Bottlebrush, Lemon-Scented Bottlebrush	Spring–December
Calytrix tetragona		August–November
Chamelaucium uncinatum	Geraldton Wax	Spring–summer
Clematis aristata	Traveller's Joy, Old Man's Beard	Spring
Correa alba	White Correa	Autumn–through year
Correa 'Ivory Bells'		April–December
Cryptandra scortechinii	Ball Cryptandra	Winter–spring
Dendrobium cucumerinum	Cucumber Orchid	November–February
Dendrobium linguiforme	Tongue Orchid	Spring–summer
Diplarrena moreae	Butterfly Flag	Late spring
Epacris microphylla	Coral Heath	Autumn–spring
Eriostemon myoporoides	Long-Leafed Wax Flower	Winter–spring
Eucalyptus curtisii	Plunkett Mallee	Summer
Eucalyptus globulus	Tasmanian Blue Gum	Winter–spring
Eucalyptus nicholii	Narrow-Leaf Black Peppermint	Autumn
Eucalyptus polyanthemos	Red Box	September–December
Grevillea australis		Spring
Grevillea banksii	Red Silky Oak	Most of the year
Grevillea biternata		Spring
Grevillea rosmarinifolia var. lutea		Winter–spring
Grevillea vestita		Winter–spring
Grevillea 'White Wings'		Winter–spring
Hakea florulenta		Summer
Hakea oleifolia		Spring
Haloragodendron racemosum		Summer
Helichrysum diosmifolium	Pill Flower, Sago Flower	Winter–summer
Helipterum anthemoides	Chamomile Sunray	Winter–spring
Hemiandra pungens	Snakebush	Spring–summer
Isotoma anethifolia		Summer
Kunzea ambigua	Tick Bush, White Kunzea	September–November
Leptospermum flavescens 'Cardwell'		Winter–spring
Leptospermum flavescens 'Pacific Beauty'		Winter–spring
Libertia paniculata		Spring
Lophostemon confertus	Brush Box	November–December
Melaleuca alternifolia		Summer
Melaleuca linariifolia 'Snowstorm'		Spring–summer
Micromyrtus ciliata	Fringed Heath-Myrtle	Winter–spring
Myoporum viscosum	Sticky Boobialla	Summer
Olearia floribunda		Spring–summer
Olearia microphylla	Bridal Daisy Bush	Winter–spring
Pandorea pandorana	Wonga Wonga Vine	Spring
Passiflora aurantia	Golden Passionflower	All year
Pimelea ligustrina	Tall Rice Flower	Summer
Pittosporum undulatum	Sweet Pittosporum	Spring
Pratia pedunculata	Trailing Pratia	Spring–summer
Pseudanthos pimeleoides		Spring
Ricinocarpos pinifolius	Wedding Bush	Spring
Rulingia hermanniifolia	Wrinkled Kerrawang	Spring
Scaevola albida		Spring
Sollya heterophylla	Bluebell Creeper	Spring–summer
Spyridium parvifolium	Dusty Miller	Spring–summer
Telopea speciosissima 'Wirrimbirra White'	White Waratah	Spring
Westringia fruticosa	Coastal Rosemary	November

Colour without flowers — Summary of plants and features

Fruits and nuts

Botanical name	Common name	Features
Banksia ericifolia	Heath Banksia	Long narrow tapered cone
Banksia integrifolia	Coastal Banksia	Brown cones with open seed follicles
Banksia robur	Swamp Banksia	Bronze-cone, red-brown velvet-like new foliage
Casuarina cunninghamiana	River Oak	Green to brown small woody cones
Ceratopetalum gummiferum	N.S.W. Christmas Bush	Masses of red calyces
Citriobatus pauciflorus	Orange Thorn	Small edible orange berries

Botanical name	Common name	Features
Dodonaea		Bronze-red winged fruits
Drymophila cyanocarpa	Turquoise Berry	Globular blue or white berries
Eleocarpus reticulatus	Blueberry Ash	Small brilliant blue fruits
Eucalyptus caesia 'Silver Princess'		Grey bell-shaped fruits
Eucalyptus erythrocorys	Illyarrie Gum	Bright red biretta-like operculums
Eucalyptus globulus	Tasmanian Blue Gum	Grey-green operculums
Eucalyptus lehmanni	Bushy Yate	Orange–yellow horn-shaped operculums, brown multi-capsule fruits
Eucalyptus robusta	Swamp Mahogany	Yellow-white operculums
Harpullia pendula	Tulipwood	Orange seed cases with shiny black seeds
Hakea bakeriana		One of the largest hakea fruits
Macadamia	Macadamia Nut	Rounded hard green fruits
Mackinlaya macrosciadia		Clusters of dark-fleshed blue-grey berries
Persoonia pinifolia	Pine-Leaf Geebung	Pale green succulent fruits
Pittosporum rhombifolium	Hollywood	Yellow capsules with two black seeds
Pittosporum undulatum	Mock Cherry	Yellow capsules with ruby-coloured seeds
Podocarpus elatus	Plum Pine	Bluish-black plum-like fruits
Rhagodia baccata	Coastal Saltbush	Long-lasting red berries
Syzygium luehmanni	Riberry, Small-Leaved Lilypilly	Small pink to red fruits
Syzygium paniculatum	Magenta Cherry	Large magenta rounded berries, dark red new growth
Xanthorrhoea preissii	Grass Tree, Black Boy	Blackened fruits on tall flower spike
Xylomelum pyriforme	Sandplain Pear	Large pear-shaped fruits

Foliage

Botanical name	Common name	Features
Acacia baileyana	Cootamundra Wattle	Grey fern-like foliage
Acacia howittii		Weeping light green foliage
Acacia podalyriifolia	Qld Silver Wattle	Rounded silver-grey phyllodes
Adiantum aethiopicum	Common Maidenhair	Delicate light green new fronds
Allocasuarina torulosa	Forest Oak	Copper-brown slender drooping new branchlets
Angophora hispida	Dwarf Apple	Velvety rust-red hair-covered young branches and flower buds
Asplenium australasicum	Bird's Nest Fern	Light green new radiating fronds
Baeckea virgata 'Howie's Feathertips'		Red-brown new foliage
Banksia conferta		Rusty-brown hairy new leaves
Callistemon salignus	Willow Bottlebrush	Copper-pink new foliage
Ceratopetalum gummiferum	N.S.W. Christmas Bush	Light green new foliage
Davallia pyxidata	Hare's Foot Fern	Fresh new light green creeping fronds
Dicksonia antarctica	Soft Tree-Fern	Light green new unfolding fronds
Doodia aspera	Prickly Rasp Fern	Rosy pink immature fronds
Drosera	Sundew	Red rosetted sticky leaves
Eucalyptus	Various species	Red tips on new leaves
Eucalyptus cinerea	Argyle Apple	Small rounded grey-green leaves
Eucalyptus globulus	Tasmanian Blue Gum	Contrasting grey-green juvenile and dark green mature leaves
Eucalyptus pulverulenta	Silver-leaved Mountain Gum	Small ovate silver-blue leaves
Gleichenia dicarpa	Coral Fern	Light green new foliage
Hakea salicifolia	Willow Hakea	Red new leaf tips
Helichrysum apiculatum	Common Everlasting	Grey felty foliage
Homoranthus flavescens		Fine grey-green foliage
Hypocalymma cordifolium 'Golden Veil'		Cream-yellow variegated foliage
Melaleuca incana	Grey Honey-Myrtle	Delicate red tips on weeping grey-green leaves
Pennisetum alopecuroides	Swamp Foxtail	Bluish-green leaves and purple flower spikes
Persoonia chamaepitys		Light green foliage, red new leaf tips

Botanical name	Common name	Features
Platycerium bifurcatum	Elkhorn	Light green new fronds
Platycerium superbum	Staghorn	Large light green pendular new fronds
Scleranthus biflorus	Cushion Bush	Soft green creeping moss-like perennial herb
Westringia fruticosa	Coastal Rosemary	Dark green leaves with silky grey underside
Woollsia pungens		Red tips on new growth

Tree trunks and barks

Botanical name	Common name	Features
Allocasuarina torulosa	Forest Oak	Rough deep brown corky bark
Angophora costata	Smooth-barked Apple	Gnarled and twisted salmon-pink pitted bark
Banksia serrata	Saw Banksia	Grey-green gnarled bark
Callistemon salignus	Willow Bottlebrush	Pink papery bark
Casuarina equisetifolia	Horsetail She-Oak, Coastal She-Oak	Smooth grey-brown bark on young trees
Casuarina glauca	Swamp Oak	Rough grey bark
Eucalyptus canaliculata		Dark brown flaky bark
Eucalyptus haemastoma	Scribbly Gum	Irregular markings on pale-coloured bark
Eucalyptus mannifera subsp. *mannifera*	Brittle Gum	White bark often mottled with patches of grey and pink
Eucalyptus nicholii	Narrow-Leaf Black Peppermint	Persistent fibrous brown bark
Eucalyptus saligna	Sydney Blue Gum	Smooth white bark with short stocking of rough bark at the base of the tree
Eucalyptus scoparia	Wallangarra White Gum	Slender white powdery bark, sometimes with light grey blotches
Eucalyptus sideroxylon	Red Ironbark	Rough almost black bark
Melaleuca quinquenervia	Broad-Leaved Paperbark	Papery white or grey textured bark
Xanthorrhoea glauca	Grass Tree	Blackened trunks

Index of Botanical Names

Index of Common Names